Education in an Altered World

Also Available from Bloomsbury

Disabled Children and Digital Technologies, *Sue Cranmer*
Education and Disability in the Global South, *edited by Nidhi Singal, Paul Lynch and Shruti Taneja Johansson*
Supporting Difficult Transitions, *edited by Mariane Hedegaard and Anne Edwards*
A New Perspective on Education in the Digital Age, *Jesper Tække and Michael Paulsen*
Navigating Teacher Education in Complex and Uncertain Times, *Carmen I. Mercado*
Developing Culturally and Historically Sensitive Teacher Education, *edited by Yolanda Gayol Ramírez, Patricia Rosas Chávez and Peter Smagorinsky*
Doing Diversity Differently in a Culturally Complex World, *Megan Watkins and Greg Noble*
Identity, Culture and Belonging, *Tony Eaude*
Issues and Challenges of Immigration in Early Childhood in the USA, *Wilma Robles-Melendez and Wayne Driscoll*
Education in Radical Uncertainty, *Stephen Carney and Ulla Ambrosius Madsen*

Education in an Altered World

*Pandemic, Crises and Young People
Vulnerable to Educational Exclusion*

Edited by
Michelle Proyer, Wayne Veck, Fabio Dovigo
and Elvira Seitinger

BLOOMSBURY ACADEMIC
LONDON • NEW YORK • OXFORD • NEW DELHI • SYDNEY

BLOOMSBURY ACADEMIC
Bloomsbury Publishing Plc, 50 Bedford Square, London, WC1B 3DP, UK
Bloomsbury Publishing Inc, 1359 Broadway, New York, NY 10018, USA
Bloomsbury Publishing Ireland, 29 Earlsfort Terrace, Dublin 2, D02 AY28, Ireland

BLOOMSBURY, BLOOMSBURY ACADEMIC and the Diana logo are trademarks of
Bloomsbury Publishing Plc

First published in Great Britain 2023
Paperback edition published 2025

Copyright © Michelle Proyer, Wayne Veck, Fabio Dovigo and Elvira Seitinger and
contributors, 2023

Michelle Proyer, Wayne Veck, Fabio Dovigo and Elvira Seitinger and contributors
have asserted their right under the Copyright, Designs and Patents Act, 1988,
to be identified as Editors of this work.

Cover design: Grace Ridge

All rights reserved. No part of this publication may be: i) reproduced or transmitted
in any form, electronic or mechanical, including photocopying, recording or by means
of any information storage or retrieval system without prior permission in writing from the
publishers; or ii) used or reproduced in any way for the training, development or operation
of artificial intelligence (AI) technologies, including generative AI technologies. The rights
holders expressly reserve this publication from the text and data mining exception as
per Article 4(3) of the Digital Single Market Directive (EU) 2019/790.

Bloomsbury Publishing Plc does not have any control over, or responsibility for,
any third-party websites referred to or in this book. All internet addresses given in this
book were correct at the time of going to press. The author and publisher regret any
inconvenience caused if addresses have changed or sites have ceased to exist,
but can accept no responsibility for any such changes.

A catalogue record for this book is available from the British Library.

A catalog record for this book is available from the Library of Congress.

ISBN: HB: 978-1-3502-8269-8
PB: 978-1-3502-8273-5
ePDF: 978-1-3502-8270-4
eBook: 978-1-3502-8271-1

Typeset by Newgen KnowledgeWorks Pvt. Ltd., Chennai, India

For product safety related questions contact productsafety@bloomsbury.com.

To find out more about our authors and books visit www.bloomsbury.com
and sign up for our newsletters.

Contents

List of Figures   viii
List of Tables   ix
List of Contributors   xi

Introduction   1
   Michelle Proyer, Wayne Veck, Fabio Dovigo and Elvira Seitinger

Part 1   Critical Understandings of Educational Exclusion and Crisis

1. The Meaning of Collective Capabilities for the Education of Refugee Children during a Pandemic   13
   Margarita Bilgeri
2. Covid-19 Exposing the Fault Lines of Inclusion: The 'Risk' and 'Vulnerability' of Disabled Children in the UK   25
   Sharon Smith

Part 2   Teaching and Learning under the Shadow of a Global Pandemic: Exclusions and Possibilities

3. The Effect of the Covid-19 Pandemic on Students in a Vulnerable Situation in Iceland   43
   Hermína Gunnþórsdóttir and Ylfa G. Sigurðardóttir
4. Increased Educational Disadvantages of Refugee Students in German Language Support Classes during Covid-19 School Closures in Austria: Perceptions and Pedagogical Reactions of Austrian Teachers   59
   Katharina-Theresa Lindner, Marie Gitschthaler, Alexandra Gutschik, Julia Kast, Julia Honcik, Rupert Corazza and Susanne Schwab
5. Distance Learning and Inclusive School: An Impossible Challenge?   75
   Ines Guerini, Giorgia Ruzzante and Alessia Travaglini

Part 3 Addressing Social Exclusion: Illuminating Possibilities for Inclusion in and through Crisis

6 A Widening Inequality Gap: Reducing Educational Inequalities in Europe by Reaching Out to Students and Families at Risk during a Time of Crisis and Beyond   93
   Pamela Marie Spiteri

7 Establishing the Medium- to Long-Term Impact of Covid-19 Constraints on the Socio-Emotional Well-Being of Impoverished Children and Young People (and Those Who Are Otherwise Disadvantaged) during, and in the Aftermath of, Covid-19   111
   Joan G. Mowat

8 Possible Contributions of the School in Preventing the Maintenance of Poverty in the Case of Some Romanian Disadvantaged Children and the Context of the Pandemic   129
   Ruxandra Folostina and Loredana Adriana Patrascoiu

Part 4 Including Excluded Individuals and Communities in Times of Crisis

9 Covid-19 and Disadvantaged Roma Communities in Romania   151
   Rosa Drown

10 Teachers Supporting Refugee Students in Canada during Covid-19: Greater Equity and a Sense of Belonging   167
    Susan Barber

11 Making a Place for Refugee Education: Routes towards Meaningful Inclusion for Refugee Teenagers in 'New-Normal' England   183
    Joanna McIntyre

12 Thinking about the Emotional Well-Being of Black Children in a Post-Pandemic World   199
    Siya Mngaza

Part 5 Disability and Crisis

13 Teach in the Mornings, Cry in the Evenings: The Impact of Covid-19 Remote Schooling on the Mothers of Emergent Bilinguals with Disabilities   223
    María Cioè-Peña

14 'We're in the Same Storm but NOT in the Same Boat': Searching for
   the Voices of Parents of Students with SEN in Covid-19 Times   243
   Elisabeth De Schauwer, Inge Van de Putte and Geert Van Hove

Conclusion

15 Out of Crisis the New Future: Concluding Thoughts on Inclusive
   and Equitable Education for All with a View from Scotland   261
   David Watt

Index   281

Figures

6.1	The HSCL as an opportunity development programme to reduce ELET risk factors by increasing capabilities and functionings	104
7.1	Illustration of key theme 'the nature, quality and strength of networks of support around communities, families and schools'	119
11.1	Sketching at Lakeside	189
11.2	Image taken during visit to New Art Exchange, Phoebe Boswell HERE exhibition	196
12.1	Stern, Barbarin and Cassidy's (2021) adaptation of Bronfenbrenner's bio-ecological systems theory	211

Tables

4.1	Item 'The students feel strongly burdened in the current situation'	65
4.2	Item 'The students believe they are on holidays'	66
4.3	Item 'The students have a weekly individual coaching with me'	66
4.4	Item 'The students have enough possibilities at home to work on a computer, laptop, or tablet'	67
4.5	Item 'The students are working actively on their tasks at home'	67
4.6	Item 'Distance learning increases educational disadvantages'	68
4.7	Item 'It will be difficult to create a collective knowledge base after the distance learning'	69
8.1	Descriptive statistics for problems identified by experts	135
8.2	Descriptive statistics for problems identified by parents	137
8.3	Ranking problems parents and experts identified during the Covid-19 pandemic	138
8.4	Descriptive statistics for solutions identified by experts/principals	139
8.5	Descriptive statistics for solutions of parents	140
8.6	Ranking solutions parents and experts identified during the Covid-19 pandemic	141
8.7	Clustering solutions identified by experts and parents	143
13.1	Participant and qualifying child demographics	228
13.2	Participant responses to question: Did your child receive a device from NYCDOE and/or school?	230
13.3	Participant responses to question: How often do you use cell phone data to access the internet at home?	231
13.4	Participant responses to question: How satisfied were you with your child's school experience before Covid-19 remote schooling?	232
13.5	Participant responses to question: How satisfied are you with your child's current school experience during Covid-19 remote schooling?	232

13.6	Participant responses to question: Since the Covid-19 pandemic started, have you experienced any of the following? Please select all that apply	234
13.7	Concern over academics versus socio-emotional concerns during Covid-19 pandemic related remote schooling	236

Contributors

Susan Barber is Senior Lecturer in Education at Simon Fraser University, Canada, and a counselling psychologist in Vancouver, Canada. Her research interests lie in the field of arts education and its alternate ways of learning and healing. Currently she is employing arts-based research as a mental health intervention for refugee students.

Margarita Bilgeri is Project Manager at the European Agency for Special Needs and Inclusive Education and lecturer at the University of Vienna. Her field of expertise is related to inclusive education in Europe and the Global South with a focus on the capability approach. Further research interests are related to poverty, socio-emotional well-being in schools and voices of learners and families.

María Cioè-Peña is Assistant Professor at The University of Pennsylvania's Graduate School of Education, USA. She examines the intersections of ableism, linguicism and racism within education policy and the school-based experiences of Latinx children with disabilities and their mothers. María's book, *(M)othering Labeled Children: Bilingualism and Disability in the Lives of Latinx Mothers*, was published in May 2021.

Rupert Corazza is an educational researcher and political advisor at the Board of Education for Vienna. As a member of the expert staff, he currently leads the implementation process of an extensive education reform in the field of special educational needs. He holds a doctorate in education and a master's degree in philosophy.

Elisabeth De Schauwer is working as Assistant Professor in the field of Disability Studies at Ghent University, Belgium. Her research focuses on intra-actions with difference in (pedagogical) relations. She works closely together with children, parents and schools in the praxis of inclusive education.

Fabio Dovigo (PhD) is Full Professor of Psychology of Education at the Danish School of Education, Aarhus University (DK). His research interests are in the area of inclusive education and early childhood education and care. He is currently working on projects investigating early childhood systems quality and refugee education. His recent publications include *Special Educational Needs and Inclusive Practices* (2016), *Challenges and Opportunities in Education for Refugees in Europe: From Research to Good Practices* (2018) and *The Social Dimension of*

Higher Education in Europe: Issues, Strategies and Good Practices for Inclusion (2020).

Rosa Drown is an independent researcher with a wide experience of providing support for disadvantaged people in Romania. As an experienced teacher, her work and research have included the educational inclusion of Roma children and the interface between school Roma parents and their children.

Ruxandra Folostina is Senior Lecturer at University of Bucharest, Faculty of Psychology and Educational Sciences, Special Education Department, Romania. Her research interests focus on autism spectrum disorder, dramatherapy for people with special needs and inclusion of children at risk. Her most recent book is *Interventions for Improving Adaptive Behaviors in Children with Autism Spectrum Disorders* (2021).

Marie Gitschthaler is Professor for Inclusive Education at the KPH Vienna/Lower Austria, playing a leading role in national and international research projects over the past twelve years. Currently coordinating an Erasmus+-KA3 project on the International Classification of Functioning for Children and Youth (ICF-CY), Marie's research focus areas are causes and consequences of early school leaving, multilingualism, students with emotional and social support needs and exclusion.

Ines Guerini (PhD) is a research at Roma Tre University, Department of Education, Italy, where she is also a member of the Research Laboratory for the Development of Scholastic and Social Inclusion. Her research interests concern inclusive processes at school and in the society as well as teachers' training and disabling mechanisms. She is the author of numerous publications on these topics.

Hermína Gunnþórsdóttir is Professor at the University of Akureyri, Iceland. She has worked in kindergarten, primary and secondary schools. Her teaching and research interest is related to social justice in education, inclusive school and education, multicultural and plurilingual education, disability studies, educational policy and practice.

Alexandra Gutschik (BEd, BA) is a master's student in the teachers program for inclusive education at the University of Vienna, Austria, and teaches at a special school in Vienna. She also works as a research assistant at the Centre for Teacher Education. Her research areas are inclusion and diversity in schools.

Julia Honcik (BEd) graduated in educational science and also has a teaching qualification for special education. She has many years of experience in support facilities for disabled people. Since 2018, she is also a diversity manager at the Vienna Board of Education. Her research focuses on inclusion and diversity.

Julia Kast (BEd) is a PhD candidate at the Centre for Teacher Education at the University of Vienna, Austria. Her research has mainly focused on inclusive education. Further topics include attitudes and self-efficacy beliefs. Her doctoral thesis is about the inclusion of students with different language abilities within the Austrian Education system.

Katharina-Theresa Lindner is a post-doctoral fellow at the Faculty of Education, University of Vienna, Austria. An educational scientist in research and teaching and co-project leader of the research project PATHWAY (Academic and Socioemotional Development of Students in Diverse School Settings, funded by Austrian National Bank), dealing with educational biographies of students with learning disabilities, her research focuses on diversity and intersectionality, discrimination-critical pedagogy, school and socio-pedagogical diagnostics.

Joanna McIntyre is Professor of Education at the University of Nottingham, UK. Jo is interested in how, through the field of education, we can understand and improve the lives of those who are marginalized or disadvantaged by society. Jo works on a range of funded research projects focusing on refugee education.

Siya Mngaza works as an educational and child psychologist in South London and is an academic tutor at the University Birmingham. Siya has researched school belonging amongst Black pupils who attend predominantly white schools, and she is currently exploring the way that Black families navigate neurodiversity, autism and learning differences.

Joan G. Mowat is Senior Lecturer in the School of Education, University of Strathclyde, Glasgow, UK. Her principal research interests are inclusion, social, emotional and behavioural needs and leadership for social justice. Her most recent research has focused on the pandemic and on the relationship between poverty, attainment and well-being.

Loredana Adriana Patrascoiu is Junior Lecturer at University of Bucharest, Faculty of Psychology and Educational Sciences, Special Education Department, Romania. Her research interests focus on quality of inclusive education. Her most recent contribution is the chapter 'The Management and Assurance of Quality in Romanian Schools', in Heidi Flavian (eds), *From Pedagogy to Quality Assurance in Education: An International Perspective* (2020).

Michelle Proyer is Associate Professor at the Center for Teacher Education and Department of Education, University of Vienna, Austria. She specializes in Inclusive Education, her research and teaching focus on inclusive schools and the disabilities migration nexus.

Giorgia Ruzzante (PhD) is a research fellow at University of Bozen, Faculty of Education, Italy. Her research interests concern inclusive education, teachers' training and philosophy for children. She is the author of numerous publications on these topics.

Susanne Schwab is University Professor of School Pedagogy with Special Focus on Social, Linguistic and Cultural Diversity at the Center for Teacher Education and the Faculty of Education at the University of Vienna, Austria, and associate professor at North-West University in Vanderbijlpark, South Africa. Her research focuses on diversity and heterogeneity in the school context, social, cultural and linguistic diversity, inclusive pedagogy, evaluation of educational policies and concepts.

Elvira Seitinger is a project assistant at the University of Vienna, Austria, and a Master's student in teacher training with a focus on Inclusive Education and German. She has experience in teaching in an inclusive school setting at Schule am Himmel, Vienna.

Ylfa G. Sigurðardóttir is supervisory teacher in elementary education at Norðlingaskóli in Reykjavík. She completed her MEd degree from the University of Akureyri, Iceland, in 2020 and her research during Covid-19 was conducted in partial fulfilment of her master's degree. Ylfa's interest is inclusive school and teaching.

Sharon Smith is a PhD research student at the University of Birmingham, UK. Her PhD approaches the subjectivity of parents of disabled children/children labelled with special educational needs in order to explore how this impacts on inclusion in education. Sharon was awarded the inaugural BERA Doctoral Fellowship in 2019.

Pamela Marie Spiteri (PhD) graduated in Education and Social Justice at Lancaster University, UK, focusing on students at risk of early leaving from education and training (ELET) and minimizing barriers due to disadvantaged family backgrounds. Pamela is the education officer leading the national Early Leaving from Education Unit (ELETU), in Malta responsible for policy monitoring, development, evaluation and implementation related to ELET and a visiting lecturer at the Institute for Education in the areas of pedagogy, assessment for learning, equity, social justice and ELET, which are her main research interests.

Alessia Travaglini (PhD) teaches human sciences in high schools and teaching strategies for special educational needs at La Sapienza University (Rome), Italy. She is a member of the Research Laboratory for the Development of Scholastic and Social Inclusion at Roma Tre University, Italy. Her research interests concern inclusive education and teachers' training. She is the author of numerous publications on these topics.

Inge Van de Putte supports children, parents and schools in the processes of inclusive education. Support for teachers and the position of special needs coordinators were the topics in her PhD and current research at Ghent University, Belgium. Her emphasis lies on the transfer of scientific knowledge in educational practices.

Geert Van Hove is Full Professor of Disability Studies at Ghent University, Belgium. He teaches and does research on narratives of inclusion/exclusion, use of creative research methods and working with parents and families of disabled kids. He is a jazz-cat and a basketball addict.

Wayne Veck started his teaching career as a teacher of English to students from Afghanistan and Iraq seeking refuge in the UK. He is now Professor of Education at the University of Winchester, UK, having been Faculty Head of Research and Knowledge Exchange from 2015 to 2018. He has given keynote addresses at the universities of Bergamo, Vienna and Winchester, Lillehammer University College and at the Polish Disability Forum's conference. He has published in leading education journals, including the *Oxford Review of Education*, *British Journal of Sociology of Education*, *Cambridge Journal of Education*, and the *International Journal of Inclusive Education*.

David Watt is a former HMI and Senior Education Officer for Inclusion and Equalities with Education Scotland. His interests are social justice in education and inclusive education. At present, David is course leader in Equity, Diversity and Inclusion in Education in the School of Education at the University of Glasgow, UK.

Introduction

Michelle Proyer, Wayne Veck, Fabio Dovigo and Elvira Seitinger

Holding this book in your hands or looking at these lines on your screen, you might probably have passed a negotiation process. Should I buy this book or not? Yet another piece on the pandemic? Do I really want to do this?

You have apparently decided to go for it and we as editors are happy about your decision but still feel we owe you an explanation. Why did we decide to put together and publish a book on crises even as we lived through the difficult times of a global pandemic?

Regardless of whether you are looking back at years of the world under the rules of a pandemic or are reading this while right in the middle of it, we aimed for setting a mark of a world that is not at the fringe of becoming a different one or bouncing back to what we assumed as normal. This holds especially true as of the time of rewriting this introduction, war in Ukraine is raging and Afghanistan sees changes in politics and societal order as a new government forms and reshapes an already crises-torn country. The list could go on.

It is safe to say that this world is already altered and will continue to change. Effects on education, educators as well as educational institutions are imminent and hold much potential for positive change even as they bring about many challenges.

At the time of writing a first draft for this introduction, we found ourselves confronted with challenging news on an hourly basis. Live tickers announcing numbers of deaths resulting from the Covid-19, peaks of cases and so on. Additionally, live feeds from sites of natural disasters and other crises that surround us make daily headlines. Though we might be used to bad news by now, the enormity and intensity of this global crisis throws education into an unprecedented situation. Hand in hand with this goes a need for ad hoc high-quality research that helps monitor and understand possible shifts in dynamics of what causes vulnerabilities (Mukumbang, Ambe and Adebiyi 2020; Obermayr et al. 2021).

Crises can add hardship to those already affected by exclusion. Research in this area is ongoing and only slowly do we understand the tolls of global impact, besides imminent health crises, this pandemic has – among these mental health (e.g. Boyraz, Legros and Tigershtrom, 2020), economic challenges (e.g. Tso et al. 2020) as well as broadening gaps in educational outcomes and access (e.g. in terms of digital divide – Coleman 2021). These might affect specific groups, such as children and young people with disabilities, those with refugee or migration experience and so on. Equally, learning remotely has meant that children need functioning digital infrastructure within their homes (Liu 2021). If this cannot be granted due to socio-economic restraints, children of families already deprived of equal educational opportunities will fall behind even more. This can be due to direct health-related or indirect impact of the pandemic, such as job and, thus, income loss (Reimers 2022). On the other hand, crises can lead to new sorts of vulnerability, for example due to loss of housing, health issues or elevated stress levels over extended periods of time. Despite these shifting dynamics, ableist and healthist ideals remain in place. Academic targets need to be met as educational institutions are slow to react to emerging needs. Inclusive developments in the context of education could offer solutions to this paradox situation by offering individualized equal and high-quality access to education, regardless of the circumstances.

Education in an Altered World

What does it mean to educate – and, in particular, to educate young people vulnerable to exclusion – in a world altered by pandemic? The contributors to this book have, each in their own way, advanced distinct answers to this question. And yet, it is possible to trace out two common themes that run through their responses. The first acknowledges that each author has reflected, researched and written their contribution in the midst of this global crisis that, despite our hopes, persists at the time of writing. In other words, we write, as we teach, learn and research, in an increasingly uncertain and insecure world. The second theme is born of the recognition that, despite all the uncertainty, this crisis presents us with an opportunity to rethink possibilities for learning and teaching. In this volume, we consider the complexities and significance of both these themes.

Teaching and Learning in an Increasingly Uncertain and Insecure World

On 25 March 2020, the UN Educational, Scientific and Cultural Organization (UNESCO) estimated that the coronavirus disease 2019 (Covid-19) pandemic had led to 'nationwide closures' of schools, affecting over 90 per cent of the world's student population (UNESCO 2020a). This meant that 184 countries had closed schools, impacting over 1.5 billion learners (UNESCO 2020b). Hence, Professor Viner and his colleagues, writing in the *Lancet*, noted: 'The scale and speed of school closures are unprecedented globally' (Viner et al. 2020: 402). As we consider the dimensions of this crisis, we are confronted by the first of the many paradoxes it has thrown into sharp contrast. It is the fact that while we all find ourselves living under the same shadow of a global pandemic, it affects us to different extents. In their report, 'Five Steps to Support Education for All in the Time of COVID-19', UNESCO observes 'the price that children and youth all over the world will pay in terms of education', incorporating:

> School closures, confinement, and psychological distress will have serious consequences on their futures and well-being, as well as on those of their teachers and families. (UNESCO 2020a)

As has been demonstrated throughout this book, the price has not and is not evenly distributed. We live not only in an altered world but also in a world more altered for some than for others.

Covid-19 has simultaneously illuminated already existing social and educational disparities and further deepened these inequalities (Giannini and Lewis 2020; Reay 2020; Stanistreet, Elfert and Atchoarena 2020). Indeed, it is precisely their awareness of these conditions that has fuelled the contributors to this book as they have engaged in critical reflection and embarked upon their research. More than crisis management at the level of distinct educational systems, the contributors to this book suggest that what is needed is a close examination of what it might mean to educate in and for a world in crisis.

Rethinking the Possibilities of Teaching and Learning

Zhao outlines two ways schools can respond to Covid-19. First, it might be conceived 'as a short-term crisis' (Zhao 2020: 29). Second, it might be viewed 'as an opportunity for reimagining education' (Zhao 2020: 30). The difference here between short-termism and the advancement of a long-term vision is, at least in part, in how we think about what it means to live in a time of crisis. In an essay first published in Germany in 1954, the philosopher and political theorist, Hannah Arendt, published an essay titled, 'The Crisis in Education', in which she wrote:

> A crisis forces us back to the questions themselves and requires from us … direct judgments. A crisis becomes a disaster only when we respond to it with preformed judgments, that is, with prejudices. (Arendt 1993: 174)

And, if every 'crisis forces us back to the questions themselves', then the global pandemic crisis requires us to return anew to the question of what demands our most serious attention in education. Pursuing an approach that looks at the opportunities latent in this crisis, this book invites us to enter into conversations with researchers and their research to consider a series of distinct difficulties, exclusions and possibilities for young people during and in the midst of enduring crisis and global pandemic and beyond, considering that the aftermath of the pandemic and other lurking crises will bring about the need to learn to incorporate specific new foci into teaching and learning.

In their various ways, the chapters in this book have situated challenges and difficulties in education within the wider dimensions of social and economic justice. In this way they fall into harmony with Reay's (2020: 320) view that 'for a fairer and more inclusive educational system to emerge from the pandemic, we need as a nation to develop a much stronger collective sense of righteous indignation at the unjust status quo, and at the myriad inequalities of class and race it generates'. Immediately, this means rejecting an individualized conception of educational difficulty. What is required of us, instead, as we attempt to come 'to terms with COVID-19' is a 'a renewed focus on solidarity, within and between nation states, and among people' (Stanistreet, Elfert and Atchoarena 2020: 633).

This, in turn, entails some reflection on the question of what it means to be 'vulnerable' and, especially, on what it means to be or to become 'vulnerable' in a time of global crisis. Hargreaves (2020) maintains that while governments may respond to the economic cost of Covid-19 by introducing and increasing austerity, what is needed most is 'counsellors, mental health specialists and learning support teachers to help our weakest learners and most vulnerable children settle down and catch up'. Whereas Reay (2020) advances a contrary understanding of what it might mean to be a 'vulnerable' young person living during a time of global pandemic. Commentating on a British Broadcasting

Corporation report from 2020 on the low attendance of young people identified as 'vulnerable' at schools closed to their non-labelled peers, Reay (2020: 316) notes: 'Labelling such children as "vulnerable children" clearly did not help with take-up and signalled a continuation of historical processes of labelling poor and working-class children.' There is a difficult balance to maintain here, between recognizing that some young people experience difficulties that make them vulnerable to exclusion, while at the same time retaining a steady and critical focus on the ways in which these difficulties, vulnerability and exclusions are conditioned by social and economic mechanisms. It is a balance that the authors of the chapters that make up this book have maintained and one which we, its editors, have attempted to sustain by pointing to the experiences of 'young people vulnerable to educational exclusion', rather than to 'vulnerable young people', in the subtitle of this book.

On 6 January 2021, the United Kingdom's Secretary of State for Education, Gavin Williamson, outlined how parents dissatisfied by the distance education offered by their children's school should communicate their concerns. Speaking in the House of Commons, Williamson suggested that concerned parents could directly contact their children's school and, if this should prove unsatisfactory, they should report their concern to Ofsted (the Office for Standards in Education, Children's Services and Skills). In response, Ofsted, which inspects educational, training and care provision in England, received over 10,000 emails from parents (from those who had access to email communication at that time), almost all of which were entirely complimentary of their children's schools (Weale, 2021). This outpouring of recognition for schools and the positive difference they make to young lives reminds us that, in Hargreaves's (2020) words: 'Teachers are among the unsung heroes of COVID-19: preparing resources and guidance for remote learning, dropping off school supplies in plastic boxes, connecting with kids and their parents to make sure they're OK – even while many have kids of their own at home.' So, in light of all the exclusion and hardship engendered by Covid-19, and in anticipation of all the global difficulties we might anticipate in future crises, it is to teachers and to their work that we will all turn. Thus, this book affirms the value of teachers as they educate, support and guide the young and so mitigate the worst consequences of global pandemic, exclusion and further diminishment into perceived vulnerability.

This matters because, having lived in a world deprived of schooling, we have been given the chance to examine the essence of what it means to educate and to be educated. This is, of course, first and foremost, a question of values. Azorín (2020: 382), for example, reflects: 'The current situation has made active forms of education such as deep learning even more essential.' Observing how 'even among very liberal media', concern has been expressed about the loss of learning time, Arnove detects an assumption 'that there is some divinely ordained amount of knowledge that must be learned in a specified amount of time', before going on to call for a move from 'concentrating on the quantity of knowledge imparted' to a 'focus on what is learned and how it is learned' (2020: 44). Zhao concluded his analysis of how Covid-19 might alter education by noting: 'If nothing else, governments can rethink whether they want to resume accountability testing, given that students have been over-tested and testing has itself become a pandemic in education' (2020: 30). Taken together, these reflections suggest that we have much to learn from the global crisis of Covid-19 as we come to think about what it means to educate in an altered world and a world constantly vulnerable to crisis. It is not enough to determine that education matters without further judging what kind of education brings value to young lives and to the world we share with each other.

In order to provide knowledge on changing learning and teaching strategies, this book presents findings from research in the broader scope of education and crises. Thus, it provides documentation and at the same time an empirical basis to develop teaching and learning in challenging times further pointing to a way ahead, beyond crises.

This book brings together researchers and scholars in the fields of inclusive education, disability studies, refugee education and special education to examine how children, already vulnerable to exclusion, might be supported and educated in and through times of global pandemic and crisis. It comprises fifteen contributions. The perspectives cover a wide geographical scope, across different locations in Europe, the UK, Canada and the United States. It is organized in five parts that focus on different aspects of education in challenging times. These cover methodological approaches and perspectives, geographical scopes and groups but also themes.

Part 1 – Critical Understandings of Educational Exclusion and Crisis – comprises two theoretical contributions to introduce a more critical understanding of educational exclusion. Bilgeri's chapter uses a capabilities' approach lens, while that of Smith critically examines definitions of risk and vulnerability in the context of crisis.

Three chapters are summarized under Part 2 of the book titled Teaching and Learning under the Shadow of a Global Pandemic: Exclusions and Possibilities. In this part, Gunnþórsdóttir and Sigurðardóttir provide insights into challenges in teaching and learning focusing on the student–teacher perspective in Iceland, while

Lindner and others outline possibilities for inclusive home-schooling in Austria, and Guerini and colleagues consider anew the possibilities of distance learning.

Addressing social exclusion and highlighting possible ways out, Part 3 – Addressing Social Exclusion: Illuminating Possibilities for Inclusion in and through Crisis – is made up of three chapters. In 'A Widening Inequality Gap: Reducing Educational Inequalities by Reaching Out to Students and Families at Risk During a Time of Crisis and Beyond', Spiteri offers insights into the advantages of working with parents to improve educational inequalities. The two other contributions look into poverty: Mowat focuses on mental health aspects, while Folostina and Patrascoiu elaborate preventive measures in the context of Romania.

The inclusion of excluded groups is at the core of the Part 4 of the book. It is titled: Including Excluded Individuals and Communities in Times of Crisis. Drown's chapter takes disadvantaged groups in Romania into consideration, while Barber, McIntyre and Mngaza each contribute important insights into the education of young people with refugee or migration backgrounds.

Part 5 refers to 'Disability and Crises' and includes chapters by Cioè-Peña and Schauwer and others, who consider a content-based focus on the issue of disability in times of crises.

Finally, the book is brought to a close by Watt in a concluding chapter that simultaneously echoes the major themes of this collection while offering a distinctive contribution to what it means to education in times of crisis and what we may still hope for in an altered world.

References

Arendt, H. (1993), *The Crisis in Education. In between Past and Future: Eight Exercises in Political Thought* (pp. 173–96). New York: The Viking Press.

Arnove, R. F. (2020), 'Imagining What Education Can Be Post-COVID-19', *Prospects*, 49: 43–6.

Azorín, C. (2020), 'Beyond COVID-19 Supernova. Is Another Education Coming?' *Journal of Professional Capital and Community*, 5(3/4): 381–90.

Boyraz, G., Legros, D. N. and Tigershtrom, A. (2020), 'COVID-19 and Traumatic Stress: The Role of Perceived Vulnerability, COVID-19-Related Worries, and Social Isolation', *Journal of Anxiety Disorders*, 76: 1–9.

Coleman, V. (2021), *Digital Divide in UK Education during COVID-19 Pandemic: Literature Review*, Research Report. Cambridge Assessment. Available at: https://files.eric.ed.gov/fulltext/ED616296.pdf (accessed 30 September 2022).

Giannini, S., and Lewis, S. (2020), 'Three Ways to Plan for Equity during the Coronavirus School Closures', *World Education Blog*, 25 March 2020. Available at: https://gemreportunesco.wordpress.com/2020/03/25/three-ways-to-plan-for-equity-during-the-coronavirus-school-closures/ (accessed 30 September 2022).

Hargreaves, A. (2020), 'What's Next for Schools after Coronavirus? Here Are 5 Big Issues and Opportunities'. (theconversation.com): 1–8 (accessed 30 September 2022).

Liu, J. (2021), 'Bridging Digital Divide amidst Educational Change for Socially Inclusive Learning during the COVID-19 Pandemic', *Sage Open*, 11(4). Available at: https://journals.sagepub.com/doi/epub/10.1177/21582440211060810 (accessed 30 September 2022).

Mukumbang, F. C., Ambe, A. N., and Adebiyi, B. O. (2020), 'Unspoken Inequality: How COVID-19 Has Exacerbated Existing Vulnerabilities of Asylum-Seekers, Refugees, and Undocumented Migrants in South Africa', *International Journal of Equity Health*, 19: 141, https://doi.org/10.1186/s12939-020-01259-4.

Obermayr, T., Subasi Singh, S., Kremsner, G., Koenig, O., and Proyer, M. (2021), 'Revisiting Vulnerabilities – Auswirkungen der Pandemie auf die (Re) Konstruktion von Vulnerabilität*en im Kontext von Bildung', in S. Krause, I. M. Breinbauer and M. Proyer (eds), *Corona bewegt – auch die Bildungswissenschaft. Bildungswissenschaftliche Reflexionen aus Anlass einer Pandemie*, 137–52, Bad Heilbrunn: Verlag Julius Klinkhardt.

Reay, D. (2020), 'English Education in the Time of Coronavirus', *Forum*, 62(3): 311–22.

Reimers, F. M. (2022), 'Learning from a Pandemic. The Impact of COVID-19 on Education around the World', in F. M. Raimers (ed.), *Primary and Secondary Education during COVID-19*, 1–37, Cham: Springer.

Stanistreet, P., Elfert, M., and Atchoarena, D. (2020), 'Education in the Age of COVID-19: Understanding the Consequences', *International Review of Education*, 66: 627–33.

Tso, W. W. Y., Rosa S. Wong, Keith T. S. Tung, Nirmala Rao, King Wa Fu, Jason C. S. Yam, Gilbert T. Chua, Eric Y. H. Chen, Tatia M. C. Lee, Sherry K. W. Chan, Wilfred H. S. Wong, Xiaoli Xiong, Celine S. Chui, Xue Li, Kirstie Wong, Cynthia Leung, Sandra K. M. Tsang, Godfrey C. F. Chan, Paul K. H. Tam, Ko Ling Chan, Mike Y. W. Kwan, Marco H. K. Ho, Chun Bong Chow, Ian C. K. Wong, and Patrick lp et al. (2020), 'Vulnerability and Resilience in Children during the COVID-19 Pandemic', *European Child & Adolescent Psychiatry*, 31: 1–16.

UNESCO. (2020a), 'COVID-19 Educational Disruption and Response'. Available: at https://en.unesco.org/covid19/educationresponse (accessed 17 May 2022).

UNESCO. (2020b), 'Five Steps to Support Education for All in the Time of COVID-19', 9 April 2020. Available at: http://www.iiep.unesco.org/en/five-steps-support-education-all-time-covid-19-13382 (accessed 17 May 2022).

Viner, R. M., Russell, S. J., Croker, H., Packer, J., Ward, J., Stansfield, C., Mytton, O., Bonell, C., and Booy, R. (2020), 'School Closure and Management Practices during Coronavirus Outbreaks Including COVID-19: A Rapid Systematic Review',

Lancet, 4: 397–404. 6 April 2020. Available at: https://doi.org/10.1016/ S2352-4642(20)30095-X (accessed 30 September 2022).

Weale, S. (2021), 'Ofsted Gets Thousands of Emails Praising Schools after Minister's Remarks', *Guardian*, 12 January. Available at: https://www.theguardian.com/world/2021/jan/11/ofsted-gets-thousands-of-emails-praising-schools-after-ministers-remarks (accessed 10 October 2022).

Zhao, Y. (2020), 'COVID-19 as a Catalyst for Educational Change', *Prospects*, 49: 29–33.

Part 1
Critical Understandings of Educational Exclusion and Crisis

1

The Meaning of Collective Capabilities for the Education of Refugee Children during a Pandemic

Margarita Bilgeri

Introduction

The chapter focuses on education in light of the capability approach. It goes on to engage in a short discussion about children and agency, and a more specific view on different forms of agency, before discussing jeopardizing aspects and new resources from a capability perspective. These aspects are then reflected and concluded on in the last part of the chapter.

The UNHCR states that the educational situation for refugee children was already highly problematic before Covid-19: '… If you were a refugee child before the pandemic, you were already at a grave disadvantage – twice as likely to be out of school as a non-refugee child' (2020b: 5). This underlines the severity of the current situation for refugee children and their education.

Looking at different challenges that have accumulated since the outbreak of the pandemic in 2020 around the world, I focus on vulnerable children who are additionally challenged by the consequences of forced migration and the Covid-19 pandemic in the context of education.

> Children are simultaneously in processes of being and becoming. This requires a balancing of their interests as vulnerable beings and as competent and active agents in their lives and those of others. The school, as a primary sphere in which many children develop, grow and learn, plays a fundamental role in framing how this balance between protection and participation plays off. (Hart and Brando 2018: 294)

The lack of possibilities to receive education and participate in the social environment which schools usually offer will lead to a general lack of possibilities of participation and protection. Children can be active agents for their own education and well-being if the circumstances are favourable. In this context Hart and Brando (2018) discuss issues around well-being and the choices of children. They ask, for instance, to what extent children are able to make thought-out decisions. At the same time, they take into consideration the fact that every child is different, and 'the possibility that children may unwittingly compromise their well-being or not fully understand the consequences of their choices and actions in the short or longer term' (2018: 296). For this chapter it is essential to consider the fact that the children in focus have experienced multiple extreme situations and that most of them will have suffered traumas. The UNHCR (2020a) states that more than half of all refugees are children and most of them are separated from their families. 'They may have witnessed or experienced violent acts and, in exile, are at risk of abuse, neglect, violence, exploitation, trafficking or military recruitment' (UNHCR 2020a). On the other hand, the UNHCR (2020a) emphasizes the resilience of children and refers to families and communities as the children's resources to cope with extreme situations. We do not have exact knowledge of the consequences which these experiences have for the children's decisions and how these affect their well-being and quality of life in the context of education. Even though most refugee children are without their families, community as such remains an essential factor that can support children in difficult situations.

Following this argumentation, this chapter concentrates on communities and groups as conversion factors and/or spaces for developing collective agency and collective capabilities. These capabilities aim at supporting children in difficult situations and focus especially on the context of education.

Education

Historically, education for all and inclusive education started with a focus on learners with disabilities. Today education for all as well as inclusive education usually refer to all learners and especially to those who experience the risk of being excluded or disadvantaged.

> Although Salamanca's rights-based anti-discriminatory stance was primarily in support of learners with special needs, the idea of an inclusive educational

system, where all were welcome and no one was excluded, had broad appeal. Over time, the conceptualisation of inclusive education was broadened to encompass anyone who might be excluded from or have limited access to the general educational system within a country. In this way Salamanca foreshadowed current ideas of inclusive education as being about everyone. (Florian 2019: 691)

From this perspective, children with a refugee background are among those students who must be especially considered in terms of inclusive education. 'Despite the existence of a general right to education for migrant children, obstacles to securing it in practice are common' (Bhabha 2009: 440). This endangers refugee children in different ways: while psychologically it is undebatable that the children live a very difficult life far away from home and family, educationally it puts their future at risk if they cannot (regularly) attend school and continue or start their education in the same way as their peers, even though children worldwide had and still have limited access to education due to the pandemic. Education does not only influence economic aspects of the future lives of these children, but it also determines and influences the children – as persons and as members of (a global) society – and their capabilities. In other words, education to a great extent sets the course for what someone will be able to do and to be. With this in mind, it is important not to reduce the purpose of education to economic achievements.

When criticizing Nussbaum's work on capabilities in her book *Creating Capabilities* (2011), Ingrid Robeyns refers to education as one example of aspects that are not considered appropriately:

> Economists typically conceptualize and value education as an investment in human capital. The capabilitarian conceptualization of education is different. It looks at what education means for a life that is composed of many different dimensions and sees education as a contribution to the development of the kind of person one will become and the types of things one will be able to do. (Robeyns 2016: 399)

Robeyns still sees the importance of skills for the labour market, but adds that skills are related to 'the formation of one's character, the cultivation of moral virtues, and an appreciation of culture in all its dimensions' (Robeyns 2016: 399). For this chapter it is important to include the dimensions which were added by Robeyns. Even though Nussbaum writes explicitly about the importance of non-economic aspects of education, she does not include it as one way of capabilitarian theorizing. Robeyns (2016: 399) suggests including the conceptualization of education as one type of the latter.

When considering education as one essential contributing factor to the development of a child, well-being must be seen as multidimensional. One of these dimensions can be found in different possibilities to choose from, which are opened up through not only education as a capability, but also education as a functioning by itself. In relation to Hart and Brando's (2018) view of children as being in a process of being and becoming at the same time, the example of education illustrates this aspect quite well. This is the reason education must receive special attention. It is a stage in the life of children (and continues throughout the different stages of life) where they are growing in the sense of acquiring knowledge, *feeding* their curiosity and learning to understand the world around them. Especially when thinking about *understanding the world*, children who are especially in danger of educational exclusion because of experiences of flight, displacement, armed conflict and so on, the world around them becomes much more complex and much more difficult to understand and to cope with. In this sense, education takes over more than 'only one' important role. In other words: 'Education is regarded as a core capability, fundamental to enhancing other capabilities and well-being. Yet, education capabilities may not necessarily be agency or well-being enhancing if they do not identify and alter the forms of social relations that marginalize young people' (Dejaeghere 2020: 17). Dejaeghere (2020) specifically points out the importance of having possibilities to influence social relations through the capability of education. This influence, in consequence, can work against marginalization of young people and towards (social) inclusion. The significance of education in the context of disadvantage and vulnerability becomes explicit here. The quotation also mentions agency in the context of education and well-being. It is not the first time that this term appears in the paper, and it might not be surprising that agency and agency freedom play an important role in the discussion around well-being, education, vulnerability, capabilities and community. The following two sections elaborate on the relationship between these terms.

Agency and Children

Amartya Sen (1992) describes agency freedom in relation to a person's values and achievements. He states that it is about the possibilities which a person has to achieve the things she values (Sen, 1992: 57). As a consequence, agency achievement defines reaching goals we value, which are not necessarily related to our own well-being (Hart and Brando 2018; Sen 1992). This argument is related to the earlier discussion about children deciding for themselves and the possible consequences of traumatic experiences for certain decisions concerning their well-being. Sen identifies different challenges related to children and decisions which are often taken for them by others:

> There is a special problem in the case of children, since they do not, frequently enough, take their own decisions. If rights are interpreted in terms of freedoms that the right-holders should have, their usefulness must depend on how those freedoms are exercised. But can children take their own decisions? If the application of human rights to children must involve the children themselves taking well-considered decisions on the exercise of those freedoms, then we would seem to be on the threshold of a manifest contradiction. Can children really take these decisions? But is that the right question? (2007: 243)

The dilemma which Sen addresses here reveals the problems we face when talking about not only the personal agency of children, but also agency that is taken by others for some groups. If it is not the right question to ask if children can take these decisions, the better question might be: 'Are the decisions taken (by children or by others) really contributing to the children's well-being and their quality of life?'

As the capability approach has a focus on possibilities and the freedom of choice in relation to well-being, we very quickly get to a point where we start discussing the appropriacy of individual values. This leads to difficult debates especially in regard to children.

Ingrid Robeyns takes a clear stance in this dilemma by referring to the concept of agency-capacity: 'If we have a strong reason to believe that agency-capacity cannot be attributed to a person, we should not let the person make decisions by herself' (Robeyns 2016: 401). As a solution, Robeyns suggests that someone make the choices for this person or support the person in the choice-making process (Robeyns 2016). One way of supporting children in their choices and agency is to focus on possibilities that are created by certain choices and on doors that close by going through others. With possible pictures of future scenarios, children can be supported in taking decisions about their own well-being in simultaneously 'being' and 'becoming'. Relational agency (Edwards 2005) is an essential capacity to be able to give this kind of support.

Different Forms of Agency: Relational Agency and Collective Agency

We can differentiate between different forms of agency, one of which is 'relational agency'. Edwards sees relational agency as 'a capacity to align one's thought and actions with those of others in order to interpret problems of practice and to respond to those interpretations' (2005: 169–70). This means that relational agency is in line with the values and needs of other people. Hence, relational agency addresses the problematic aspect of agency that might oversee or fail to follow the individual or collective needs and values of other persons. Edwards speaks of negotiations that take place while the individual constantly enriches her understanding. At the same time learning is seen as systemic change. 'The argument, in summary, is that we transform the world through first interpreting and then acting on the basis of our interpretations' (Edwards 2005: 173). But how can we relate this theoretical perspective to the educational needs of a refugee child? As this chapter focuses on groups and communities as the basis of educational support for refugee children and the development of capabilities during the pandemic, it emphasizes the importance of collective actions and the additional values of communities.

Edwards argues that relational agency puts an emphasis on joint action rather than on the system. Joint action, as a consequence, enables a focus on individual learning. Edwards also identifies certain possibilities: 'In joint action a wider range of concepts or other resources are likely to be deployed on the object or problem space than is the case with individual action and it is more likely that the object is expanded' (Edwards 2005: 174). What is essential here is that finally the focus is not placed on individual change but on the transformation of a system. In other words, through relational agency we activate more resources, concepts and possibilities for the child by focusing on joint action than we would if we were to focus on individual ways regarding the problem of education for refugees during the pandemic.

Adding the concept of collective capabilities at this point enriches the argumentation for including a capabilitarian perspective in relation to the problematic situation created by the pandemic and forced migration for lots of children.

> Gaining the freedom to do the things that we have reason to value is rarely something we can accomplish as individuals. For those already sufficiently privileged to enjoy a full range of capabilities, collective action may seem superfluous to capability, but for the less privileged attaining development as freedom requires collective action. (Evans 2002: 56)

Education can be seen as one important aspect in the context of development as freedom. Evans puts an emphasis on the importance of communities and groups for achieving certain goals which are usually valued by all members. He later also mentions the intrinsic importance and the intrinsic satisfaction that comes through social interaction with family, community and groups which share values and interests (Evans 2002).

D'Amato (2020) in his recent paper on collectivist capabilitarianism discusses very comprehensively the aspects of individual agency and other individualistic features of the capability approach and criticism related to the individualism in the approach. The part which is relevant for the chapter at hand starts with his conceptualization of a collectivist capabilitarianism. The capabilities referred to by D'Amato are collectivist capabilities in the sense that they are of value for a group and not for an individual. 'Some contemporary social justice movements explicitly frame their key values in collective terms, rejecting the individualism of the (neo-)liberal practices they oppose in favour of a stronger communal ethic. This matters to collectivist capabilitarianism insofar as such movements seek to increase the capabilities of entire collectives' (2020: 110).

When looking at refugee children during the pandemic, it seems indispensable to act collectively for ensuring regular quality education. This would help prevent them from further negative experiences. The capabilities that can be created through acting collectively can be related to education, to possibilities of receiving education and to possibilities of demanding quality education. Thereby, a group is by no means restricted to refugee children only, but can be composed of individuals from different (vulnerable) backgrounds.

'Since the poor suffer from limitations on their individual capabilities and agency, they engage in acts of collective agency to generate new collective capabilities that each individual alone would not be able to achieve' (Ibrahim 2017: 197). Talking about 'the poor' as one group must be viewed critically. The argument could be rephrased into 'groups of vulnerable people'. However, Ibrahim in her paper asks how these processes can be initiated, supported and sustained. This question will also be addressed in the following section.

Jeopardizing Aspects and New Resources

In the introduction it was mentioned that I will be concentrating on jeopardizing aspects and at the same time focusing on new resources to support educational efforts for refugee children. These new resources should, as a consequence, enable children to use their own resources in new ways or activate certain new resources.

To start with jeopardizing aspects, some were already discussed earlier. We know that the environmental conditions for refugee children during the pandemic have a negative influence on their education in many ways. Looking at a literature review covering publications from the year 2020 (European Agency 2021) about the influence of Covid-19 on education in Europe conducted in the year 2020, we find only a few mentions of refugee children. Identified aspects from the literature were related to higher risks of dropping out (especially for girls), the problem of low probabilities of returning to school and issues of language (European Agency 2021). As for recommendations, the review only found 'support for immigrant/refugee learners through WhatsApp groups' as a suggestion that was directly related to refugee children (European Agency 2021: 37).

We know that households with poor socio-economic backgrounds faced more difficulties in providing students with the necessary digital environments than other households. In June 2020 the UNHCR organized a conference on 'the impact of COVID-19 on refugee education' (2020b). But already before the pandemic, the UNHCR reported about the low chances of refugee children attending school at all (UNHCR 2019). This, together with the effects of the Covid-19 crisis, makes education for refugee children an enormous challenge.

However, a crisis usually also offers – albeit limited – new possibilities, which lead us to new resources. Digitalization, for instance, can offer the possibility of automated translations of text material. It also opens possibilities for a Universal Design for Learning approach (e.g. Hall, Meyer and Rose 2012) which can enhance accessibility.

From a capability perspective, the environmental conversion factors play an essential role in this context as they convert resources into capabilities. In the case of digitalization of education, collective capabilities can support (refugee) children in overcoming the digital divide in matters of digital skills, digital environments and digital learning. Rosignoli (2018) makes a clear distinction between collective and external capabilities. External capabilities can be achieved, for instance, with the support of others (Foster and Handy 2008). In the case of children, it is usually a parent who will support them to reach certain capabilities. Collective capabilities are capabilities that are of value for the whole group and that can only be reached by the group as a whole.

Hence, children might already have resources or capabilities through their different experiences with digital tools. However, a community might be able to develop collective capabilities and use peer learning to support accessibility and so on. Groups and communities might also be able to organize digital devices and in this way support access to education for individuals, which might be more difficult to organize for parents or caretakers alone. The UNHCR states: 'Engagement with communities is also key to understanding the extent to which refugees have access to the home-based learning programmes introduced by governments' (2020c: 2). Such an exchange with communities makes problems and challenges more transparent and enables the wider community to act and support children appropriately.

The collective capabilities that are created through this support can be identified as general possibilities to participate in educational, social and political processes. In other words, it leads to having knowledge and a standing in society, being able to contribute to political discussions and working towards the change of structures and systems. Thereby, it is by no means to be taken for granted that a community exists of people with refugee background only. A community in this context may consist of different stakeholders, including not only refugee children, but also NGOs, social workers, people from the local community and so on. This, in turn, enhances the accessibility of further valuable collective, and individual, capabilities through quality education.

Also, Stewart (2005) argues in favour of giving groups a more central role in the capability approach. His arguments follow aspects of empowerment, efficiency and reducing inequalities through adequate policies to finally enhance valuable capabilities. For him there are three reasons why groups are important for the individual well-being:

- 'Because group membership and group achievements affect people's sense of well-being.
- Because groups are important instrumentally in determining efficiency and resource shares.
- Because groups influence values and choices, and hence the extent to which individuals choose to pursue valuable capabilities for themselves and for others' (Stewart 2005: 190).

These three reasons are meaningful for the education of refugee children during the pandemic, above all because groups can ensure that children give importance to their own education (influencing values and choices), by opening up possibilities to participate in education (sharing resources) and by having the necessary basis (well-being) for pursuing education in a sustainable way.

Groups and communities provide lots of possibilities for individuals to enhance their well-being. It is important, however, to clearly differentiate between the positive effects which being part of a group can have as such – external capabilities and collective capabilities. The feeling of belonging to a group clearly has positive effects on refugee children also. It can enhance their well-being and self-esteem. This in consequence can influence their capabilities. External capabilities, like supporting capabilities of parents or friends, can enhance the transformation of individual resources into capabilities and in that way contribute to a person's well-being. Groups, for example, can influence the values which someone thinks are important. These values again will determine which capabilities are important to that person. Collective capabilities can enhance the well-being of a whole group and in this way also enhance the individual quality of life.

Rosignoli (2018) defined two categories of collective capabilities: resistant capability and resilient capability. The first one refers to the 'collective ability to resist to structural injustices, such as top-down decisions imposed by authorities upon groups'. The second one is defined as the 'collective ability to react constructively to structural injustices, including collective actions taken by groups aimed at expanding their freedoms' (Rosignoli 2018: 830). The author kept these definitions very broad to allow community-based definitions of 'concrete actions realizing collective capabilities' (Rosignoli 2018: 830). Thus, collective capabilities can provide new resources to refugee children to receive quality education, which is a human right. Thereby, resisting and reacting to structural injustices is one of the most important steps towards implementing the right to education for refugee children.

Conclusion

The Covid-19 pandemic made disadvantages in education even more visible. Refugee children are especially vulnerable in such an extreme situation where the intersection of forced migration, most likely poverty, trauma, health and other factors limit children's capabilities and functionings. For their well-being in the present and in the future, receiving education is of utmost importance. School is not only a place to learn different subjects, but also a place where socio-emotional development takes place. Education influences very strongly what someone will be able to do and to be.

By looking at collective capabilities, collective agency and relational agency, this chapter focused on a theoretical perspective of how to open up educational possibilities for refugee children in times of pandemics or other extreme situations through the lens of the capability approach. Using the resources of different groups to reactivate (educational) possibilities is a necessary capability to which children with a refugee background must be enabled.

This chapter hence identified the possibility of being part of a group or community and contributing to, as well as benefiting from, collective capabilities as an essential capability for refugee children.

The Covid-19 pandemic on the one hand challenged an already very difficult situation. On the other hand, it opened some doors. Taking the example of digitalization, the pandemic challenged the educational system to find new ways for implementing the teaching–learning process. One of the problems that goes hand in hand with the pandemic is the unpreparedness of educational systems for remote teaching and learning. In the future, however, the use and development of digital tools, didactics and methods could be seen as a positive development that was accelerated through the pandemic. Nonetheless, attending school in person and possibilities of face-to-face interaction must be considered as a priority in the teaching–learning process. Personal interaction and the satisfaction of socio-emotional needs cannot be compensated online.

The capability approach with its focus on possibilities to choose from, on beings and doings which one has reason to value, opens a new perspective on educational possibilities for refugee children when groups are put into focus instead of the individual. Referring to resistant and resilient capabilities, collective capabilities can provide refugee children with the necessary basis for the opportunity to receive quality education. Changing structural injustices through the development of collective capabilities creates spaces where disadvantaged groups can gain ground. Collective actions as well as collective and relational agency can establish an environment for refugee children in which quality education is possible, even during a pandemic.

References

Bhabha, J. (2009), 'Arendt's Children: Do Today's Migrant Children Have a Right to Have Rights?', *Human Rights Quarterly*, 31: 451.

D'Amato, C. (2020), 'Collectivist Capabilitarianism', *Journal of Human Development and Capabilities*, 21(2): 105–20.

Dejaeghere, J. G. (2020), 'Reconceptualizing Educational Capabilities: A Relational Capability Theory for Redressing Inequalities', *Journal of Human Development and Capabilities*, 21(1): 17–35.

Edwards, A. (2005), 'Relational Agency: Learning to Be a Resourceful Practitioner', *International Journal of Educational Research*, 43: 168–82.

European Agency for Special Needs and Inclusive Education. (2021), *The Impact of COVID-19 on Inclusive Education at the European Level: Literature Review*. (C. Popescu, ed.). Odense, Denmark.

Evans, P. (2002), 'Collective Capabilities, Culture, and Amartya Sen's *Development as Freedom*', *Studies in Comparative International Development*, 37: 60.

Florian, L. (2019), 'On the Necessary Co-existence of Special and Inclusive Education', *International Journal of Inclusive Education*, 23: 704.

Foster, J. E., and Handy, C. (2008), 'External Capabilities', OPHI working paper No. 08, Oxford: Oxford University Press.

Hall, T. E., Meyer, A., and Rose, D. H. (2012), *Universal Design for Learning in the Classroom: Practical Applications*. New York: Guilford Press.

Hart, C. S., and Brando, N. (2018), 'A Capability Approach to Children's Well-Being, Agency and Participatory Rights in Education', *European Journal of Education*, 53(3): 293–309.

Ibrahim, S. (2017), 'How to Build Collective Capabilities: The 3C-Model for Grassroots-Led Development', *Journal of Human Development and Capabilities: Special Issue on Social Innovation for Human Development*, 18: 222.

Nussbaum, M. C. (2011), *Creating Capabilities: The Human Development Approach*. Cumberland: The Belknap Press of Harvard University Press.

Robeyns, Ingrid. (2016), 'Capabilitarianism', *Journal of Human Development and Capabilities*, 17(3): 397–414.

Rosignoli, Francesca. (2018), 'Categorizing Collective Capabilities', *Partecipazione e Conflitto*, 11: 813–37.

Sen, A. (1992), *Inequality Reexamined*. New York: Oxford University Press.

Sen, A. (2007), 'Children and Human Rights', *Indian Journal of Human Development*, 1: 235–45.

Stewart, F. (2005), 'Groups and Capabilities', *Journal of Human Development*, 6(2): 185–204.

UNHCR. (2020a), 'Children', UNHCR. Available at: https://www.unhcr.org/children-49c3646c1e8.html (accessed 2 September 2020).

UNHCR. (2020b), 'Coming Together for Refugee Education. Education Report 2020', UNHCR. https://www.unhcr.org/5f4f9a2b4 (accessed 15 October 2020).

UNHCR. (2020c), 'Supporting Continued Access to Education during COVID-19. Emerging Promising Practices', UNHCR https://www.unhcr.org/5ea7eb134.pdf (accessed 20 April 2021).

UNHCR. (2019), '"Flüchtlingsbildung in der Krise": Mehr als die Hälfte aller Flüchtlingskinder kann nicht in die Schule gehen', UNHCR. Available at: https://www.unhcr.org/dach/de/34228-fluechtlingsbildung-in-der-krise-mehr-als-die-haelfte-aller-fluechtlingskinder-kann-nicht-in-die-schule-gehen.html (accessed 3 December 2020).

2

Covid-19 Exposing the Fault Lines of Inclusion: The 'Risk' and 'Vulnerability' of Disabled Children in the UK

Sharon Smith

Introduction

The idea of some children being 'at risk' is now an accepted part of schooling in the UK. With Covid-19, every pupil is suddenly at risk of actual harm, of future underachievement and their physical presence potentially increases risk to others, resulting in an explicit focus on risk management in education. The 'at-risk' label can no longer be relied on alone to justify specialist interventions or separate school placements. Therefore, those previously deemed to be 'at risk' have additionally been labelled as 'vulnerable', even though they might be no more vulnerable to Covid-19. The combination of being 'at risk' and vulnerable provides further justification for individual intervention and separate forms of education, under the guise of protection. Simultaneously, schools are introducing risk-management practices or policies, designed to protect the whole school population, which can lead to the further isolation or exclusion of pupils categorized as having Special Educational Needs or Disabilities (SEND).

Brown claims that the 'deployment of vulnerability' in policy remains uninterrogated and receives little scrutiny, despite a more complicated picture being revealed when there is closer attention given to the 'exceptional treatment' of individuals labelled as vulnerable (Brown 2017: 2). During the Covid-19 crisis, there was a noticeable shift in UK education policy, moving from referring to some pupils as 'at risk' to a pandemic response which focused on protective measures to keep 'vulnerable' students safe. Education settings were required to identify 'vulnerable' children and young people in their setting, and if these pupils also had Education, Health and Care Plans (EHCPs) they needed to undertake individual risk assessments (DfE 2020b). This shift in discourse from 'at-risk' to 'vulnerable' pupils could therefore present an opportune moment to not only critique the use of risk in relation to students categorized as having SEND, but also to think about the implications of the use of the vulnerable label in relation to their education too. The concept of vulnerability also 'stretches well beyond the UK', as a 'vital ingredient for understanding care and social control mechanisms across local, national, regional and global contexts' (Brown 2017: 173). Therefore, while this chapter specifically draws on interventionist UK policy and practice, its theoretical approach has significance for thinking about the inclusion of all disabled children and those categorized with Special Education Needs (SEN) in its call for a rethinking of approaches to risk and vulnerability in education.

The chapter is split into five sections. In the first two sections, I explore risk and vulnerability as seen during the Covid-19 pandemic. I then discuss the risk discourse and how this leads to a temporal shift in power over the future of pupils with SEND, followed by a discussion about risk and vulnerability, which argues that a shift in emphasis from risk to vulnerability – as seen during the Covid-19 pandemic – allows even greater control over futures, as it is more pervasive while being hidden under a veil of concern. The final section will discuss ethical responses to vulnerability and how it is necessary to understand the conditions that create risk and vulnerability within education.

Covid-19 Risk-Based Responses

During the Covid-19 pandemic, discussions and calculations of risk have become commonplace. Through an understanding of the heterogeneities of risk, the Covid-19 response could 'focus resources and actions on those most susceptible to severe disease, who are a fraction of the total number of people considered at risk' – allowing targeted interventions rather than a one-size-fits-all approach centred on the 'misconception that everyone is at equal risk of severe illness' (Schwalbe, Lehtimai and Gutiérrez 2020: 974). This risk-based approach was evident within the UK government's response to the pandemic, as protection measures were based on understandings of 'risk levels in different parts of the population – both risk to self and risk to others' (HM Government 2020: 36). To target social restrictions, the government relied on scientific 'data and evidence' to determine which groups of people might be more vulnerable to Covid-19 and who therefore should take additional precautions to reduce their risk of catching the virus (HM Government 2020: 36). Within the UK, approximately 2.5 million people were identified as 'most at risk of severe illness if they contract COVID-19' due to underlying health conditions. Accordingly, they were classified as 'clinically extremely vulnerable' and were required to 'shield', which meant to stay at home and avoid all face-to-face contact (HM Government 2020: 36). Additionally, a significant number of people were classed as 'clinically vulnerable' and should minimize contact with people outside of their household (HM Government 2020: 37).

The UK government also set out wide-ranging guidance to help 'support people to understand their risk' (HM Government 2020: 36). Individuals were encouraged to 'take responsible risk judgements and operate in a way that is safe for themselves and for others' (HM Government 2020: 45), with a range of measures based on the 'best available scientific theory' (HM Government 2020:4 1). As Dryhurst and others describe, 'we know from past pandemics that the success of policies to slow down the rapid transmission of a highly infectious disease rely, in part, on the public having accurate perceptions of personal and societal risk factors' (Dryhurst et al. 2020: 995). Risk perception is therefore seen as a significant determinant of the public's willingness to make sacrifices in adopting health-protective behaviours, such as social distancing and staying at home (Dryhurst et al. 2020: 995,1003).

During the pandemic, everyone is at risk and simultaneously presents a risk and a threat to the safety of others. Risk factors came to inform how we think about ourselves and our relationship and interactions with others, as we negotiate different risks to protect ourselves and others from harm. However, this focus on risk management is neither new nor unique to the pandemic. Instead, the pandemic has merely highlighted how pervasive the concept of risk is in society and education today, through its now explicit and widespread use during the Covid-19 crisis. Beck describes how we now live in a 'risk society' where the 'basis and motive force' is safety and the need to protect everyone from the worst (Beck 1992: 49). Moving away from the driving force of need, fear and anxiety have become the driving force in our social epoch (Beck 1992: 49). Furedi describes how fearfulness has 'become our normal state' and is regarded as a 'sensible and responsible orientation towards the world' and furthermore this leads to the creation of the 'fearful subject', as the ascendency of fear has consequences both on behaviour and what it means to be a person (Furedi 2018: 177). He further claims that individuals are educated to become preoccupied with safety (Furedi 2018: 177–8). Individuals are expected to assess risks and decide how to respond to them, within a culture that emphasizes the need for protection (Furedi 2018: 179–88).

Vulnerable and At-Risk/Risky Pupils during Covid-19

Within the education response to Covid-19, the language of vulnerability and risk were entwined. In March 2020, schools were closed until further notice 'except for children of key workers and vulnerable children' (DfE, 2020a). Pupils specifically highlighted as being 'vulnerable' included those allocated to a social worker, looked-after children, young carers and pupils with the most complex SEND who have an EHCP. Schools were asked to identify their 'vulnerable' students and additionally were required to undertake an individual 'risk assessment' for students with SEND who had an EHCP (DfE 2020b).

Despite the automatic categorization of all pupils with an EHCP as 'vulnerable', instead of strengthening the legal protections relating to their education, health or care provision, the government diluted the statutory duties set out within this act. Consequently, the new reduced 'reasonable endeavours' duty was frequently interpreted as 'an optional extra' by schools, resulting in respite, therapies, equipment, direct payments/personal budgets, school transport and one-to-one support being withdrawn, which had a significant impact on the education of children with SEND during the Covid-19 pandemic (NNPCF 2020; SEND Community Alliance 2020). Parents of pupils categorized under SEND reported concern, confusion and anxiety due to the lack of clarity about how the 'vulnerable' label was being applied in practice, with some schools being reluctant to include their child in school (NNPCF 2020). Despite government guidance encouraging the attendance of 'vulnerable' pupils, the notion of safety and risk was frequently used in practice to justify the prevention of 'vulnerable' children from attending. School leaders described how they 'had to make very difficult decisions' about who to offer available places to, as they had to 'balance the risks of pupils being in school with the risks of them remaining at home' (Skipp 2021).

For schools that offered places during the lockdown, most 'said their focus was on childcare' rather than teaching (Skipp 2021). Additionally, for pupils with SEND who remained at home, there was an enormous disparity in the level and type of support that was offered (Smith 2021). Schools reported finding it 'more challenging' to provide a remote support offer for pupils with EHCPs, and parents found supporting home learning difficult (Skipp 2021). While some schools provided significant levels of differentiated and tailored support, many parents of children with SEND reported that their child was not receiving suitable remote education, and they felt 'utterly abandoned' as their children were unable to be educated with, or to the same standard, as their peers who do not have SEND (Smith 2021). Furthermore, risk assessments that detailed concerns about social distancing, personal care, transport and staffing ratios were being used by schools to justify why pupils with EHCPs were unable to attend education in person, despite the government guidance encouraging attendance in school (Skipp 2021; Tirraoro 2020a). Indeed, this practice has continued after schools have reopened, resulting in some children being unable to return to school after lockdown has ceased (Tirraoro 2020b). The educational response to the Covid-19 pandemic has therefore highlighted how the inclusion and education of pupils with SEND can be contingent on an individual setting's approach risk and vulnerability. Indeed, despite the rhetoric of protection, many students were left unsupported and without a suitable education due to risk management approaches during the Covid-19 pandemic lockdowns and beyond.

Risk-Free Education and the Calculable Future

The term 'risk' is understood, in everyday language, as a synonym for danger or peril; it 'designates an objective threat' (Ewald 1991: 199). Risk used to be associated with danger embodied within individuals capable of violent and unpredictable actions, insane people who carried a threat and who were subject to preventative technologies of confinement, excluded from society (Castel 1991: 283). However, during the 1990s, there was a shift in concern in UK child welfare policy and practice from those who were previously identified as being at high risk of abuse, to wider concerns about safeguarding and promoting the welfare of children to ensure optimum life chances and a successful transition to adulthood (Parton 2010: 53). Interventions are now required, not just to prevent harm, but to prevent a range of problems in later life, such as low educational achievement, crime, antisocial behaviour or unemployment (Parton 2010: 54).

In 2003, the Every Child Matters Green Paper was published, which led to a national programme designed to 'maximise opportunity and minimise risk' for all children from birth to nineteen (Ainslie et al. 2010: 24; DfES 2003: 2). The proposals were later implemented in policy and legislation in England through the 2004 Children Act. This represented a 'considerable broadening of the objects of concern from child abuse and significant harm to children and young people who are at risk of not fulfilling their potential' (Parton 2010: 59–60). The proposed reforms of children's services within Every Child Matters were based on a model derived from the public health approach of risk and protection-focused prevention, whereby a number of 'risk factors' are identified, and characteristics which forecast the probability of future negative outcomes (Parton 2010: 54) and interventions are provided to 'avoid future problems' (Parton 2010: 55). This demonstrates a shift in seeking to identify deficits or problems located within an individual, which require help and intervention to be overcome, to identifying a potential risk, which needs addressing before there is a deficit or problem. Interventions are no longer put in place to correct or train an individual now, but to manage their future.

Following Every Child Matters, a vast apparatus was 'erected to secure the well-being of the general population' (Tremain 2015: 14–15), and the 'risk factor model' became 'instrumental in promoting an interventionist strategy of risk reduction to be delivered by cross-agency childhood' (Armstrong 2005: 144). The 'at-risk' subject has emerged into discourse and social existence, through the idea of inclusive education, which 'is used to justify the growth of surveillance and management of troublesome populations' (Rose and Miller, cited in Armstrong 2005: 148). The idea of some children being 'at risk' is therefore now an accepted part of schooling in the UK, and risk has come to replace need as the core principle of educational policy (Armstrong 2005: 148–9). Policymakers, politicians, international organizations and the public are now seen to desire an education that is 'strong, secure, predictable, and risk-free' (Biesta 2016: 1–2). Rather than an education that recognizes that the future is undetermined and students are still becoming, which offers infinite possibilities – both positive and negative – there is currently an attempt to eradicate risk and a desire for 'total control over the educative process' (Biesta 2016: 146). The need for a risk-free education means some pupils have become caught within a discourse that marks them out as being 'at risk', leading to 'the adoption of risk averse policies and practices' (Seale 2015: 2). Potential risks need addressing *before* there is a problem, providing justification for interventions based on predicted future outcomes.

Beck describes how risks 'must always be imagined, implied to be true, believed' (Beck 1992: 28). This is because nothing 'is a risk in itself; there is no risk in reality', meaning that anything can be a risk, depending on what is determined as being a dangerous or unwanted outcome (Ewald 1991: 199). Therefore, to be a focus of any intervention to reduce risk, it is no longer necessary for an individual to 'manifest symptoms of dangerousness of abnormality, it is enough to display whatever characteristics the specialists responsible for the definition of preventative policy have constituted as risk factors' (Castel 1991: 288). Ewald asserts that 'there is no such thing as an individual risk', instead risk can only be determined by looking at the whole population and calculating an individual's risk relative to that of the rest of the population (Ewald 1991: 203). Each individual pupil will be observed, assessed and judged, following which their risks can be calculated (Foucault 1990: 143), distributing individuals in a 'network of relations' (Foucault 1990: 146), where they are compared to each other based on their determined level of risk. Therefore, there are always winners and losers in risk definitions (Beck 1992: 23), and it appears that children with SEN are often the losers, as they are identified as being at greatest 'risk' of negative outcomes in the future, as they struggle to meet the ever-increasing demands that are placed on them in a one-size-fits-all education system that is designed to produce a productive and autonomous workforce. Indeed, the SEND and 'at-risk' labels are often synonymous. Pupils who do not learn as quickly as the majority, or fail to meet the expected levels of progress, who are labelled as having SEND, are identified as being 'at risk of marginalisation, exclusion or underachievement', which results in them being 'carefully monitored' and necessary interventions introduced to 'ensure their presence, participation and achievement in the education system' (Ainscow 2004: 9). Risk has therefore become an established part of the vocabulary relating to children labelled with SEND. Any move from assessing need to assessing risk means that it is not necessary for a pupil to have existing 'deficits', or to be in immediate danger of harm from others; instead the use of risk allows the future to be predicted and interventions put in place to avoid potentially negative futures.

It is the specific nature of risk that allows the future to now be calculated, known and managed. Bialostock describes how risk thinking 'brings the future into the present and makes it calculable' and furthermore describes how the language of risk 'creates the belief in the transformability of a radically indeterminate world into a manageable one' (Bialostock 2015: 564). This creates an 'illusion of scientific objectivity' that implies that 'risks and the likelihood of their effect upon future behaviour can be measured and therefore controlled by appropriate early interventions' (Armstrong 2005: 145). Risk can therefore be understood as a 'primary technique of government' and 'form of disciplinary power', which works through and upon individuals to control their conduct (Bialostock 2015: 569). This shift has led to a new mode of 'systematic predetection' (Castel 1991: 288) within education that anticipates and prevents the emergence of undesirable outcomes. Disciplinary power has therefore extended temporally. It is no longer a case of 'advancing their progress by correcting their defects' (Foucault 1991: 179); rather the normalizing judgement has extended over what progress a child may make, based on their future being calculated and 'known' now, according to predetermined risk factors. This new risk-based approach has resulted in a new form of disciplinary power which has extraordinary scope (Castel 1991: 288), as it not only attempts to control the child in their actuality, but it now also focuses on what is becoming or might become.

Risk and Vulnerability

There are 'close links among the notions of risk, identity and vulnerability' (Delor and Hubert 2000: 1560). Indeed, vulnerability is 'a close conceptual cousin to risk' (Brown 2017: 15) and it too 'has become a sign of our times' (Rozmarin 2021: 1). Indeed, Beck describes how 'vulnerability and risk are two sides of the same coin' (Beck, in Brown 2017: 15). It is therefore not surprising that alongside risk discourses, vulnerability discourses have been evident in UK policy for many years, and that they likewise took on 'a new significance' from the late 1990s (Brown 2017: 9). For example, the notion that all children are vulnerable, but some are 'more vulnerable than others' featured heavily in the Every Child Matters initiative, and this continues to inform welfare services today (Brown 2017: 10,56,173).

However, despite the concepts of risk and vulnerability frequently being used interchangeably, Brown claims that the differences between the two have received little scholarly or critical attention, due to the 'somewhat porous and ill-defined dimensions of both concepts', which frequently overlap or have blurred boundaries (Brown 2017: 41). Unlike risk narratives, 'policies and practices that seek to help those who are considered to be vulnerable' speak to 'narratives of empathy and inclusion' and have 'strong moral overtones' as they are seen primarily as being based on a duty to 'assist and protect' those who are deserving of help and support (Brown 2017: 2,179). As a result, vulnerability 'appears to speak to a sense of social inclusion, empathy and sympathy in a way that risk does not' (Brown 2017: 16). As Brown explains, 'calling young people "vulnerable" is "better than saying the child is stupid or is neglected or deviant"' (Brown 2017: 179).

Hollomotz describes how approaching risk through the notion of vulnerability 'calls for exceptionalistic solutions, namely for the protection of the 'vulnerable' individual' (Hollomotz 2009: 110). The implication is that this population needs help and a cure, and individual responses to their vulnerability, which, of course, can serve to divert attention from the structural forces that are creating disadvantage and exclusion. This too can be attributed to the specific temporal nature of vulnerability, with its inherent suggestion of precariousness in the future as well as in the present (Brown 2017: 45). As a result, because 'of its determinedly prospective temporality, vulnerability lacks urgency and makes no immediate demand' (Cole 2016: 273). It is the emphasis of 'vulnerability as "potentiality"' that Cole claims 'obscures the (temporal) distinction between a general susceptibility to harm and the actual injuries that specific individuals and communities already endure' (Cole 2016: 265). As Scully describes, 'concentrating on the generality of vulnerability may distract from identifying with empirical rigour the particular conditions that make some people more vulnerable to harms than others, and this in turn makes it harder to do anything to change those particular conditions for the better' (Scully 2014: 206).

Furthermore, rather than vulnerability being a mechanism that requires a societal response that prioritizes resources for this population, it can simply trigger a sense of 'sympathy' (Brown 2017: 194). Vulnerability is also associated with immaturity, weakness, helplessness and passivity, which impacts on other people's attitudes towards disabled people (Scully 2014: 210). The danger of this is a sense that disabled people need to be looked after and protected, which Morris claims can take us 'back to those days when to be disabled was to be shut out, shut away from society, the object of pity, not part of mainstream society' (Morris 2015). Vulnerability can therefore trigger discriminatory social responses, as those labelled as such are segregated and treated differently from the majority who are seen as 'sufficiently invulnerable' to be able to make decisions about their own lives (Scully 2014: 206). While vulnerability might be a more 'palatable' concept than risk, identifying the 'vulnerable' can therefore be seen as a 'process of otherizing and essentializing' (Marino and Faas 2020: 34–6), as it operates to exclude those who are seen as the most vulnerable (Brown 2017: 174).

Individuals who are seen as situationally vulnerable – which implies they are deserving of help – are also simultaneously constructed as a problem to be managed in a 'juxtaposition of threat and vulnerability' (Brown 2017: 32). Indeed, this was possibly evident in relation to the education of students with SEND during the Covid-19 related school closures, as previously discussed. While all pupils were vulnerable to Covid-19, those identified as 'vulnerable' pupils were encouraged to attend school, where they faced increased risks of encountering Covid-19, suggesting that it was other vulnerabilities that were of concern to policymakers. Brown describes how, in practice, the notion of vulnerability 'reinforces and reaffirms concerns about those who do not conform to standards of the self-regulating, active and responsibilised citizen' (Brown 2017: 195). The implication is that these individuals not only require extra support and help, but also that they require extra control (Brown 2017: 33). As a result, this can lead to unwarranted and unjustified paternalistic policies based on notions of protection and safety (Rogers 2014).

Vulnerability has 'even more pronounced ethical connotations than risk' due to its links with compassion and responsibility (Brown 2017: 42). Despite its connotations of empathy and tenderness, vulnerability potentially has more 'controlling undertones' which 'could extend further than risk', as vulnerability is broader in scope and does not relate to a specific negative outcome that needs to be avoided (Brown 2017: 42). Therefore, the use of vulnerability rather than at-risk label could result in an even greater extension of power and control over an individual's future than if the concept of risk alone is relied on. However, like risk, it is this temporal dimension to vulnerability that might also provide us with the opportunity to approach vulnerability differently, with a more ethical response, which I will now discuss.

Vulnerability, Risk and an Ethical Response

As Beck describes, risks do not exist in and of themselves, instead they 'must always be imagined, implied to be true, believed' (Beck 1992: 28). Risks are constructed depending on what society deems to be undesirable future outcomes. Therefore, as risks are 'mathematical condensations of wounded images of a life worth living', Beck argues that it is necessary to ask, 'how do we wish to live?' which requires an 'ethical point of view' if risks can be discussed meaningfully at all (Beck 1992: 28-9). Given that students with SEND are not at risk because of anything that exists inherently within them, rather risks are determinations based on socially 'prescribed expectations and values' (Beck 1992: 29) which they are struggling to conform to, it is necessary to consider the use of risk in relation to pupils with SEND from an ethical perspective. Given its close links to risk, the same can be argued for the label of vulnerability.

Some theorists have argued that vulnerability is a universal feature of being human, something that we will all experience at various points in our life. Rather than seeing some groups as 'vulnerable' and in need of 'special safeguards, supports or services to protect them' it is possible to understand vulnerability as a feature of human ontology, where all humans are vulnerable to illness, injury or death (Scully 2014: 204–5). Indeed, it is such a notion of vulnerability that Kittay uses as the basis of her ethics of care (Kittay 1999: 54–5). Kittay argues that Goodin's 'vulnerability model with its emphasis on the response to need is the appropriate one for moral relations' (Kittay 1999: 73). Kittay's ethics of care expands the understanding of vulnerability that requires a moral response, to not only include the person 'in need of protection' but also to include the vulnerability of the person caring for them (Kittay 1999: 128). She argues that society has an obligation to support the 'dependency relationship' and the individuals within it, within a public ethic of care (Kittay 1999: 128). This ethical approach would require a 'commitment to the equality of *all*' based on a 'shared humanity which lies as much in our need to care for others and be attended to in caring relationships as in properties we possess as individuals' (Kittay 1999: 183). She further argues that it is necessary for 'genuine equality' to create a new vision and political will to recognize ourselves as both dependents and dependency workers, based on the relatedness of all citizens (Kittay 1999: 188). This approach to vulnerability 'shift[s] the focus from an ideal image of a hyper-individual to an image of a human subject who is part of embodied social relationships' and 'add[s] an important dimension to the understanding of care relations by regarding them as a site of interwoven vulnerabilities' (Rozmarin 2021: 2). However, Rozmarin argues, 'highlighting vulnerability as a shared human condition can lead to the banalisation and de-politicization of power structures and relations that yield vulnerabilities' (Rozmarin 2021: 2).

Cole presents a convincing argument that such an approach, which upholds 'vulnerability-as-harm and the more inclusive vulnerability-as-interconnectivity under a single designation … exacerbates the risk of conflating the two' (Cole 2016: 266). She further argues how an ethics of care, which foregrounds ontological vulnerability, can displace political claims and action (Cole 2016: 272). Grounding an ethical approach on 'the generality of vulnerability', as Scully also describes, 'may distract from identifying with empirical rigour the particular conditions that make some people more vulnerable to harms than others, and this in turn makes it harder to do anything to change those particular conditions for the better' (Scully 2014: 206). As Rozmarin describes, 'in the context of neoliberal ideologies that point to certain populations as vulnerable, this focus might lead to paternalism, and further marginalization of these groups through labelling them as "the vulnerable"' (Rozmarin 2021: 2). Furthermore, Scully argues that dependency should not be seen as vulnerability, rather individuals can become vulnerable when whatever they depend on is withdrawn (Scully 2014: 211).

In the case of pupils with SEND during the Covid-19 crisis, the lack of accessibility features in online learning, the withdrawal of vital therapies and the downgrading of legal protections were all factors which created greater vulnerabilities, while under a rhetoric of care and protection. Vital services and support that children, young people and their families relied on were withdrawn during Covid-19 lockdowns and school closures, and have been slow to return to pre-pandemic levels, resulting in worsening conditions and more complex needs (Lunt 2021: 9). Lunt (2021) reports how the continuation of approaches that were introduced during the Covid-19 pandemic as protective measures are having a longer-term impact on pupils with SEND, for instance the continued use of 'bubbles', social distancing, staff absences and reduced or part-time timetables (Lunt 2021: 19–23). Furthermore, she describes how there is an increase in anxiety, a lack of trust, poor communication and ongoing delays in diagnosis and assessment (Lunt 2021: 19–23). The UK government has set up an education recovery plan to support education recovery and children and young people's well-being, which includes a tutoring programme to address impacts on progress and attainment, summer schools and training for teachers (DfE 2021). The focus for those with SEND is to 'catch up' (DfE 2021: 11), within a recovery plan that continues to focus on vulnerable pupils, rather than any consideration of why some pupils are labelled as vulnerable, or the inaccessible barriers in society that children, young people and their families face or how Covid-19 responses might have increased barriers and inequalities within education and wider society.

It is evident that we currently lack a clear understanding of 'which vulnerabilities are important, or exactly what duties are thereby entailed' (Rogers 2014: 76). Therefore, while 'everyone is vulnerable to harm by virtue of human embodiment' it is necessary for us to recognize how 'this harm may be caused or exacerbated by social, political, and environmental features' (Rogers 2014: 76). It is clear that many students with SEND and their families lacked suitable education and support during the Covid-19 crisis and this is having a longer-term impact (Lunt 2021). Indeed, it could be argued that the pandemic merely shone a light on existing inequalities within the education system. When vulnerability seems to be inherent within an individual, it is possible for the wider society to dismiss the issue as an individual problem that simply requires additional protections to be put in place for that person. However, when vulnerability is understood as harm from an interaction of social, political and environmental features that result in inequalities it becomes a priority to understand and address these harms.

Marino and Faas argue that it is necessary to 'begin to articulate vulnerability in terms of the relationships and assemblages, which produce inequitable risk' (Marino and Faas 2020: 41). It is necessary to pose new questions which recognize different articulations of risk and vulnerability as 'contested sites of struggle' for different futures, alternative ways of being and versions of good to be pursued (Marino and Faas 2020: 41–2). They further argue that instead of seeing vulnerability as a subject or group of people who are at risk of harm, it is necessary to map out the assemblage of 'diverse subjects, institutions, materials, and meanings which produce inequitable risk' which perpetuates marginalization – a process which might not be comfortable but will allow alternative paths to come into view and alternative responses to risk to be conceived (Marino and Faas 2020: 34,43). Given the increased focus on risk and vulnerability during the Covid-19 pandemic, this feels more urgent than ever, especially in relation to how these concepts are used to mark out – and treat differently – vulnerable populations within education.

Conclusion

While being mindful of the fact that some people may well be more vulnerable during the Covid-19 pandemic and beyond due to impairment or existing health conditions – for instance, some pupils would face greater difficulties if they could not access specialist equipment and trained staff during the pandemic, or families might need access to respite to ensure their continued well-being – a blanket ascription of risk and vulnerability to all pupils with SEND can be a harmful process which results in the justification of interventions based on the rhetoric of safety and protection.

This chapter has therefore argued that it is necessary for us to see beyond labels of risk and vulnerability, to think about the wider societal conditions that create risky or uncertain subjects within education and to understand how the use of these concepts leads to a temporal extension of power over some pupils' futures, particularly those categorized with having SEND. We should not be using labels of risk and vulnerability unproblematically without this ethical discussion and debate, and without understanding the way that risk and vulnerability are labels attached to some pupils and not others. Rather, we need to recognize the implications of the growth of naming groups as vulnerable and the identification and management of risk and understand what social realities and possible futures they are creating for students with SEND.

References

Ainscow, M. (2004), *Developing Inclusive Education Systems: What Are the Levers for Change?* Available at: https://pdfs.semanticscholar.org/56b3/4d5a3c37c59cd25a3 14981afa9e88fa4cf1f.pdf (accessed 17 April 2018).

Ainslie, S., Foster, R., Groves, J., Grime K., Straker, K., and Woolhouse, C. (2010), '"Making Children Count": An Exploration of the Implementation of the Every Child Matters Agenda', *Education 3–13*, 38(1): 23–38.

Armstrong, D. (2005), 'Reinventing "Inclusion": New Labour and the Cultural Politics of Special Education Source', *Oxford Review of Education*, 31(1): 135–51.

Beck, U. (1992), *Risk Society: Towards a New Modernity.* Translated by M. Ritter. London: Sage Publications.

Bialostock, S. (2015), 'Risk Theory and Education: Policy and Practice', *Policy Futures in Education*, 13(5): 561–76.

Biesta, G. J. J. (2016), *The Beautiful Risk of Education.* Abingdon: Routledge.

Brown, K. (2017), *Vulnerability & Young People: Care and Social Control in Policy and Practice.* Bristol: Policy Press.

Castel, R. (1991), 'From Dangerousness to Risk', in G. Burchell, C. Gordon and P. Miller (eds), *The Foucault Effect: Studies in Governmentality.* Chicago: University of Chicago Press, 281–98.

Cole, A. (2016), 'All of Us Are Vulnerable, But Some Are More Vulnerable than Others: The Political Ambiguity of Vulnerability Studies, an Ambivalent Critique', *Critical Horizons*, 17(2): 260–77.

Delor, F., and Hubert, M. (2000), 'Revisiting the Concept of "Vulnerability"', *Social Science & Medicine,* 50: 1557–70.

Department for Education (DfE) (2020a), 'Schools, Colleges and Early Years Settings to Close', GOV.UK. 18 March 2020. Available at: https://www.gov.uk/government/news/schools-colleges-and-early-years-settings-to-close (accessed 11 July 2021).

Department for Education (DfE) (2020b), 'Supporting Vulnerable Children and Young People during the Coronavirus (COVID-19) Outbreak – Actions for Educational Providers and Other Partners'. Updated 15 May 2020. Available at: https://www.gov.uk/government/publications/coronavirus-COVID-19-guidance-on-vulnerable-children-and-young-people/coronavirus-COVID-19-guidance-on-vulnerable-child ren-and-young-people (accessed 29 April 2021).

Department for Education (DfE) (2021), 'Education Recovery: Support for Early Years Settings, Schools and Providers of 16–19 Education – June 2021'. Available at: https://assets.publishing.service.gov.uk/government/uploads/system/uploads/atta chment_data/file/993053/Education_recovery_support_June-2021.pdf (accessed 16 November 2021).

Department for Education and Skills (DfES) (2003), *Every Child Matters: Change for Children.* London: DfES Publications.

Dryhurst, S., Schneider, C. R., Kerr, J., Freeman, A. L. J., Recchia, G., Marthe van der Bles, A., Spiegelhalter, D., and van der Linden, S. (2020), 'Risk Perceptions of COVID-19 around the World', *Journal of Risk Research*, 23(7–8): 994–1006.

Ewald, F. (1991), 'Insurance and Risk', in G. Burchell, C. Gordon and P. Miller (eds), *The Foucault Effect: Studies in Governmentality*. Chicago: University of Chicago Press, 197–210.

Foucault, M. (1990), *The History of Sexuality: An Introduction*. London: Penguin Books.

Foucault, M. (1991), *Discipline and Punish: The Birth of the Prison*. London: Penguin Books.

Furedi, F. (2018), *How Fear Works: Culture of Fear in the 21st-Century*. London: Bloomsbury Publishing.

HM Government. (2020), 'Our Plan to Rebuild: The UK Government's COVID-19 Recovery Strategy', May 2020. Available at: https://assets.publishing.service.gov.uk/government/uploads/system/uploads/attachment_data/file/884760/Our_plan_to_rebuild_The_UK_Government_s_COVID-19_recovery_strategy.pdf (accessed 29 April 2021).

Hollomotz, A. (2009), 'Beyond "Vulnerability": An Ecological Model Approach to Conceptualizing Risk of Sexual Violence against People with Learning Difficulties', *The British Journal of Social Work*, 39(1): 99–112.

Kittay, E. F. (1999), *Love's Labor: Essays on Women, Equality and Dependency*. New York: Routledge.

Lunt, C. (2021), 'Then There Was Silence: The Impact of the Pandemic on Disabled Children, Young People and Their Families', Disabled Children's Partnership. Available at: https://disabledchildrenspartnership.org.uk/wp-content/uploads/2021/10/Then-There-Was-Silence-Full-Policy-Report-10-September-2021.pdf (accessed 16 November 2021).

Marino, E. K., and Faas, A. J. (2020), 'Is Vulnerability an Outdated Concept? After Subjects and Spaces', *Annals of Anthropological Practice*, 44(1): 33–46.

Morris, J. (2015), 'Please Don't Talk about the "Most Vulnerable"'. Available at: https://jennymorrisnet.blogspot.com/2015/09/please-dont-talk-about-most-vulnerable.html (accessed 7 March 2021).

NNPCF. (2020), 'Evidence to Inform the Education Commons Select Committee Impact of COVID-19 on Education and Children's Services Inquiry CIE0113'. Available at: https://committees.parliament.uk/writtenevidence/5745/html/ (accessed 11 July 2021).

Parton, N. (2010), '"From Dangerousness to Risk": The Growing Importance of Screening and Surveillance Systems for Safeguarding and Promoting the Well-Being of Children in England', *Health, Risk & Society*, 12(1): 51–64.

Rogers, W. (2014), 'Vulnerability and Bioethics', in C. Mackenzie, W. Rogers and S. Dodds (eds), *Vulnerability: New Essays in Ethics and Feminist Philosophy*, 60–87. New York: Oxford University Press.

Rozmarin, M. (2021), 'Navigating the Intimate Unknown: Vulnerability as an Affective Relation', *NORA – Nordic Journal of Feminist and Gender Research*. Available at: https://doi.org/10.1080/08038740.2021.1899284 (accessed 28 July 2021).

Schwalbe, N., Lehtimai, S., and Gutiérrez, J. P. (2020), 'COVID-19: Rethinking Risk', *The Lancet,* 8(8): 874–975. Available at: https://www.thelancet.com/journals/langlo/article/PIIS2214-109X(20)30276-X/fulltext (accessed 10 July 2021).

Scully, J. L. (2014), 'Disability and Vulnerability on Bodies, Dependence, and Power', in C. Mackenzie, W. Rogers and S. Dodds (eds), *Vulnerability: New Essays in Ethics and Feminist Philosophy*, 204–21. New York: Oxford University Press.

Seale, J. (2015), 'Negotiating Risk and Potential: What Role Can Positive Risk Taking Play in Promoting Excellent, Inclusive Partnerships'? Conference on Education 2015 <Partners in Excellence>. Available at: https://www.researchgate.net/publication/277346624_Negotiating_risk_and_potential_What_role_can_positive_risk_taking_play_in_promoting_excellent_inclusive_partnerships (accessed 8 December 2017).

SEND Community Alliance. (2020), 'Coronavirus and SEND: Current Issues of Concern'. Available at: https://sendcommunityalliance.org.uk/2020/06/04/coronavirus-and-send-current-issues-of-concern/ (accessed 29 April 2021).

Skipp, A. (2021), 'Special Education During Lockdown: Provider and Parent Experiences', *Journal of Research in Special Educational Needs*, 21(2): 171–5.

Smith, S. (2021), 'Parents' Perspectives: What Can We Learn from COVID Crisis Education for Students Labelled with SEND', *Journal of Research in Special Educational Needs*, 21(2): 175–9.

Tirraoro, T. (2020a), 'SEND Risk Assessments and Preparing for a Return to School (or Not)'. *Special Needs Jungle*. 8 September 2020. Available at: https://www.specialneedsjungle.com/send-risk-assessments-preparing-return-to-school/ (accessed 11 July 2021).

Tirraoro, T. (2020b), 'The Scandal of the Children with Complex Needs Told They're Not Welcome Back at School'. *Special Needs Jungle*. 8 September 2020. Available at: https://www.specialneedsjungle.com/scandal-children-complex-needs-not-welcome-back-school/ (accessed 11 July 2021).

Tremain, S. (2015), 'Foucault, Governmentality and Critical Disability Theory Today: A Genealogy of the Archive', in S. Tremain (ed.), *Foucault and the Government of Disability*, 9–23. Ann Arbor: University of Michigan Press.

Part 2

Teaching and Learning under the Shadow of a Global Pandemic: Exclusions and Possibilities

3

The Effect of the Covid-19 Pandemic on Students in a Vulnerable Situation in Iceland

Hermína Gunnþórsdóttir and Ylfa G. Sigurðardóttir

Introduction

The Coronavirus disease/Covid-19 (WHO 2020) appeared in educational settings at a very short notice and required schools to rearrange their operation. Teachers had to react by changing their teaching practices overnight. In this regard, it is important to keep in mind that all children in Iceland aged between six and sixteen years are obliged to attend school according to the Compulsory School Act (The Compulsory School ActNo. 91/2008). Therefore, teachers were expected to maintain the education level in accordance with acts and curricula as much as possible. The official education policy in Iceland is based on the principles of inclusive education but all children are entitled to 'attend their compulsory schools where the educational and social requirements of each pupil are met with emphasis on respect for human values and social justice' (Ministry of Education, Science and Culture 2012: 41). Recent research in Iceland has shown that many teachers are insecure in implementing the policy of inclusion (Óskarsdóttir 2017) and at all levels teachers claim to receive insufficient support. It can thus be argued that in the Covid-19 situation it must have been extremely challenging for Icelandic teachers to maintain an inclusive focus in their teaching.

In this chapter we will report on research conducted in cooperation with thirteen Icelandic classroom teachers during the first wave of the Covid-19 pandemic. First, we provide an overview of the Icelandic context followed by a literature review as well as sections on methodology and data processing. The findings focus on two main issues; firstly, changes in regular and additional support and how it affected vulnerable students; and secondly, communication with students and their parents. The chapter ends with a discussion and conclusions, giving insight into how teachers responded to this new and challenging situation. In the chapter it is argued that more systematic and coordinated reactions towards students in a vulnerable situation would have been needed to avoid disruption of their schooling with consequences such as a cutting off additional support and personal communication.

The Icelandic Context

Legal Framework and Obligations of Compulsory Schools and Teachers in Iceland

Compulsory schools in Iceland operate with the aim of preparing students as well as possible for their own future in a democratic society with a focus on the ideology of inclusive education (Ministry of Education, Science and Culture 2012). Primary schools in Iceland have numerous responsibilities; first and foremost, however, it should be a place where children feel safe, have the opportunity to allow their talents to flourish and develop and, above all, to enjoy their childhood (Ministry of Education, Science and Culture 2012). The education system has developed towards increasing the independence of each school and centralization has been systematically reduced since the authority over compulsory schools was transferred from the state to municipalities in 1995 (Hansen, Jóhannsson and Lárusdóttir 2008). As each municipality is the official authority of its local school, reactions to an unpredicted situation as Covid-19 can vary as indeed was the case in Iceland. Schools in Iceland remained partly open during the pandemic but there were no common guidelines from the Ministry of Education as to how to implement restrictions within schools. Thus, even within the same municipality, schools implemented the restrictions in various ways. In most schools the day became a mixture of home-schooling and class attendance, but arrangements could vary depending on students' age and available resources, including the number of teachers (Jónsdóttir 2020). One of the main roles of a primary school teacher is being a leader in the classroom. According to the Compulsory School Act No. 91/2008, Art. 13, each student should have a supervising teacher who closely monitors their learning and development, emotional state and general well-being, and who guides them in their studies and work.

Literature Review

The Inclusive School and Social Justice

In terms of student placements in mainstream schools, Iceland can be considered an inclusive school system with 0.3 per cent of the overall student population registered in three special schools, and 1.3 per cent registered in special departments attached to primary schools (Statistics Iceland 2021). Thus, mainstream primary schools cater to almost 99 per cent of all students. Iceland is considered to have a solid policy in place on inclusive education (European Agency for Special Needs and Inclusive Education 2017); however, discussion for the past year has focused on implementation – or lack of implementation – and that actions taken in schools have not been inclusive enough (Gunnþórsdóttir 2021). If inclusive practices are not institutionalized as the regular routine in schools, situations as Covid-19, with consequent irregularity and imbalance, might not have supported such a regimen. A recent US review article, Morgan (2020), points out that the measures schools had to take during the first wave of Covid-19 could have increased inequality. It has proved difficult to meet the needs of both poor children, with limited access to electronic devices, and children who need special education, which has not been provided as effectively through distance education as it is on-site. New Icelandic research findings (Björnsdóttir and Ásgrímsdóttir 2020) indicate that the sudden shift to remote teaching due to the Covid-19 situation could have led to some unexpected inequality among students as teachers, for example, identified homes ill-equipped for digital technology requirements. Other studies also found signs of inequality among immigrant children and children with weaker social background relating to internet access and technology. Those children were more often absent from school than their classmates (Jónsdóttir 2020).

Teacher Professionalism

The concept of teacher professionalism involves a threefold commitment to students: skills, knowledge and devotion (Kristinsson 2013). Teacher professionalism is largely related to attitudes and ambitions, respecting themselves and others and reflecting on themselves and their work with the guiding principle that it is always possible to do better, increase one's own knowledge and be open to innovation (Aðalbjarnardóttir 2002). Professionalism means not least being ready to respond to the challenges that come with the job and being able to assess which innovations are suitable for teaching and learning materials.

With the changing spirit of the times and technological innovations, teaching methods have undergone major adjustments in a short period of time. Therefore, teachers face the challenge of assessing which technologies are suitable at any given time, as well as preparing students for the future by guiding them in the use of technology and assessing its origin and quality (Cortes et al. 2016). Diversity is a key aspect of a teacher's job because the job can change constantly, from day to day and from year to year. Every autumn, teachers face a new beginning with new challenges.

Responsive Teachers, Responsibilities and Requirements

Iceland's primary schools were given a free rein how to reorganize schooling due to the impact of Covid-19, although the response was guided by school administrators and education authorities in the municipalities, in accordance with the guidelines of the Ministry of Health and Epidemiology. The criteria were mainly for teaching to take place in smaller groups than usual, and efforts were to be made for the groups to mix as little as possible in order to slow down the spread of Covid-19 (Government of Iceland 2020). In a recent article Jónsdóttir (2020) states that in many countries, the response to Covid-19 in schools has been more centralized than in Iceland, for example in Norway which has a similar school system to Iceland. Jónsdóttir (2020) points out that the closures entailed an increased risk of inequality between children in social, economic and health terms. Icelandic schools and their teachers were, therefore, more or less free to decide how to change teaching methods within prescribed group size limits. Teachers were required to use a variety of methods and approaches in their teaching as no particular procedure suited everyone (Gunnþórsdóttir 2016). Teachers must, therefore, be responsive which means being able to adapt students' learning environment to their needs for them to flourish socially as well as academically (Guðjónsdóttir and Óskarsdóttir 2016).

Cooperation between Homes and Schools

It is important for students that their home life support their studies. The National Curriculum Guide for Compulsory Schools (Ministry of Education, Science and Culture 2012) emphasizes that the well-being of children and their successful academic progress is based on parents supporting their children's schooling and safeguarding their interests. Both teachers and parents, therefore, need to maintain good communication with the student to the best of their ability, which includes regular conversations between them. One of the most important prerequisites for successful schoolwork is a steady flow of information between the home and the school (Ministry of Education, Science and Culture 2012).

According to a study by Jónsdóttir and Björnsdóttir (2014), constant cooperation between home and school, with parental involvement, enhances the child's academic achievement, contentment and well-being. A number of studies (Christiansen 2010) have shown that in order for students to achieve maximum results, their emotional state must be supported by trying to prevent anxiety, encouraging students to control their behaviour, to persevere and pursue their studies on a regular basis as well as inspiring diligent work, creative expression and moral values.

Methods and Data

In this chapter we present findings from research conducted in Iceland during the first wave of Covid-19. This was a qualitative semi-structured interview study with thirteen teachers, eight classroom teachers and five special education teachers in three Icelandic primary schools. The aim of the study was to gain an understanding and shed light on the experience of primary school teachers of their teaching in times of population constraints due to Covid-19. For the purpose of this chapter the focus will be on how teachers responded to the situation regarding students who need additional support and are entitled to receive special education. The interviews were conducted in April; that is, before 4 May 2020 when the first 'gathering ban' was lifted and schools could operate normally again. Two of the schools are in the capital area and one in the countryside. They differ in terms of size and practices and the pandemic affected them differently as one of them had to close temporarily due to the number of Covid-19 cases. To ensure anonymity and prevent the participants' results from being traced, they were all given pseudonyms: Agla, Anna, Ester, Elva, Eva, Góa, Hallur, Heiða, Karen, Lára, Olga, Sara and Soffía. There is also a reference to the primary schools under pseudonyms which are: Blómaskóli, Fjallaskóli and Skýjaskóli. Due to the group size and distance restrictions in force at the time, all the interviews took place via the account of one of the researchers on the communication programme Google Meet, which has been assessed specifically with regard to privacy (Þorsteinsdóttir 2020). The interview framework contained open-ended questions in accordance with the objectives of the study and was pretested on two other teachers. Preliminary analysis of the data began in parallel with copying, and then thematic analysis was used to complete the data analysis (Creswell 2012).

Findings

The findings will be discussed according to two main issues: firstly, changes in regular and additional support and how these affected vulnerable students and secondly, communication with students and their parents.

Changes in Regular and Additional Support – Effects on Vulnerable Students

When group size restrictions were imposed at short notice, Iceland's primary schools had to react quickly and change learning and teaching arrangements. As time went on, it became clear that there was a notable difference between schools in the way the schoolwork was run; for example, the amount of time children attended their classes differed significantly from school to school. It was entirely up to the administrators of each school to organize the school day and students' schedules. Some of the teachers interviewed wondered whether this was the right thing to do and whether equality was maintained in light of the fact that compulsory schooling in the country stipulates the number of minimum hours in certain subjects. The regulation on students with special needs in compulsory schools (No. 585/2010) also stipulates that these students are entitled to support in their studies.

Anna pondered this from a perspective of equality and access to education since attendance at her school was possible every day, but her grandchildren in other parts of the country only attended every other day for two hours at a time and on the days when they were not at school, there was no emphasis on studies. Sara also noticed how different the student presence was among schools and found it 'amazing how everyone has something so different'.

Thus, the main changes during this period related to reduced attendance of students at the school. Ester at Blómaskóli said this about the situation:

> There were big changes that had to happen very fast, we had to limit schoolwork, you were suddenly with the children for 3 hours per day and had to consider the disease control rules ... you got a shorter day.

Heiða, who works at the same school, added:

> We shifted gear completely, we have put the main emphasis on the foundation and tried to take everything else out ... we had to let go of the fact that not all goals would be achieved but at the same time just be in the basics, math, Icelandic and sociology.

Due to reduced attendance and disease control rules, which required fewer students in each group, the number of groups had to be increased and thus more teachers were needed to take responsibility for each group. Most schools, therefore, took the path of removing special needs teachers from their traditional work and placing them in charge of regular groups of students, which were divided into separate compartments on the school premises. This measure entailed two fundamental changes in schoolwork: on the one hand, special needs teachers took on supervision teaching in regular classes, which they do not normally do, and on the other hand, regular special needs education or support for students that special needs teachers had provided was abolished.

A large part of the supervising teacher's work is collaboration with colleagues within the school, parents and guardians and the specialists that each student needs at any given time. Olga pointed out that collaboration and communication at Blómaskóli changed because many specialists within the school were removed from their regular posts and put in charge of a group. Agla described the situation in his school as follows:

> The collaboration became completely different, the study counsellor dropped out and all the collaboration with psychologists or others than parents just turned to nothing. ...

When the group size restrictions were imposed, school employees, apart from teachers, were taken off their regular jobs and placed in a certain group. Heiða said: 'We do not have the support we should have, and I find it a little difficult ... there are students who need this very good support network.' Góa talked about the students not getting the services they needed, and the diagnostic processes were halted and would most likely continue until the next autumn.

Lára was one of the special needs teachers who was placed in charge of a group and as a result had no direct involvement with the students she usually followed. She described her situation as follows:

> I have not been able to enter all the compartments ... my special education students just slipped away from me. I find it very sad. I have been trying to keep

in touch by phone and hear from the supervising teacher at least in different cases, but I think they have slipped away from me.

Here, Lára describes how she lost sight of her students, whom she had previously worked with as a special needs teacher, and her only recourse is to be in telephone contact with their parents and the teachers who handle the students in their supervision group.

Communication with Students and Their Parents

Both special needs teachers and tutors had the same story to tell about communication with students – they were encouraged to find ways to stay in touch with students and provide them with support. Teachers found it a challenge to be in electronic communication with students, but at Skýjaskóli, the situation became even more demanding when the school was completely closed due to the infection. Soffía said: 'Teaching went from much reduced, strict communication rules to 100% distance learning.' She related how the teaching took place through telecommunication means, Mentor and Facetime. Special needs teacher Anna placed great emphasis on positivity as well as finding ways to keep track of all students. Regarding further teaching methods, she said:

> I had regular meetings twice a week and individual meetings by request. I met students one-on-one or the whole group ... we made a lesson plan for each day and the meetings were mostly to have social interaction ... just so they could help themselves, so we were just chatting. Then they, hopefully, did the assignments themselves at home.

Anna's description above is in line with what most teachers said about relying on students to take extra responsibility for themselves because of the limited opportunity they had to pursue their studies.

The teachers were aware that the situation in children's homes was different, and some parents could not support their children with their schoolwork. Lára said the nature of the cooperation with the households had changed. She had the rule of being in touch at least once a week with the homes. Sara also commented on the change in communication: 'It was just incredibly different, just the situation in the home and maybe you were just being comforted and so on.' Soffía said that if it had not been for the special teachers who kept in touch with the foreign parents, she would probably have 'lost' two children at this time, as the parents only replied to the special teacher who spoke Polish and not to her. The emphasis on communication with the home at this time was not to 'lose' children and therefore try to follow up with students.

Karen, who works as a special needs teacher at Skýjaskóli and teaches Icelandic as a second language, had to leave that teaching post, because it was no longer allowed to mix students from various classes (second language groups are often formed across classes). She also said that they were lucky enough to have a Polish teacher who contacted their parents.

Some of the students were at home at this time, at the request of parents and Heiða's experience was as follows:

> What I find worst about this is students who do not come to school. I feel like I've completely lost them, I have tried to meet the child at a Meet meeting, but this has not come off … I kind of feel like I've completely lost track.

Elva talked about how difficult it was to reach students, and they had engaged in little or no study. Agla had this to say: 'The kids who did not show up because of the situation were also kids who have a hard time at school; it's strange that they were allowed to be on holiday. A very easy way, nothing can be done, and we were not allowed to make demands.' Agla and other teachers also talked about the need to consider more deeply how to react if there is a break in schooling and students do not work on their study material at home.

There was a difference in the teachers' answers regarding the supervision of students who showed up at the school. About half of the teachers felt that they had as good or even better management at that time than they had before, as Agla observed 'I have my kids all day, so you had it all figured out.' Sara, on the other hand, found it difficult to keep track of their students, as it was not possible to be completely immersed in them, and said, 'I ask how it goes and they answer just fine but then you realize it's not right, so I was relying on them to tell me the truth because I could not watch them closely.' Heiða agreed with Sara and also said, 'I clearly do not have as much management … I only get them for 1½ hours a day and have not looked in a reading book for a long time and I think it's awful.' In traditional schooling, students who need increased assistance receive it, but at that time most teachers were the only ones in their group who felt most strongly about the students who usually receive increased assistance, as Karen said, 'There is a student in my group who has lost a lot because he has not received any special education and he needs it so much.'

Some of the participants were worried about next autumn, mainly due to the expected situation of many families, as many have lost their jobs and were afraid that the financial situation of many could be bad. Sara said about this:

> I think it is very important for us as teachers that it is perhaps noted that we are able to provide students with the spiritual support they need. Their mental well-being needs to be taken into account because many parents are unemployed, and you feel that some students are quite apprehensive about it.

What many participants also felt and missed was a hug and not being able to comfort their students in times of need, especially the younger students. Soffía thought it was the hardest thing, as she said, 'not being able to be in proper contact with the kids because there are so many people there who need a hug so badly'.

Two participants were concerned about distance learning in terms of student safety. Eva said, 'I found it uncomfortable, as if it were a bit of an invasion of students' homes.' Iva expressed her concern in great detail:

> They are there visually, audibly, they are usually inside their rooms and there is usually no other adult watching the class. This is not a public area like the school is. Although I find this fun and exciting, I am worried about the security aspect, because it was done without having reviewed security aspects, introducing them to the parents, ensuring that the parents have access to all of this ... I also found that the kids felt very uncomfortable being on a screen, they were worried that the other kids were taking pictures ... But it's a great way to reach this vulnerable group.

Discussion

The purpose and focus of this chapter are aimed at how teachers responded to the Covid-19 situation regarding students who need additional support and are entitled to receive special education. The discussion will highlight which interventions or non-intervention could have long-term consequences for students in a vulnerable position.

According to the interviewees almost all formal support for students was dropped. This applies to general support in the classroom – special education in the classroom or in separate facilities, the work of developmental therapists, study counsellors, psychologists and other professionals who often provide support services to students. In addition, students' diagnostic processes (e.g. dyslexia,

ADHD, autism, etc.), which are handled by external specialists, were stopped. It is clear that the decision to emphasize basic subjects such as mathematics, Icelandic and sociology, in effect cancelling everything else, does not comply with the compulsory schooling agenda that stipulates a certain number of minimum hours in certain subjects (reference timetable) (Ministry of Education, Science and Culture 2012). The goal of the regulation on students with special needs in compulsory schools (No. 585/2010) is, among other things, to meet the learning, physical, social and emotional needs of students and thus promote equal opportunities in primary schools in accordance with international conventions on the rights of children and the disabled. Many of the results of this study show that schools failed to fulfil their statutory role in terms of students needing special educational support, and in fact they received less support than others, their support network was torn out, as one of the teachers put it, and those who had the role of supervising students in need of special support, who are usually special needs teachers, had to abandon their regular work and attend to general education. None of the thirteen teachers interviewed mentioned that the schools had tried to compensate students for this loss in a formal and systematic way. An important fundamental value that must be present in schoolwork based on social justice is that students are not discriminated against in any way and that the prevailing mentality is characterized by equality (Banks 2013).

The teachers were strongly aware of the vulnerable position of these students and of their responsibility towards students (Ministry of Education, Science and Culture 2012). Thus, they did their best to keep in touch with students and support them informally through electronic communication. However, their efforts may not have been sufficient in all cases, since they describe how students have 'slipped' away from them and they even 'lost' students. As Aðalbjarnardóttir (2002) has pointed out, teacher professionalism largely relates to the attitudes and ambitions of individual teachers, their respect for themselves and others and how willing they are to respond to new challenges. The teachers in this study have all these traits, but it is clear that the project was too extensive for them to carry out without support. The system behind them does not seem to have focused on students in a vulnerable position, apart from being in contact with students and parents as much as possible (Christiansen 2010). The framework that has been built around this group of students was almost completely set aside and focused on core subjects without the students receiving appropriate support.

The schools' response was primarily to transfer traditional learning to an electronic format and due to cuts in student attendance, either electronically or on school premises (when conditions allowed), teachers relied on students to fend for themselves – to supervise their own studies and work at home on projects that usually took place at school. The group of students under discussion here is those who receive additional support in their studies, for example because they find it difficult to take charge and manage their studies on their own (Regulation on Students with Special Needs in Compulsory School, no. 585/2010). One of the teachers specifically mentioned students who did not come to school at all, and no contact was made with the parents, so that the teacher did not know whether these students attended the class at all. In order for students to succeed in their studies, it is necessary to promote their well-being by preventing anxiety and giving them the opportunity to participate in the school's democratic activities (Christiansen 2010). The conditions imposed upon the teachers placed some restrictions on them, as they had limited resources to make demands for attendance and return of students' work, with the final decision on student attendance and participation being put in the hands of parents.

The teachers stated that special teaching for students who do not have Icelandic as their mother tongue was cancelled and teachers often found it difficult to reach the foreign parents of these students. One of the teachers describes the solution that a teacher of Polish origin was hired to reach out to Polish parents and thus ensure follow-up with students and communication with the home. In this case, the school shows a certain initiative for communication and seeks solutions that have possibly not been used before (Jónsdóttir and Björnsdóttir 2014) but these are examples of networks that the school can make better use of in the future.

It can be said that teacher professionalism and their threefold commitment to students regarding skills, knowledge and devotion have been tested in these demanding situations (Kristinsson 2013). Due to the rapid response to changing circumstances, there was little time to reflect on priorities and responses, or to evaluate actions, and it was not until later in the season that teachers considered the legitimacy of various interventions and the consequences for students in vulnerable situations. In the case of some students, little or no learning has taken place, and in fact there has been a disruption of schooling that would otherwise have been met by systematic intervention. This situation is not unique to Iceland, no less than the whole world was in the same situation but reactions differed in various countries (Jónsdóttir 2020).

The results of the study show that teachers' reactions were shaped primarily by their efforts to manage their group of students and maintain contact with students and their homes. They were aware that conditions were difficult for students in vulnerable situations and that the support they needed was no longer available. They also saw that there were differences between schools and school districts in how responses were formulated, and that consequently some students may have been the victims of inequality (Morgan 2020) as actions were not coordinated (Jónsdóttir 2020). In the long term, the group of students who became outsiders in the school system due to Covid-19 may be at an even greater disadvantage. The legal framework for schooling in Iceland takes into account the emphasis of inclusive education (Ministry of Education, Science and Culture 2012; The Compulsory School Act No. 91/2008) and thus it will perhaps be even more important than before to ensure that future schooling clearly adheres to the principles of democracy and equality.

Conclusion

The findings show that schools responded to the Covid-19 situation in very different ways, such as regarding students' attendance at school, online lessons and whether additional support was delivered or not. Teachers wondered whether equality was maintained in this regard. In general, emphasis was laid on core subjects and everything else cut off, such as art and craft and sport lessons. Most schools decided to transfer special needs teachers from their traditional work to oversee regular groups of students. This meant that students who are usually entitled to additional support did not receive these hours during the restriction period. Teachers describe this as a missing student support network and simultaneously the diagnostic processes that had started were put on hold.

Teachers were encouraged to find ways to stay in touch with students and provide them with support. They found it a challenge to maintain electronic communication with students and for many of them this was a new reality. Most teachers relied on students to take extra responsibility for their learning because of the limited opportunity they had to pursue their studies. For students who had limited support at home or had difficulties in managing their own learning this could mean that their participation and learning was insufficient. In some instances, communication with parents of foreign origin was interrupted but there were also examples where teachers who spoke Polish, for example, reached out to the Polish parents. In some cases, there were students who did not come to school and teachers felt as if they had 'lost' them since there was no communication with them or their parents. Teachers worried about the homes that could not be reached. In most cases, teachers reported that the kids who did not show up were also kids who have a hard time at school. They called for more systematic action if a break in schooling happens due to a situation such as Covid-19 and students do not attend school either locally or electronically. Many participants missed the social part of teaching and not being able to hug and comfort their students in times of need, especially the younger students.

In general, it can be argued that more systematic and coordinated responses to students' needs in a vulnerable situation would have been required to avoid disruption of their schooling with consequences such as interrupted additional support and personal communication. There is good reason to pay special attention to this group of students as time goes by and schoolwork reaches an equilibrium.

References

Aðalbjarnardóttir, S. (2002), 'Í eilífri leit – virðing og fagmennska kennara'. *Netla – Veftímarit um uppeldi og menntun*. Available at: http://netla.hi.is/greinar/2002/005/03/index.htm. Accessed 14 July 2020.

Banks, J. A. (2013), 'Multicultural Education: Characteristics and Goals', in J. A. Banks and C. A. M. Banks (eds), *Multicultural Education. Issues and Perspectives*, 8th edn, 3–23. New York: John Wiley.

Björnsdóttir, K., and og Ásgrímsdóttir, E. E. (2020), COVID bjargaði mér". Störf kennara í fyrstu bylgju heimsfaraldurs *Netla – Veftímarit um uppeldi og menntun*. Available at: https://netla.hi.is/serrit/2020/menntakerfi_heimili_covid19/04.pdf. Accessed 15 January 2021.

Christiansen, N. K. (2010), *Skóli og skólaforeldrar, ný sýn á samstarfið um nemendur*. Reykjavík: Iðnú.

Cortes, S. B., Guðbrandsson, B. Í., Hugadóttir, M., and Hjartarson, T. (2016), *Skapandi skóli. Handbók um fjölbreytta kennsluhætti og starfræna miðlun*. Kópavogur: Menntamálastofnun.

Creswell, J. W. (2012), *Educational Research*, 4th edn. Boston: Pearson.

European Agency for Special Needs and Inclusive Education. (2017), 'Education for All in Iceland. External Audit of the Icelandic System for Inclusive Education'. Available at: https://www.stjornarradid.is/media/menntamalaraduneyti-media/media/frettatengt2016/Final-report_External-Audit-of-the-Icelandic-System-for-InclusiveEducation.pdf. Accessed 10 October 2022.

Government of Iceland. (2020), Leiðbeinandi viðmið um íþrótta- og æskulýðsstarf í ljósi takmörkunar á skólastarfi og samkomum'. Available at: https://www.stjornarradid.is/efst-a-baugi/frettir/stok-frett/2020/03/20/Leidbeinandi-vidmid-um-ithrotta-og-aeskulydsstarf-i-ljosi-takmorkunar-a-skolastarfi-og-samkomum/. Accessed 2 May 2020.

Guðjónsdóttir, H., and Óskarsdóttir, E. (2016), 'Inclusive Education, Pedagogy and Practice', in S. Markic and S. Abels (eds), *Science Education towards Inclusion*, 7–22. New York: Nova Science Publisher.

Gunnþórsdóttir, H. (2016), 'Fjölbreytileiki nemenda og kennarastarfið', in D. S. Bjarnason, H. Gunnþórsdóttir and Ó. P. Jónsson (eds), *Skóli margbreytileikans*, 259–82. Reykjavík: Háskólaútgáfan.

Gunnþórsdóttir, H. (2021), 'The Path towards Inclusive Education in Iceland', in N. B. Hanssen, S. E. Hansén and K. Ström (eds), *Dialogues between Northern and Eastern Europe on the Development on Inclusion. Theoretical and Practical Perspective*s, 66–82. London: Routledge.

Hansen, B., Jóhannsson, Ó. H., and Lárusdóttir, S. H. (2008), 'Breytingar á hlutverki skólastjóra í grunnskólum', *Uppeldi og menntun*, 17(2): 87–104.

Jónsdóttir, K., and Björnsdóttir, A. (2014), 'Foreldrasamstarf', in G. G. Óskarsdóttir (ed.), *Starfshættir í grunnskólum við upphaf 21. Aldar,* 197–216. Reykjavík: Háskólaútgáfan.

Jónsdóttir, K. (2020), 'Tengslin við heimilin trosnuðu merkilega lítið í fyrstu bylgju COVID-19 Sjónarhorn stjórnenda og grunnskólakennara'. *Netla – Veftímarit um uppeldi og menntun: Sérrit 2020 – Um Covid 19*. https://doi.org/10.24270/serritne tla.2020.21. Accessed 2 November 2021.

Kristinsson, S. (2013), 'Að verðskulda traust. Um siðferðilegan grunn fagmennsku og starf kennara', in R. Sigþórsson, R. Eggertsdóttir and G. H. Frímannsson (eds), *Fagmennska í skólastarfi: skrifað til heiðurs Trausta Þorsteinssyni*, 238–43. Reykjavík: Háskólinn á Akureyri og Háskólaútgáfan.

Ministry of Education, Science and Culture (2012) 'The Icelandic National Curriculum Guide for Compulsory School: General Section'. Available at: https://www.governm ent.is/library/01-Ministries/Ministry-of-Education/Curriculum/adskr_grsk_ens_2 012.pdf. Accessed 10 October 2022.

Morgan, H. (2020), 'Best Practices for Implementing Remote Learning during a Pandemic', *Clearing House: A Journal of Educational Strategies, Issues and Ideas*, 93(3): 134–40.

Óskarsdóttir, E. (2017), 'Constructing Support as Inclusive Practice: A Self-Study'. (Doctoral thesis). Reykjavik: University of Iceland, School of Education.

Statistics Iceland. (2021), *Nemendur sem njóta sérkennslu eða stuðnings 2004–2020*. Available at: https://px.hagstofa.is/pxis/pxweb/is/Samfelag/Samfelag__ skolamal__2_grunnskolastig__0_gsNemendur/SKO02107.px/table/tableViewLayo ut1/?rxid=42836191-e6cf-43d4-b930-6962dac44720. Accessed 10 October 2022.

The Compulsory School Act No. 91/2008.

The Regulation on Students with Special Needs in Compulsory Schools no. 585/2010.

WHO. (2020), *Coronavirus*. Available at: https://www.who.int/health-topics/coronavi rus#tab=tab_1. Accessed 15 May 2021.

Þorsteinsdóttir, Þ. (2020), 'Nám og frístundastarf í gegnum rafræna miðla'. Available at: https://reykjavik.is/frettir/nam-og-fristundastarf-i-gegnum-rafra ena-midla. Accessed 10 April 2020.

4

Increased Educational Disadvantages of Refugee Students in German Language Support Classes during Covid-19 School Closures in Austria: Perceptions and Pedagogical Reactions of Austrian Teachers

Katharina-Theresa Lindner, Marie Gitschthaler, Alexandra Gutschik, Julia Kast, Julia Honcik, Rupert Corazza and Susanne Schwab

Introduction

The integration of students with a migration biography into the national school and education systems is prioritized by several countries across the world (Bešić et al. 2020; Hilt 2017). However, such a drive for ensuring inclusive educational opportunities for all students varies from one school system to another. The interpretations of the conceptual meaning of inclusive education do not always correspond to the understanding of inclusion as equal access to high-quality education for each learner, regardless of their characteristics. This is especially true in the case of refugee students or those having a (forced) migration biography.

When German Language Support Classes and Courses (GLSCCs, *Deutschförderklassen*, or *Deutschförderkurse*) got instated in Austria in the school year 2018/2019 (BMBWF 2019), they provided a new base for understanding the inclusive and exclusive practices within the educational processes of the Austrian school system. The government's decision to introduce GLSCCs ignores the diversity of (refugee) students' first languages and fails to use multilingualism as an aid for teaching. Although this measure was introduced under the guise of inclusion, it can be classified as an exclusionary practice (Horvath 2018; Rheindorf and Wodak 2018). Except for Slovene and Croatian, the official minority languages, the Austrian School Instruction Act only allows German as the language of instruction (School Instruction Act §16). In GLSCCs, children should learn German as fast as possible to be better integrated into mainstream education in due course. It is worth noting that among all legal provisions concerning the promotion of German, those dealing with GLSCCs and the testing of children with a first language different from German completely disregard possible disabilities in children. For example, it is required that a child with a sensory disability and a child with a mental disability go through the same selection procedure, even if they face barriers by taking the designated test due to their disability.

Education and Schooling of Refugee Students

Given the context of the unpredicted arrival in 2015 of more than one million people who sought safety and protection within the European countries in just a few months, there have been public and political debates about the integration of these asylum seekers and refugees. Educational policies have been altered to accommodate the large number of school-aged children who had fled their countries of origin (Kremsner, Proyer and Obermayr 2020; Proyer et al. 2021). According to the Austrian education legislation, all children irrespective of their nationality or ethnicity have the right to compulsory education until the age of fifteen. As the provisions of this law also extend to children having a forced migration biography or asylum-seeking status, the education sector needed to react to new educational demands (Proyer et al. 2021).

> Since 2015, the refugee status of children has become a major concern in some documents provided by the Federal Ministry of Education (2017). Frequently, diversity dimensions linked to this status are of a linguistic nature, on the one hand, but also differences in culture, as well as experienced trauma, on the other hand. (Messiou et al. 2020: 8)

Specially designated accommodations were established for refugees. One of the very first political reactions to the influx of children having a forced migration biography in 2015 was the establishment of separate special classrooms called 'New to Vienna Classrooms' (Hawlik and Varol 2019; Kremsner, Proyer and Obermayr 2020; Proyer et al. 2021). These reception classes were set up only in Vienna, the capital of Austria. In addition to these classes, nationwide on-site parallel schooling was carried out (Kremsner, Proyer and Obermayr 2020;

Proyer et al. 2021). Both measures were taken up as transitional solutions. At the beginning of the school year 2018/19, GLSCCs were established, and they replaced these existing solutions (BMBWF 2019). Therefore, it can be assumed that students attending GLSCCs are mostly children with refugee experiences and equipped only with beginner-level German language skills operationalized via standardized testing (Kremsner, Proyer and Obermayr 2020; Proyer et al. 2021).

German language support classes and courses in Austria

According to the Austrian Ministry of Education, the aim of the German language support classes and courses (GLSCCs) is as follows: 'the early and intensive learning of these students of the language of instruction, German, so that they can be taught together in the class as quickly as possible according to the curriculum of the respective school type and grade' (BMBWF 2019, translation by the authors).

If eight or more students at one school have little or no German language competence, it is mandatory to set up a GLS class. These classes can also be organized across different classes, school grades or schools.

The decision regarding students who have to attend the GLSCCs is based on the results of a standardized test – the MIKA-D test. On the day of school enrollment, principals decide on which students have to take the MIKA-D test after a personal interview with every newly enrolled student. Based on the results of the MIKA-D test, one of the following three scenarios will ensue:

1. Students are perceived to have sufficient language competence and get to attend regular classes.
2. Students, whose German language competence is perceived to be 'emerging' get to attend regular classes and receive additional language support for six hours a week in a 'pull-out course'.
3. Students' who are perceived to have inadequate German language competence need to attend a GLS class (fifteen hours/week in primary school, twenty hours/week in lower-secondary school).

In the contexts of scenarios 2 and 3, students get the status of 'irregular students', which implies that they don't receive marks in subjects in which scoring marks depends on their German language skills. The presence of GLSCCs entails the separation of student groups due to language competence. As such, for students in GLSCCs the opportunity to learn from peers who are more linguistically proficient in German remains denied.

Once students are enrolled either in the GLS classes or 'pull-out courses', they have to remain in the specific setting for at least one semester, but no longer than four semesters. At the end of each semester, the students are tested again.

If the students in GLSCCs do not manage to transfer to regular classrooms after one or two semesters, they have to repeat the grade they are in, which means that they change their class teacher and their classmates. In the case of students who are perceived to have sufficient language competence after being tested again, the language support stops after they have transitioned to the regular classrooms. Furthermore, their status as being 'irregular students' is revoked, which means that they are graded according to the same guidelines as their peers who do not need language support.

At present, there is little empirical evidence regarding the effects of the current support model. However, studies that have been published levelled significant criticism against GLSCCs (see e.g. Erling et al. 2021; Schwab, Kast and Lindner 2020; Schweiger and Müller 2021). There are significant concerns about the learning progress within the GLS classes as language seems to be taught and learned in what appears to be a laboratory-like scenario disregarding the chance of natural social language exchange. Further, students' social participation becomes limited, and many teachers are concerned that the students in GLS classes are stigmatized.

Covid-19 and Its Impact on School Operations in Austria

Due to the global Covid-19 pandemic, school life in Austria has changed dramatically, and there have been several phases of distance learning since spring 2020. The first phase of distance learning took place from March 2020 until mid-May/June 2020 (depending on the type of school and the age of the students). During this time, the teaching and learning process was transferred from face-to-face lessons at school to the digital platform(s) at home. After this first phase of distance learning, shift teaching took place in schools (i.e. the students of each class were divided into two groups) until the end of the school year 2019/20 to prevent further spread of Covid-19 (BMBWF 2020a). The following school year 2020/21 started in September 2020 under special circumstances – with hygiene protocols and social distancing rules in place. However, due to another drastic increase in the number of positive Covid-19 cases in Austria, the schools had to switch again to distance learning in November 2020 and January 2021. However, by this time, some special regulations were in place for certain types of schools and classes (e.g. special schools and GLSCCs), which continued to have face-to-face teaching and only switched to distance learning sporadically, while the remaining school types were consistently in distance learning (BMBWF 2020b). In the weeks after the Easter holidays in the spring of 2021, the last lockdown to date was implemented, and all the schools were closed again. Since May 2021, all students, regardless of their school type and level, have returned to their classrooms (BMBWF 2021b).

At the institutional level, distance learning has led to a massive upgrade in the digitalization of schools, and a wide variety of technical and didactic strategies were introduced such as (a)synchronous online teaching, digital tasks and paper–pencil tasks. Due to this dependence on digital resources during the distance learning phase and the different (learning) situations in the students' home environments such as those relating to adequate learning space and the presence of family members at home, concerns have emerged about the possibility of distance learning causing a widening of the social gap (e.g. Huber and Helm 2020; Huber et al. 2020; Schober et al. 2020). In particular, it was noted that the educational disadvantage of students from low socio-economic backgrounds would get reinforced because of distance learning.

The Study

This section highlights the increased educational disadvantage experienced by the refugee students in GLS classes due to school closures. The greater disadvantage experienced by these students resulted from two main factors and their reciprocal relation: First, GLSCC are segregating and excluding measures, which reinforce the structural disadvantage of certain groups of students, especially refugee students and those having a (forced) migration biography. Second, the Covid-19 pandemic posed major challenges for education systems worldwide. As a result, the key stakeholders of the education systems in different countries of the world were confronted with new tasks and problems while attempting to ensure quality education for all (Kast et al. 2021).

In this context, this study asks and answers the following research question: In terms of equity in education, what risks and barriers do the teachers in GLSCCs perceive for their students due to the Covid-19 induced school lockdowns in Austria?

Procedure

To answer the said research question, a quantitative study on teachers' perspectives has been conducted. The data considered for this study were collected in November 2020 during the second lockdown from all the nine federal states of Austria. For this survey, primary, middle and special schools from all over Austria were invited via email to participate in the study and fill out the online survey.

Participants

In all, 2,651 in-service teachers (18 per cent male and 82 per cent female) participated in the study. Their mean age was 43.95 years (SD = 11.66). Most of them were born in Austria (96.5 per cent) and spoke German as a first language (97.7 per cent). Furthermore, 39.2 per cent of the study participants were primary school teachers, 33.3 per cent were secondary school teachers, 22 per cent were vocational school teachers and 5.6 per cent worked in special schools. The majority (62 per cent) worked in mainstream classes, 12.1 per cent in integration classes, 3.3 per cent in special classes, 1.3 per cent in GLS classes and 0.8 per cent in GLS courses. The duration of the participants' teaching experience ranged from 1 to 45 years (M = 17.89; SD = 12.32).

Results

In the online survey, the participating in-service teachers indicated what they perceived regarding their students' learning behaviour during school closures. The aspects covered in the survey detail the possible consequences of distance learning for students. The results for the presented items are shown for the total sample encompassing all the participating teachers (n = 2,651), in-service teachers of regular classes (n = 1,536), those of GLS classes (n = 32) and those of GLS courses (n = 19). In addition to this, the analyses of variance were calculated for the three subgroups (regular-class teachers and teachers in GLSCCs). In this context, it must be stated that the number of participating teachers who work in GLSCCs is lower compared to the teachers of regular classes. Nevertheless, the results allow insights into GLSCCs' teachers' experiences and perceptions during Covid-19.

Table 4.1 Item 'The students feel strongly burdened in the current situation'

	Not at all true	Somewhat not true	Somewhat true	Certainly true	Mean score
Total sample	2.2%	28.3%	51.0%	18.5%	2.86 (.73)
Regular classes	2.0%	28.0%	52.0%	17.9%	2.86 (.72)
GLS classes	35.7%	0.0%	42.9%	21.4%	2.86 (.76)
GLS courses	18.8%	0.0%	62.5%	18.8%	3.0 (.63)

Teachers' Perceptions of Students' Burden

Regarding this item, the teachers' ratings of all subgroups are rather similar. There seems to be a consensus among the participants that students feel much burdened due to distance learning (see Table 4.1). The mean values and the analysis of variance showed no significant differences between the teachers' ratings of the subgroups ($F_5 = 1.154$; n.s.), which implies that the teachers of all sample groups perceived almost the same degree of burden for their students due to the distance learning situation induced by the Covid-19 pandemic.

Teachers' Ratings of Students' Perceptions regarding Being on Holidays

Regarding this item, the GLS class teachers' agreement (by rating 'Somewhat true' and 'Certainly true') was above average compared to that of the other subgroups (GLS classes: 46.4 per cent, GLS courses: 12.6 per cent regular classes: 16.4 per cent; see Table 4.2). The analysis of variance revealed significant differences between the sample groups ($F_5 = 5.363$; $p < .00$). This means that the teachers of GLS classes perceive their students significantly more likely to believe that they are on holiday(s) than their colleagues in regular classes, followed by teachers of GLS courses.

Provision of Weekly Individual Coaching for Students

Within all the sample groups, about the same proportion of teachers certainly agreed with the statement that the students must be provided weekly individual coaching sessions. However, the results proved to be interesting for the GLS

Table 4.2 Item 'The students believe they are on holidays'

	Not at all true	Somewhat not true	Somewhat true	Certainly true	Mean Scores
Total sample	32.8%	49.5%	15.8%	1.8%	1.87 (.74)
Regular classes	34.6%	49.0%	14.6%	1.8%	1.84 (.73)
GLS classes	14.3%	39.3%	32.1%	14.3%	2.46* (.92)
GLS courses	18.8%	68.8%	6.3%	6.3%	2.0* (.73)

Table 4.3 Item 'The students have a weekly individual coaching with me'

	Not at all true	Somewhat not true	Somewhat true	Certainly true	Mean scores
Total sample	19.5%	21.7%	29.0%	29.8%	2.69 (1.1)
Regular classes	21.6%	23.7%	29.3%	25.4%	2.58 (1.1)
GLS classes	22.2%	11.1%	37.0%	29.6%	2.74 (1.13)
GLS courses	42.9%	14.3%	14.3%	28.6%	2.29 (1.33)*

courses as they aligned with the opposite extreme: GLS teachers' negation of this item was above average compared to that in the other subgroups (GLS classes: 22.2 per cent, GLS courses: 42.9 per cent, regular classes: 21.6 per cent; see Table 4.3).

The analysis of variance showed significant differences in teachers' ratings since the teachers of GLS courses provide significantly less weekly individual coaching than the teachers of regular classes and GLS classes ($F_5 = 9.224$; $p < .00$).

Teachers' Perceptions about Students' Opportunities to Work with Digital Devices

The teachers of GLS classes especially, followed by teachers of GLS courses, perceived that their students have no opportunity at all to use a computer, a laptop or a tablet for schoolwork or while home schooling (GLS classes: 32.1 per cent, GLS courses: 18.8 per cent, regular classes: 4.6 per cent; see Table 4.4). Regarding the mean scores, the analysis of variance showed significant differences between the specific groups ($F_5 = 40.779$; $p < .00$).

Table 4.4 Item 'The students have enough possibilities at home to work on a computer, laptop, or tablet'

	Not at all true	Somewhat not true	Somewhat true	Certainly true	Mean score
Total sample	7.6%	23.5%	52.5%	16.5%	2.78 (.81)
Regular classes	4.6%	20.2%	57.5%	17.7%	2.88* (.74)
GLS classes	32.1%	46.4%	10.7%	10.7%	2.0 (.94)
GLS courses	18.8%	62.5%	0.0%	18.8%	2.0 (.63)

Table 4.5 Item 'The students are working actively on their tasks at home'

	Not at all true	Somewhat not true	Somewhat true	Certainly true	Mean scores
Total sample	1.0%	10.7%	64.1%	24.2%	3.12 (.61)
Regular classes	0.4%	8.5%	65.4%	25.7%	3.17 (.57)
GLS classes	7.1%	32.1%	42.9%	17.9%	2.71 (.85)*
GLS courses	6.3%	18.8%	50.0%	25.0%	2.94 (.86)*

Teachers' Perceptions about Students Working Actively at Home

The mean scores and results from the analysis of variance revealed a significant difference between the subgroups ($F_5 = 11.963$; $p < .00$; see Table 4.5) in the teachers' perceptions as to whether their students work actively to complete their school tasks at home. The teachers of GLSCCs perceived their students to be less actively working on the tasks assigned to them by their schools compared to the teachers in regular classes (sum of 'Not at all true' and 'Somewhat not true': GLS classes: 39.2 per cent, GLS courses: 25.1 per cent, regular classes: 8.9 per cent; see Table 4.5).

Teachers' Perceptions about whether Distance Learning Increases Educational Disadvantages

The survey revealed that 27.4 per cent of the regular-class teachers perceived that distance learning increases educational disadvantages. The proportion almost doubled in the case of GLSCCs' teachers (GLS classes: 42.9 per cent, GLS courses: 46.7 per cent; see Table 4.6). Nevertheless, while the teacher

Table 4.6 Item 'Distance learning increases educational disadvantages'

	Not at all true	Somewhat not true	Somewhat true	Certainly true	Mean scores
Total sample	12.4%	25.9%	33.8%	27.8%	2.77 (1.0)
Regular classes	12.6%	26.2%	33.8%	27.4%	2.76 (1.0)
GLS classes	14.3%	17.9%	25.0%	42.9%	2.96 (1.16)
GLS courses	20.0%	0.0%	33.3%	46.7%	3.27 (.80)

ratings account for significant differences, the analysis of variance revealed no significant differences between the ratings of the three subgroups ($F_5 = 2.692$; n.s.), which implies that all the subgroups similarly perceived home schooling to be a risk for increased educational disadvantages.

Teachers' Perceptions about whether It Will Be Difficult to Create a Collective Knowledge Base after Distance Learning

The survey suggested that 11.6 per cent of the regular-class teachers thought that it would be difficult to create a collective knowledge base after distance learning. In contrast, a significantly higher percentage of teachers in the GLSCCs agreed with this statement – 25 per cent and 33.3 per cent respectively (see Table 4.7). The results of the analysis of variance showed that the contrasting ratings of the teachers in the different subgroups are significant, which implies that the teachers of GLSCCs perceive a significantly higher risk of facing difficulties in creating a collective knowledge base after the distance learning phase ($F_5 = 2.692; p < .05$).

Discussion

As the Covid-19 induced school lockdowns have significantly affected students' lives – especially of those having a refugee biography – this study investigated the situation of Austrian students attending GLSCCs with a special emphasis on students having a refugee biography, as it is these students who are often placed in these educational settings owing to their limited German language competence. For this purpose, teachers' perspectives on students' educational

Table 4.7 Item 'It will be difficult to create a collective knowledge base after the distance learning'

	Not at all true	Somewhat not true	Somewhat true	Certainly true	Mean scores
Total sample	16.5%	40.0%	31.0%	12.6%	2.40 (.91)
Regular classes	16.7%	40.6%	31.1%	11.6%	2.38 (.90)
GLS classes	7.1%	28.6%	39.3%	25.0%	2.82* (.91)
GLS courses	6.7%	26.7%	33.3%	33.3%	2.93* (.96)

conditions and disadvantages have been investigated in this quantitative study. Covid-19 related research covering aspects of how education systems have been affected all over the world has pointed out that students who face linguistic barriers in their education are more at the risk of experiencing further educational disadvantages during school lockdowns (e.g. Gornik et al. 2020; Uro, Lai and Alsace 2020). These results can be underpinned for the Austrian education system. By investigating the perceptions of various teachers in regular classes as well as in GLSCCs, it was concluded that the teachers of GLSCCs emphasized increased risk factors and inequalities for students in GLSCCs vis-à-vis distance learning when compared to students in regular classes. The results of this large quantitative online survey highlight the barriers caused by several factors to the learning of the students attending GLSCCs. Some of these factors relate to the teachers, some to the students' personal domains and the rest to institutional conditions and circumstances. Concerning the aspects covered in the survey related to the personal circumstances, the teachers of GLSCCs see a higher risk for their students than regular class teachers. This is evident, for example, from the results regarding students' access to digital devices to be used as facilitating tools of distance learning. Teachers in GLSCCs are more likely than teachers in regular classrooms to perceive that their students tend to believe that they are on holiday(s). This can lead to appalling consequences. It can be assumed that students who think they are on holiday(s) may also conclude that they have no schoolwork to do. Such students then end up not being stimulated either socially or intellectually, and consequently, they feel emotionally and cognitively disconnected from the school. In line with this, the teachers in GLSCCs are more likely to perceive that their students work less actively during distance learning when compared to regular-class teachers. This problem seems to be even more profound when the teachers' answers regarding the provision of weekly individual coaching sessions were analyzed. The teachers in GLSCCs are significantly less likely to report that they provide weekly individual coaching sessions to their students compared to teachers in regular classrooms. Surprisingly in this context, the teachers in GLSCCs consider it significantly more likely that it will be difficult to have a common knowledge base of all the students in the class because of a lack of in-person contact and shared learning in school.

Although Austrian policies state that students' learning development has to be independent of their individual characteristics, the school closures due to the pandemic are likely to exacerbate the already existing divide in academic achievement where students having a refugee biography end up at a significant disadvantage (see e.g. Keddie 2012). As a first empirical (subjective) indicator, the quantitative study showed that nearly half of the teachers think that educational disadvantage has increased during distance learning. To bridge this gap, the Austrian government has introduced short-term summer schools (BMBWF 2021b) for students from GSLCC, which provide intensive support for around two weeks. However, it is not highly expected that this minor measure will adequately allow students having a refugee biography to catch up. On the one hand, language learning is a long-term process that is best started at the preschool level and allowed to last until the end of secondary schooling (see Erling et al. 2021). On the other hand, the staff of these summer schools does not seem to be adequately trained, as the courses are taught by pre-service teachers who have received very limited training at the time of the internships during their studies.

As explained in the introduction, all students from GSLCCs must pass the MIKA-D test to move forward in the regular programme of education. However, if they do not pass, they have to repeat the school level they are assigned to. Grade repetitions can be detrimental to the further development of students and can even lead to them quitting school early (Lessard et al. 2014; De Witte et al. 2013). As MIKA-D was not suspended in the current semesters, what would happen in the future remains uncertain. The status of 'irregular student' will not be extended, which means that those students who have already received two years of support measures will probably not get any additional language support thereafter. Moreover, there is a possibility that students might not be able to pass the MIKA-D even after four semesters owing to learning difficulties or because they require the aid of special needs education programmes. At the moment, there are few plans or guidelines on how to deal with students who cannot be included in the mainstream classrooms based on their MIKA-D test results within two school years. Thus, an urgent solution is needed to ensure that these children are not left behind.

German language skills are also criteria for the assessment of school readiness when children transition from kindergarten to primary school (BMBWF 2019: 9). Children who are perceived as 'not school ready' have to attend preschool classes for one year even if they pass the MIKA-D test during the respective school year. Due to this regulation, these children lose one year of their schooling. This is especially problematic for the so-called *late borns*. In Austria, there is a special regulation that children who complete six years of age after 1 September can rather enroll in preschool. The result of these regulations is that students who attended preschool are at least one or two years older than their peers. This age gap can cause problems within the peer group in a way that older students are socially less accepted. Further, the related career loss disadvantages the students having German as their second language who are often concerned with this problem. This is also against the guideline of the Ministry of Education which says, 'Grade repetition and career losses should be prevented as far as possible' (BMBWF 2021a, authors' translation). It is important to note that such regulations increase the possibility of these students being diagnosed as having a learning disability, especially for those who still struggle with the German language even after their status as 'irregular students' has been revoked, and language support is no longer provided to them. Even though the Austrian law is against diagnosing students as having special educational needs (SEN) merely because of language barriers, the increased number of students having a migration biography having SEN can be observed in some of Austria's federal states.

In terms of further research, it would be necessary to examine the number of students with a refugee biography who are attending GLSCCs in order to find out the actual proportion of those students in segregated educational settings. In this way, it would be possible to verify whether GLSCCs are indeed mainly composed of students with a (forced) migration biography and therefore excluded not only because of learning disability but also owing to social, linguistic and cultural segregation at institutional and legal levels.

It can be concluded from the results of this study that teachers in GLSCCs perceived that distance learning hinders the active use of the German language. Further, the communication barrier that the teachers perceive between them, their students in GLSCCs and the students' parents must also be mentioned as an aggravating factor. Qualitative findings from previous research (see Erling et al. 2021; Schwab, Kast, and Lindner 2020; Schweiger and Müller 2021) have indicated that there is a lack of integration in the mainstream class and that students in GLS classes experience more social isolation. It can be assumed that these existing problems become worse during distance learning. The socio-emotional situation of the students having a refugee biography might be especially worrying as they have not had the same opportunities to get into contact with their peers during the Covid-19 pandemic because of having limited access to technical devices in addition to the language barriers that continue to exist.

References

Bešić, E., Paleczek, L., Rossmann, P., Krammer, M. and Gasteiger-Klicpera, B. (2019), 'Attitudes towards Inclusion of Refugee Girls with and without Disabilities in Austrian Primary Schools', *International Journal of Inclusive Education*, 24(5): 463–78.

Bundesministerium für Bildung, Wissenschaft und Forschung (2019), Deutschförderklassen und Deutschförderkurse. Leitfaden für Schulleiterinnen und Schulleiter [German Support Classes and German Support Courses. Guideline for School Principals]. Available at: https://www.bmbwf.gv.at/dam/jcr:f0e70 8af-3e17-4bf3-9281-1fe7098a4b23/deutschfoerderklassen.pdf (accessed 25 September 2022).

Bundesministerium für Bildung, Wissenschaft und Forschung (2020a), Umsetzung des Etappenplans für Schulen. Richtlinien für die Unterrichtsorganisation und die pädagogische Gestaltung [Implementation of the Stage Plan for Schools. Guidelines for the Organisation of Lessons and Pedagogical Design]. Available at: https://www.bmbwf.gv.at/Themen/schule/beratung/corona_info (accessed 28 June 2021).

Bundesministerium für Bildung, Wissenschaft und Forschung (2020b), Schulbetrieb ab dem 17. November 2020 [School Operation from 17 November 2020]. Available at: https://www.bmbwf.gv.at/Themen/schule/beratung/corona/schulbetrieb_20201 207 (accessed 28 June 2021).

Bundesministerium für Bildung, Wissenschaft und Forschung (2021a), Erlass: Schulbetrieb ab dem 17. Mai 2021 vom 10. Mai 2021 [Decree: School Operation from 17 May 2021 Dated 10 May 2021]. Available at: https://www.bmbwf. gv.at/dam/jcr:080907d8-ea67-4bd3-afd1-2ebbd7dfa795/schulbetrieb20210517 (accessed 28 June 2021).

Bundesministerium für Bildung, Wissenschaft und Forschung (2021b), Sommerschule 2021 [Summer School 2021]. Available at: https://www.bmbwf.gv.at/Themen/schule/ zrp/sommerschule.html (accessed 27 July 2021).

De Witte, K., Cabus, S., Thyssen, G., Groot, W. and Van den Brink, H. M. (2013), 'A Critical Review of the Literature on School Dropout', *Educational Research Review*, 10: 13–28.

Erling, E. J., Foltz, A., and Wiener, M. (2021), 'Differences in English Teachers' Beliefs and Practices and Inequity in Austrian English Language Education: Could Plurilingual Pedagogies Help Close the Gap?', *International Journal of Multilingualism*, 18(4): 570–85. DOI: 10.1080/14790718.2021.1913170.

Gornik, B., Dežan, L., Sedmak, M., and Medarić, Z. (2020), 'Distance Learning in the Time of the Covid-19 Pandemic and the Reproduction of Social Inequality in the Case of Migrant Children', *Druzboslovne Razprave*, 36(94/95): 149–68.

Hawlik, R., and Varol, Z. (2019), 'Ankommen in einer fremden Stadt: Kinder mit Fluchterfahrung in Primarschulen Wiens.' [Arriving in a Foreign City: Children with Refugee Background in Primary Schools in Vienna], in E. Furch, O. Gruber, K. Kremzar, W. Swoboda and M. Wiedner (eds), *Ankommen – Bleiben – Zukunft gestalten*, 56–62. Vienna: AK Verlag.

Hilt, L. T. (2017), 'Education without a Shared Language: Dynamics of Inclusion and Exclusion in Norwegian Introductory Classes for Newly Arrived Minority Language Students', *International Journal of Inclusive Education*, 21(6): 585–601.

Horvath, K. (2018), 'Entrechtung als politisches Projekt. "Migrations- und Integrationspolitik" in Zeiten von Schwarz-Blau II' [Deprivation of Rights as a Political Project. 'Migration and Integration Policy' in Times of Schwarz-Blau II], *Kurswechsel*, 3(18): 83–90.

Huber, S. G., Günther, P. S., Schneider, N., Helm, C., Schwander, M., Schneider, J. A. and Pruitt, J. (2020), *COVID-19 – aktuelle Herausforderungen in Schule und Bildung. Erste Befunde des Schul-Barometers in Deutschland, Österreich und der Schweiz* [COVID-19 – Current Challenges in Schools and Education. First Findings of the School Barometer in Germany, Austria and Switzerland]. Münster: Waxmann.

Huber, S. G., and Helm, C. (2020), 'COVID-19 and Schooling: Evaluation, Assessment and Accountability in Times of Crises – Reacting Quickly to Explore Key Issues for Policy, Practice and Research with the School Barometer', *Educational Assessment, Evaluation and Accountability*, 32: 237–70. DOI: 10.1007/s11092-020-09322-y.

Kast, J., Lindner, K. T., Gutschik, A. and Schwab, S. (2021), 'Austrian Teachers' Attitudes and Self-Efficacy Beliefs regarding At-Risk Students during Home Learning due to COVID-19', *European Journal of Special Needs Education*, 36(1): 114–26.

Keddie, A. (2012), 'Pursuing Justice for Refugee Students: Addressing Issues of Cultural (Mis)recognition', *International Journal of Inclusive Education*, 16(12): 1295–310.

Kremsner, G., Proyer, M. and Obermayr, T. (2020), 'Die Ausgangslage und die Einrichtung des Zertifikatskurses „Bildungswissenschaftliche Grundlagen für Lehrkräfte mit Fluchthintergrund"' [The Initial Situation and the Establishment of the Certificate Course 'Educational Science Fundamentals for Teachers with a Refugee Background'], in G. Kremsner, M. Proyer and G. Biewer (eds), *Inklusion* von Lehrkräften nach der Flucht. Über universitäre Ausbildung zum beruflichen Wiedereinstieg, 17–45. Bad Heilbrunn: Verlag Julius Klinkhard.

Lessard, A., Butler-Kisber, L., Fortin, L. and Marcotte, D. (2014), 'Analyzing the Discourse of Dropouts and Resilient Students', *The Journal of Educational Research*, 107(2): 103–10.

Messiou, K., and Ainscow, M. (2020), 'Inclusive Inquiry: Student-Teacher Dialogue as a means of Promoting Inclusion in Schools', *British Educational Research Journal*, 46: 670–87. DOI: 10.1002/berj.3602.

Proyer, M., Biewer, G., Kreuter, L. and Weiß, J. (2021), 'Instating Settings of Emergency Education in Vienna: Temporary Schooling of Pupils with Forced Migration Backgrounds', *International Journal of Inclusive Education*, 25(2): 131–46. DOI: 10.1080/13603116.2019.1707299.

Rheindorf, M., and Wodak, R. (2018), 'Borders, Fences, and Limits – Protecting Austria from Refugees: Metadiscursive Negotiation of Meaning in the Current Refugee Crisis', *Journal of Immigrant & Refugee Studies*, 16(1–2): 15–38.

Schober, B., Lüftenegger, M., Spiel, C., Holzer, J., Ikanovic, S. K., Pelikan, E. and Fassl, F. (2020), 'Lernen unter COVID-19-Bedingungen. Erste Ergebnisse Schüler*innen' [Learning under COVID-19 Conditions. First Results Pupils]. Available at: https://lernencovid19.univie.ac.at/fileadmin/user_upload/p_lernencovid19/Zwischenergebnisse_Schueler_innen.pdf. (accessed 28 June 2021).

Schwab, S., Kast, J., and Lindner, K.-T. (2020), 'Deutschförderklassen und Deutschförderkurse. Ergebnisse zur Befragung von Lehrer*innen' [German Support Classes and German Support Courses. Results of the Survey of Teachers]. Available at: https://lehrerinnenbildung.univie.ac.at/fileadmin/user_upload/p_lehrerinnenbildung/Arbeitsbereiche/Bildungswissenschaft/Projekte/DFK_Deutschfoerderklassen/Ergebnisse_DFK_Dez_2020.pdf (accessed 22 September 2022).

Schweiger, H., and Müller, B. (2021), 'Mangelhaft und Unzureichend. Deutschförderklassen aus der Sicht von Lehrerinnen und Lehrern' [Deficient and Inadequate. German Support Classes from the Teachers' Perspective], in K. Resch, K. Lindner, B. Streese, M. Proyer and S. Schwab (eds), *Inklusive Schulentwicklung*, 43–54. Münster: Waxmann.

Uro, G., Lai, D., and Alsace, T. (2020), *Supporting English Learners in the COVID-19 Crisis*. Council of the Great City Schools. Available at: http://files.eric.ed.gov/fulltext/ED607280.pdf (accessed 25 September 2022).

5

Distance Learning and Inclusive School: An Impossible Challenge?

Ines Guerini, Giorgia Ruzzante and Alessia Travaglini[1]

Introduction

As is widely known, the Covid-19 pandemic has caused the closing of schools all around the world – in addition to other restrictive measures (e.g. that concerning the closure of gyms) – for several months in 2020 and some in 2021 in order to contain the spread of the virus (UNESCO, 2021). From time to time, depending on the progress of the virus spread, the governments of different countries – and the different areas within the countries too – have approved the return of students to schools. For instance, in Italy there has been partial or full opening of schools during the scholastic year 2020/21.

Therefore, closing schools has inevitably involved a widespread use of distance learning[2] (Schneider and Council 2020) – changing the traditional teaching strategies – it has also revealed some critical aspects of the Italian schools which have been broadly analyzed by national studies and researches (Bocci 2020; Fondazione et al. 2020; Guerini et al. 2020; Nirchi 2020; Pireddu 2020).

Consequently, new questions and doubts emerged from the large use of distance learning. For instance, how has the learning context changed? What challenges and what weaknesses is this new model displaying? What kind of parenting involvement is requested? How are support teachers involved in distance learning?

---

[1] This chapter is a six-handed work. Just to give credit, we wish to specify that Ines Guerini has written the introduction and the conclusion, Alessia Travaglini has written the first section and Giorgia Ruzzante has written the second.

[2] That in Italy has involved the use of synchronous and asynchronous teaching activities.

For these reasons, starting from the analysis of current national research data, we intend to propose a reflection on the use of online learning in the Italian schools with regard to inclusion. Particular attention will be paid to discuss how distance learning was used with disabled students and with those who live in situations of social, educational and material poverty. Moreover, some possible good practices will be presented in order to allow the participation of all students in this new learning context, in case we would have to use it again.

Before proposing the above-mentioned reflection, we think it is important to briefly summarize the historical path of school inclusion in Italy in order to let the reader understand the reasons we believe talking about inclusion does not necessarily mean being inclusive in the building of the educational environments. Italy has a long tradition of integrative practices at school (as well as in society), thanks to which the country is known as *positive exception* (Dovigo 2016) among the other European countries. For instance, we look at the deinstitutionalization that began in the 1980s after Franco Basaglia denounced the *inhuman conditions* (Cutrera 2016) in which people lived in the Italian asylums.

School inclusion – which is one of the topics of this chapter – was started in the early half of the 1970s[3] on some teachers' initiative with the so-called insertion phase.

In fact, teachers progressively felt the need to let disabled pupils leave the margins of society intended for them: 'special schools' and 'different classes'. The first special schools were educational institutions – just for the first level of instruction – for children with impairments. The second were classrooms of public schools where pupils defined as too 'restless, hyperactive' for the 'normal' school were educated.

Therefore, during the insertion phase Italian schools began to see 'a progressive participation of students with disabilities in common classes' (Bocci 2017: 14; our translation) on the basis of what Falcucci Commission stated

> even people with developmental, learning and adaptation difficulties must be considered protagonists of their own growth (MPI 1975: our translation).

It is not by chance that the Falcucci Commission is known as a cornerstone of the path that has led Italy towards inclusion.

The next phase was that of 'integration' which started during the second half of the 1970s with the enactment of the Law 517/77, according to which all students

---

[3] On the contrary, the neighbouring Switzerland, Germany and Austria have decided to close the special schools only in the last years after the ratification of the 2006 UN Convention (Hascher 2017; Lütje-Klose et al. 2017; Melzer 2019).

with disabilities can be educated in the mainstream. Finally, the third phase of the historical path of school inclusion started in the 2000s – when attention was focused not only on disabled students but also on those with learning difficulties (we look, for instance, at the Law 170/2010) – and is ongoing.

The major theoretical difference between 'integration' and 'inclusion' is that according to the first perspective disability is a 'personal tragedy' (Oliver 1990), and is, therefore, conceptualized by the medical model of disability. On the contrary, according to the inclusive perspective, the context must be transformed for welcoming people with disabilities.

Unfortunately, as stated before this is just a theoretical difference which still struggles to become praxis. In fact, Italian researchers on inclusion stress the presence of the phenomenon of micro-macro exclusion of students with disabilities (Bocci 2016; D'Alessio et al. 2015; Demo 2014), which highlights the importance of setting up learning contexts that suit all students (d'Alonzo 2012). Otherwise, disability is still interpreted through medical lenses.

It is our view that the so-called *pull and push phenomena* (Demo 2015) at school happen because the concept of inclusion itself needs to be disambiguated. In fact, we believe that 'inclusion' does not mean just 'insert/include' students in the school environment (D'Alessio 2011; Gardou 2012), but should involve a transformative process of the context (both educational and social) in order to welcome all and thus become really inclusive (Booth and Ainscow 2014; 2016). After all, as we argue in what follows, the educational institution is a privileged place for the encounter with the *other* and, therefore, capable of triggering the inclusive process.

Educational Poverty, Covid-19 Pandemic and Inclusion

It is undeniable that school presents an essential opportunity for the improvement of a society: education doesn't concern children only and can be considered as the way to reduce inequality and injustice in a community.

This is the reason its closure – although compensated by the introduction, in many cases too late, of distance learning – deeply affects not only the present time but also people's future perspectives. Moreover, it is quite clear that the school is not 'only' a place where students can intellectually and culturally grow up, because it affects the psychological, the emotional and, last but not least, the relational development of young people. These are variables that make up personal identity and co-construct the student's self-image, acting on the area of self-efficacy and, ultimately, of self-esteem. These considerations are even more relevant when compared to students in conditions of fragility and/or with Special Educational Needs (disability and/or learning disabilities, in particular).

Several researchers have aimed at identifying whether and how the pandemic has contributed to widening the social gap. First of all, it should be emphasized that widespread situations of poverty and social exclusion are still present in Italy. According to Save the Children (2015), in Italy over one million minors – about 10 per cent of the total – live in situation of absolute poverty and deprivation of adequate services. Alongside this kind of poverty, there are still widespread forms of educational poverty. They consist, for example, in fewer opportunities for 0–17-year-old people to take part in sports and cultural challenges; this inequality has a negative impact on the level of learning (Save the Children 2015).

According to Mario Rossi Doria, street teacher and expert in educational policies as well as an activist and president of the association named 'Con i bambini' (With Children),[4] educational poverty affects about 34 per cent of minors. Moreover, he thinks educational poverty is caused by factors of different nature that do not necessarily address the economic field. In fact, the social environment where a child lives plays a crucial role in causing educational poverty. According to the activist, factors such as extended school time programmes, a school canteen, the existence of classrooms connected to internet or the presence of cultural and sporting opportunities could reduce situations of educational poverty.

The core assumption from which Doria starts is that learning does not only concern the classroom life but also involves the entire community.[5] For this reason, also taking in mind the perspective adopted and theorized by Maria Montessori, Paulo Freire and Don Milani, we think that a deep social inclusion cannot be developed if children are not allowed to have access to learning opportunities.

Their educational models and practices, albeit in different ways, share the common vision that education is a powerful tool for social justice. Just to briefly remember their doing, we can affirm that Montessori (1909), by educating children, urged mothers to emancipate themselves, pushing them to find employment. According to Freire (1973), Brazilian peasants could make decisions about their political life and have a chance to change their condition if they could defeat illiteracy and ignorance. Finally, Don Milani (1967) believed

[4] It is an association that aims to fight childhood inequalities.
[5] https://www.invalsiopen.it/poverta-educativa-intervista-marco-red-doria/.

that education represented the main way to guaranteeing equity and equal opportunities for all.

Therefore, it is clear that, in the absence of a supportive social network and community, if a school does not fulfil its mission, regardless of the set of possible causes, a society could be forced to face great risks such as those caused by the Covid-19 pandemic in terms of educational poverty.

There has been vast research recently on the effects of the pandemic. For instance, a study carried out by the Community of S. Egidio, as part of a project entitled 'Valori in circolo' (Values in Circle), reports that about 25 per cent of children belonging to the suburbs of Rome are at risk of dispersion. This phenomenon is further stressed in the south of the city, in which about one out of three pupils does not receive appropriate care.[6] Specifically, these children have seldom attended school and did not take part in distance learning: as a consequence, they have received lower quality of training opportunities.

A similar situation is found in other countries: a report published in 2020 by the Centre for Learning and Life Chances in Knowledge Economies and Societies (LLAKES) highlights the existence of inequalities among children in the UK. Just to have an idea, during the lockdown period 31 per cent of private schools guaranteed about four hours a day of online teaching, compared to 6 per cent of public schools. In addition, 97 per cent of the pupils in private schools had a computer, while one in five of the students who enjoyed free meals in public schools did not (Green 2020).

According to the Department of Pediatrics at the University of Missouri-Kansas City, the closure of schools has negatively impacted the physical, nutritional and emotional needs of students, especially those belonging to families in difficulty who cannot adequately support the needs of children (Masonbrink and Hurley 2021). Lancker and Parolin (2020) highlight, in particular, that the suspension of face-to-face lessons had negative repercussions on infant feeding. According to Eurostat, 6.6 per cent of the families with children in the European Union and 14.4 per cent of the American families cannot have a full meal. Furthermore, they live in inadequate homes, poorly heated and lacking adequate outdoor spaces. In New York City, for example, during the pandemic one out of ten students was homeless or without a permanent home since the year before the spread of Covid-19.

These considerations acquire particular relevance if we consider the pupils identified with Special Education Needs. To this purpose, the report of the

---

[6] santegidio.org.

National Institute of Statistics (Istat), published on 9 December 2020, titled 'The Scholastic Inclusion of Students with Disabilities – s.y. 2019–2020', highlights that in Italy 23 per cent of pupils with disabilities (about seventy thousand students) did not take part in distance learning, with a significant difference between the different geographical areas (the most positive trend is associated to the central geographical area, where 'just' 5 per cent of the students were excluded from lessons vs. 9 per cent of the southern regions). Further significant findings emerged from research carried out in Italy. For example, according to the survey conducted by the SIRD – Italian Educational Research Society (2020) – 8 per cent of the students did not use the distance learning and 18 per cent used it only partially.

These data are further stressed within the urban neighbourhoods that present a poor socio-economic background, such as the Spanish Quarters in Naples, Quarto Ogiaro in Milan or Bastogi in Rome. These parts of the cities are also defined as distressed urban areas in which the economic, social and environmental conditions are worse than the national average and the average of the city as a whole (OECD 1998). Within them, we can find inequalities of all kinds, which mark 'biographies, limit opportunities and frustrate the ambitions of a significant part of the residents of big cities' (Chiodini and Milano 2010: 19; our translation).

The effects on minors are devastating: Iavarone and Girardi (2018), for example, observe that minors who have a past characterized by educational neglect more frequently run the risk of becoming deviant. Furthermore, they develop the conviction that 'being born in a "certain" family, living in a certain neighborhood, having seen the police getting in the house at dawn to arrest a parent, having met their father almost exclusively in prison, living with relatives involved in legal matters, have convinced them that they can't avoid an ineluctable destiny' (Iavarone 2019: 2; our translation).

According to UNICEF (2017), in order to improve life conditions, it is necessary to strengthen social policies, promoting access to work as much as possible for all people. However, this measure is not sufficient in itself; it is essential to develop – as much as possible – resilient communities, which are able to face critical issues, transforming difficulties into opportunities.

Following this perspective, many social initiatives have been undertaken in Italy to support families in their educational path. For instance, we refer to the Foundation Quartieri Spagnoli onlus (FOQUS), which started in Naples a process of regeneration of a highly marginalized district. In particular, it started specific measures aimed at promoting minors and their families. Another important association is Maestri di Strada (Street Teachers), whose motto is the famous Danilo Dolci's quotation 'Each Grows only if Dreamed'. Since 2003, the year his foundation was established, it has promoted numerous projects aimed at promoting active citizenship, seeking new resources and opportunities. On the other hand, in Rome we have to keep in mind the central role of Rampi Centre, which aims at promoting 'a civil society that respects human rights, first of all that relate mainly to security, safety, health, protection'.[7]

These experiences – although they cannot fully remove social problems – deserve credit for developing a sense of belonging among people in a community. Thus, they give special support to build social inclusion, understood as 'the condition in which all individuals live in one state of equity and equal opportunities, regardless of the presence of disability or poverty' (Ortigosa 2017: 78).

This definition is inspired by the main values of the Index for Inclusion (Booth and Ainscow 2014; 2016): according to it, the achievement of success by all students requires the synergy of measures that affect, in their whole, culture, politics and practices developed by an entire community, nationally and locally.

In fact, regulations alone do not produce far-reaching social changes. In a similar way, actions and challenges undertaken by a community have to be enhanced by legislative provisions capable of giving a strong and ongoing support to people's actions.

The Impact of Covid-19 on School Inclusion

The worldwide crisis caused by the pandemic has highlighted a large number of shortcomings that do not exclusively concern the healthcare sector (Guerini et al. 2020). In fact, in Italy – despite the full inclusion system – the closure of schools highlighted specific problems in terms of inclusion and school accessibility.

For instance, during the first lockdown[8] no specific legislative measures were adopted for students with disabilities. Consequently, disabled pupils – regardless of the complexity of their impairment – participated together with their classmates in distance learning, sometimes using a different virtual classroom, separated from classmates and shared only with the support teacher.

---

[7] centrorampi.it.
[8] Lockdown which lasted from the beginning of March 2020 until the end of the school year.

These circumstances remind us of that already mentioned *push and pull out phenomena* (Demo 2015), in which students with disabilities are only apparently included in the school system, since they are in fact excluded as they undertake lessons other than those of their classmates and in separate spaces. These events have made it very difficult to develop a strong relationship with their classmates. We also refer to the fact that only a small number of schools have organized synchronous online learning activities.

Particular difficulties were highlighted in kindergartens and in the first years of primary school, where it is more complex to devise didactic proposals with distance learning, given that due to the particular age of the group the body and the relation with teachers are the first mediators for learning.

The traditional school environment has been disrupted by the pandemic, which introduced an extensive use of virtual classrooms, using platforms. Different levels of instruction chose different paths: high schools started with online lessons first, while k-14 schools gradually built the digital infrastructure in the institutes over a few weeks, choosing one of the platforms for school use. They also lent devices for free to students who didn't have them. Educational poverty and socio-economic hardship did not allow all students to access distance learning, particularly in the southern areas of the country (ISTAT-National Institute of Statistics 2020).

In distance learning, times, teaching strategies, tools and evaluation practices change. Every aspect of the usual school lesson is revolutionized by distance learning: planning, didactic action and evaluation. Online learning has therefore created difficulties for the different actors in the educational field: pupils and their families, teachers and school principals. Students with disabilities were the most penalized ones. In fact, the possibility of sharing common spaces and activities allows teachers to work for full inclusion and to obtain high-level school performance (Giangreco, Doyle and Suter 2012). This challenge allows Italian students to perform better than their peers with disabilities from other countries.

Surely, the pandemic has made clear that schools are asked to use technology in their teaching practices. In a similar way, it has stressed that nowadays digital illiteracy has a negative impact on socialization. Moreover, the role of families was fundamental during the pandemic, and allowed in positive situations the strengthening of the bond with the school in order to allow the continuation at least at a minimum level of educational and didactic activities, allowing a deeper communication between the two main educational agencies. In situations of educational poverty, with low-income families and scarce cultural resources, it was instead much more complex to be able to adequately support children during remote school activities. Censis-Center Study of Social Investments (2020) found that foreign pupils were particularly disadvantaged.

In the first phase of the lockdown, the support teachers worked to develop the most effective distance teaching methods in order to continue to advance students in learning. In Italy, Ianes (2020) proposed to form *partner ropes*, for not interrupting the bonds between the students with disabilities and their classmates, including them in the virtual classroom or in small groups in mixed presence, composed of students with and without disabilities. Nevertheless, the legislation relating to the regulation of the pandemic has started a heated debate at national level as the presence in the classroom of only students with special educational needs during the lockdown, considering this to be exclusive and therefore in contrast with the principles and practices of school inclusion present in Italy. Certainly, for some students to attend the school physically is the only way to learn, but many times students have asked the question why they were alone in their class, sometimes only with the support teacher, reproducing the negative dual relation between the support teacher and students with disabilities. In this way, the impression was given of dividing in two dimensions that are intrinsically connected – learning and socialization – the two aims to which inclusive schooling tends.

Furthermore, even the network connection is not always stable and widespread throughout the national territory. Only towards the end of the first lockdown of spring 2020 were the educators/assistants allowed to carry out their service at the students' homes, losing for a long time the possibility of having important and significant educational figures for the students' life. Moreover, it is difficult for some pupils to spend their entire life inside their homes, without being able to go outside: we are thinking, for example, about pupils with autism or attention deficit and hyperactivity.

All students with Special Educational Needs were disadvantaged as their attendance in the school environment is an important facilitator to overcome the obstacles they encounter to learning and participating. This point is highlighted by the International Classification of Functioning (WHO 2001), according to which disability is conceptualized by the bio-psycho-social model (instead of the medical model). Namely, interacting with others or working on projects and participating in activities in the community reduce the condition of disability. At school, there are environmental facilitators such as classmates and teachers with whom it is possible to build a relationship, while in distance learning it is only mediated by a screen.

Distance learning has proved to be a barrier for many students, especially those with more complex disabilities such as autism spectrum disorders. In fact, these students cannot learn using the PC, but only through the physical presence of the teacher or educator. We look at, for example, education for personal autonomy and the establishment of socio-relational skills, which are precisely the most important skills to be learnt by pupils with autism. Particularly penalized were students who had just started or were finishing a school cycle. In fact, research (Bocci 2020; Fondazione et al. 2020; Guerini et al. 2020; Nirchi 2020; Pireddu 2020) carried out on school inclusion and distance learning has shown that only about under half of the students with disabilities have been fully included in distance learning activities. In fact, for some students it was very difficult to be able to continue working on the objectives set up by their individualized educational plan through forms of distance learning.

The pandemic has therefore helped to highlight the already known criticalities of the Italian school system, such as the separation of the pupil with disabilities from their classmates, and the marginal and separate role played by the support teacher. These topics represent open questions that are still widely detected by research in pedagogy and special education (e.g. Cottini 2014; Guerini 2020; Montanari and Ruzzante 2020).

The use of learning models that refer to UDL (Universal Design for Learning) principles allows to rethink teaching–learning processes from an inclusive perspective, for a profound renewal of teaching and to find creative solutions to new problems. To reach this goal, schools need to go beyond the format of the frontal lesson which is still the most frequently used methodology within the classroom today (Cavalli and Argentin 2010).

Morin (2020) wonders what lessons the pandemic has given us: certainly, the *lesson of digital,* as it is called by the scholar himself.

Technology has become an integral part of everyday life for children, teenagers and adults and all teachers must learn to use it for educational purposes. Technological tools must become allies in the teaching–learning process; they can also be considered from a UDL perspective as tools capable of allowing accessibility and personalization, enhancing the potential of socio-constructivism.

It is necessary to renew and rethink the teaching practices in place in the school, both at present and in the distant future; this step can be reached by proposing methodologies capable of being inclusive for all students, providing students with a plurality of didactic mediators to match different cognitive styles. An inclusive school should be a more flexible school, from the organizational and the didactic points of view, and able to always find new solutions to solve old and new problems.

Conclusions: About Future Implications of Covid-19

This chapter has argued that the Covid-19 pandemic can become an opportunity for Italy to invest again in education and to put school back at the centre – introducing, for instance, essential technological, organizational and didactic changes for the school of the twenty-first century – or it can become yet another lost opportunity to reform this institution.

Referring to the changes that schools could bring about, the Recovery Plan envisaged by the European Union for the relaunch of the economies of the adhering countries can be a valuable opportunity to invest resources in education, which is the most important engine of economic as well as social revival that a country can have. It would be important to improve school approaches because prolonged closure of educational institutions has led to multiple effects and probably will bring some additional ones. We looked, for example, at some possible problems linked to the psychological conditions of children and youth, especially as regards the age group of adolescents.

Moreover, as already affirmed above, Covid-19 has accentuated the preexisting situations of educational poverty and social inequality. At the same time, the pandemic situation has brought back an interest in outdoor teaching practices, as outdoor spaces significantly reduce the risk of contagion. These didactic practices, offer not only multisensory, but also inclusive perspectives. In fact, these kinds of didactic methodologies also guarantee more autonomy than the classical one in the learning process. Just to mention a kind of methodology which moves in this direction, open learning (Demo 2016; Jürgens 2009; Peschel 2006a,b) offers high levels of choice to the students. Therefore, students take part in the learning process more easily and with more motivation than in the traditional lesson. Finally, open learning pays attention to the individual characteristics of students, who become aware protagonists of their own learning process. In fact, students can experiment with the various activities and understand which ones are suitable for them at that specific moment and which ones, on the other hand, need additional time to be carried out.

References

Bocci, F. (2016), 'Didattica inclusiva. Questioni e suggestioni', in F. Bocci, B. De Angelis, C. Fregola, D. Olmetti Peja and U. Zona (eds), *Rizodidattica. Teorie dell'apprendimento e modelli inclusivi*, 15–82. Lecce: Pensa Multimedia.

Bocci, F. (2017), 'I protagonisti dell'inclusione', in A. Morganti and F. Bocci (eds), *Didattica inclusiva nella scuola primaria. Educazione socio-emotiva e Apprendimento cooperativo per costruire competenze inclusive attraverso i 'compiti di realtà'*, 24–33. Firenze: Giunti Edu.

Bocci, F. (2020), 'Disabilità e Didattica a Distanza a scuola durante la Pandemia Covid-19. Una riflessione intorno alle narrazioni dei diversi protagonisti', *Nuova Secondaria Ricerca*, 2: 321–42.

Booth, T., and Ainscow, M. (2014), *Nuovo Index per l'Inclusione. Percorsi di apprendimento e di partecipazione a scuola*. Italian Edition. Roma: Cartocci.

Booth, T., and Ainscow, M. (2016), 'Index for Inclusion: A Guide to School Development Led by Inclusive Values'. Cambridge: Index for Inclusion Network Limited.

Cavalli, A., and Argentin, G., eds. (2010), *Gli insegnanti italiani: come cambia il modo di fare scuola. Terzo rapporto Iard sulla situazione docente*. Bologna: Il Mulino.

CENSIS. (2020), 'Italia sotto sforzo. Diario della Transizione 2020-1. La scuola e i suoi esclusi'. Available at: https://www.censis.it/sites/default/files/downloads/Diario%20della%20Transizione.pdf (accessed 2 July 2021).

Chiodini, L., and Milano, R. (eds) (2010), *Le città ai margini: povertà estreme e governo delle aree urbane: analisi e linee di orientamento per lo sviluppo di politiche locali sulla marginalità sociale e le povertà estreme*. Ministero del lavoro e delle politiche sociali: Roma.

Cottini, L. (2014), 'Editoriale-Promuovere l'inclusione: l'insegnante specializzato per le attività di sostegno in primo piano', *Italian Journal of Special Education for Inclusion*, 2(2): 10–20.

Cutrera, S. (ed.) (2016), *Stop ai crimini d'odio contro le persone con disabilità*. Roma: PG PrimeGraf srl.

D'Alessio, S. (2011), *Inclusive Education in Italy. A Critical Analysis of the Policy of Integrazione Scolastica*. Rotterdam: Sense Publishers.

D'Alessio, S., Medeghini, R., Vadalà, G., and Bocci, F. (2015), 'L'approccio dei Disability Studies per lo sviluppo delle pratiche scolastiche inclusive in Italia', in R. Vianello and S. Di Nuovo (eds), *Quale scuola inclusiva in Italia? Oltre le posizioni ideologiche: risultati della ricercar*, 151–79. Trento: Erickson.

d'Alonzo, L. (2012), 'Questioni, sfide e prospettive della Pedagogia Speciale', in L. d'Alonzo and R. Caldin (eds), *Questioni, sfide e prospettive della Pedagogia Speciale. L'impegno della comunità di ricerca*, 7–20. Napoli: Liguori.

Demo, H. (2014), 'Il fenomeno del push e pull out nell'integrazione scolastica italiana', *L'integrazione scolastica e sociale*, 13/3: 202–17.

Demo, H. (2015), 'Dentro e fuori dall'aula: che cosa funziona davvero nella classe inclusiva? Alcuni risultati di 13 studi di caso nella scuola primaria italiana', *Italian Journal of Special Education for Inclusion*, 3(1): 53–70.

Demo, H. (2016), *Didattica aperta e inclusione. Principi, metodologie e strumenti per insegnanti della scuola primaria e secondaria*. Trento: Erickson.

Don Milani e la Scuola di Barbiana. (1967), *Lettera a una professoressa*. Firenze: Libreria Editrice Fiorentina.

Dovigo, F. (2016), 'Introduzione', in F. Dovigo, C. Favella, A. Pietrocarlo, V. Rocco and E. Zappella (eds).*Nessuno escluso. Trasformare la scuola e l'apprendimento per realizzare l'educazione inclusiva. Atti del Convegno*, 23–47. Bergamo: Bergamo University Press.

Fondazione Agnelli, Università di Bolzano, Università LUMSA, and Università di Trento. (2020), 'OLTRE LE DISTANZE. L'indagine preliminare'. Available at: https://www.fondazioneagnelli.it/wp-content/uploads/2020/05/OLTRE-LE-DISTANZE-SINTESI-RISULTATI-QUESTIONARIO-1.pdf (accessed 29 June 2021).

Freire, P. (1973), *L'educazione come pratica di libertà*. Milano: Mondadori.

Gardou, C. (2012), *La société inclusive, parlons-en! Il n'y a pas de vie minuscule*. Toulouse: Édition Érés.

Giangreco, M. F., Doyle, M. B., and Suter, J. C. (2012), 'Demographic and Personnel Service Delivery Data: Implications for Including Students with Disabilities in Italian Schools', *Life Span and Disability*, 15(1): 97–123.

Green, F. (2020), 'Schoolwork in Lockdown: New Evidence on the Epidemic of Educational Poverty'. Centre for Learning and Life Chances in Knowledge Economies and Societies (LLAKES), Research Paper, 67.

Guerini, I. (2020), 'La formazione degli insegnanti specializzati per il sostegno. Esiti della rilevazione iniziale sul profilo dei corsisti dell'Università Roma Tre', *Education Sciences & Society*, 1: 169–85.

Guerini, I., Montanari, M., Ruzzante, G., and Travaglini, A. (2020), 'Disabilità ed emergenza sanitaria: quale inclusione scolastica'? *Nuova Secondaria*, 2: 304–20.

Hascher T. (2017), 'Die Bedeutung von Wohlbefinden und Sozialklima für Inklusion', in B. Lütje-Klose, S. Miller, S. Schwab and B. Streese (eds). *Inklusion: Profile für die Schul- und Unterrichtsentwicklung in Deutschland, Österreich und der Schweiz. Theoretische Grundlagen – Empirische Befunde – Praxisbeispiele*, 69–80. Münster: Waxmann.

Ianes, D. (2020), 'Le cordate tra compagni: valorizzare l'apprendimento formale e informale'. Available at: https://eventi.erickson.it/convegno-didattiche-2020-erickson/session-detail/1559/le-cordate-tra-compagni-valorizzare-lapprendimento-formale-e-informale (accessed 14 October 2022).

Iavarone, M. L. (2019), 'Curare i margini. Riprendersi il senso dell'educazione per prevenire il rischio', *Annali online della Didattica e della Formazione Docente*, 11(18): 1–5.

Iavarone, M. L., and Girardi, F. (2018), 'Povertà educativa e rischio minorile: fenomenologia di un crimine sociale', *Rivista di Studi e Ricerche sulla criminalità organizzata*, 4(3): 23–44.

Istituto Nazionale di Statistica (ISTAT). (2020), 'Spazi in casa e disponibilità di computer per bambini e ragazzi'. Available at: https://www.istat.it/it/files//2020/04/Spazi-casa-disponibilita-computer-ragazzi.pdf (accessed 2 February 2021).

Jürgens, E. (2009), *Die «neue» Reformpädagogik und Bewegung offener Unterricht: Theorie, Praxis und Forschungslage*. Sankt Augustin: Academia Verlag.

Lütje-Klose, B., Miller, S., Schwab, S., and Streese, B. (2017), 'Einleitung: Schulische Inklusion in den deutschsprachigen Ländern', in Lütje-Klose, B., Miller, S., Schwab, S., and Streese, B. (eds), *Inklusion: Profile für die Schul- und Unterrichtsentwicklung in Deutschland, Österreich und der Schweiz. Theoretische Grundlagen – Empirische Befunde – Praxisbeispiele*, 9–13. Münster: Waxmann.

Masonbrink, A. R., and Hurley, E. (2020), 'Advocating for Children during the COVID-19 School Closures', *Pediatrics*, 146(3): 1–4.

Melzer J. (2019), 'Eine Schule für alle oder Wie inklusive Bildung gelingen kann – Ableitungen aus der Existenziellen Pädagogik', *Pädagogische Horizonte*, 3(1): 129–48.

Ministero della Pubblica Istruzione. (1975), 'Relazione conclusiva della Commissione Falcucci concernente i problemi scolastici degli alunni handicappati'. Available at: https://www.edscuola.it/archivio/didattica/falcucci.html (accessed 5 June 2021).

Montanari, M., and Ruzzante, G. (2020), 'Formare l'insegnante specializzato: l'esperienza inclusiva dei laboratori nel corso di specializzazione per il sostegno', *Italian Journal of Special Education for Inclusion*, 8(1): 335–49.

Montessori. (1909), *Il metodo della pedagogia scientifica applicato all'educazione infantile nelle Case dei Bambini*. Città di Castello: Casa Editrice S. Lapi.

Montessori, M. (2000), *Il metodo della pedagogia scientifica applicato all'educazione infantile nelle Case dei Bambini*. Roma: Opera Nazionale.

Morin, E. (2020), *Changeons de voie: Les leçons du coronavirus*. Paris: Denoel.

Nirchi, S. (2020), 'La scuola durante l'emergenza COVID/19. Primi risultati di una indagine sulla Didattica a distanza (DaD)', *QTimes, anno XII*, 3: 127–39.

OECD. (1998), 'Integrating Distressed Urban Areas'. Paris: OECD.

Oliver, M. (1990), *The Politics of Disablement: A Sociological Approach (Critical Texts in Social Work and the Welfare State)*. London: Macmillan.

Peschel, F. (2006a), *Offener Unterricht: Idee, Realität, Perspektive und ein praxiserprobtes Konzept zur Diskussion. Teil I*. Baltmannsweiler: Schneider Verlag Hohengehren.

Peschel, F. (2006b), *Offener Unterricht: Idee, Realität, Perspektive und ein praxiserprobtes Konzept zur Diskussion. Teil II*. Baltmannsweiler: Schneider Verlag Hohengehren.

Pireddu, M. (2020), 'Didattica online: presenza e prossimità nell'era della "nuova normalità"', *QTimes, anno XII*, 3: 5–19.

Ranci Ortigosa, E. (2017), 'Il costo della povertà', *Mondoperaio*, 1/2017: 75–83.

Save the Children Italia Onlus. (2015), 'Illuminiamo il Futuro 2030. Obiettivi per liberare i bambini dalla povertà educativa'. Roma: Save the Children Italia.

Schneider, S. L., and Council, M. L. (2020), 'Distance Learning in the Era of COVID-19', *Archives of Dermatological Research*, 313: 389–90.

SIRD. (2020), 'Per un confronto sulle modalità di didattica a distanza adottate nelle scuole nel periodo di emergenza Covid-19'. Available at: https://www.sird.it/wp-content/uploads/2020/07/Una_prima_panoramica_dei_dati.pdf (accessed 2 July 2021).

UNESCO. (2021), 'Education: From School Closure to Recovery'. Available at: https://en.unesco.org/covid19/educationresponse#schoolclosure (accessed 14 October 2022).

UNICEF. (2017), 'Inclusive Education – Including Children with Disabilities in Quality Learning'. Available at: https://www.unicef.org/eca/sites/unicef.org.eca/files/IE_summary_accessible_220917_brief.pdf (accessed 14 October 2022).

Van Lancker, W., and Parolin, Z. (2020), 'COVID-19, School Closures, and Child Poverty: A Social Crisis in the Making', *The Lancet Public Health*, 5(5): e243–4.

World Health Organization (WHO) (2001), *International Classification of Functioning, Disability and Health*. Geneva: WHO.

Part 3

Addressing Social Exclusion: Illuminating Possibilities for Inclusion in and through Crisis

A Widening Inequality Gap: Reducing Educational Inequalities in Europe by Reaching Out to Students and Families at Risk during a Time of Crisis and Beyond

Pamela Marie Spiteri

Introduction

The issue of students at risk of early leaving from education and training (ELET)[1] has been widely discussed as a European challenge during the past decade (Van Praag et al. 2018). ELET refers to those students who drop out of compulsory schooling or finish compulsory education without an upper secondary qualification and are consequently at a great disadvantage in progressing in their education or career (European Commission 2013). Within the field of education, ELET can be considered as a main marker of an inequality gap that reduces social justice within society (Popovici 2019; Tarabini et al. 2019). ELET is considered as a phenomenon brought about by a number of risk factors, mainly, achievement, behaviour, chronic absenteeism, disability, engagement, family disadvantage, gender and health (Gonzalez-Rodriguez, Vieira and Vidal 2019; Kallip and Heidmets 2017; Popovici 2019).

Some of these main risk factors have been strongly amplified by the educational crisis of school closure brought about by the worldwide pandemic Covid-19, which not only impacted learning, but also students' well-being (Bayrakdar and Guveli 2020; Drane, Vernon and O'Shea 2020; Eivers, Worth and Ghosh 2020; Engzell, Frey and Verhagen 2021; Masonbrink and Hurley, 2020). During the pandemic, several families ended up without income and community support

---

[1] ELET was selected and used in this chapter since, as opposed to early school leaving (ESL), ELET encompasses not only academic training, but also vocational pathways.

thereby precipitating increased poverty and family disadvantages. These are strong markers of ELET and the risk of education progression or deprivation of higher education. Consequently, this increased disadvantage has affected other risk factors, such as absenteeism and academic achievement also. Moreover, health issues, mitigation measures and distance learning within the home environment, rather than at school, had a significant impact on learning. This has serious implications within the field of education, including greater numbers of ELET students due to increased risk factors, which would therefore continue to widen the inequality gap. The recent European Commission's review on ELET has recommended that early identification of risk factors and whole-school support measures should be in place from the early years of schooling, hence supporting preventive policy measures (Donlevy, Andriescu and Downes 2019).

This chapter brings to the fore a preventive policy measure, namely, the Home School Community Liaison (HSCL) programme (Department Education and Skills, 2019), which aims to identify and target social and educational risk factors from the early years of schooling in an attempt to minimize a widening inequality gap. This strategic measure supports salient adults within students' lives (mainly parents and teachers), and findings from pre- and post-pandemic obtained from a wider doctoral study[2] will be discussed. Although each educational context is unique, through a case study of the HSCL programme in Ireland as a strategic preventive ELET measure, and by utilizing the Sen–Bourdieu Analytical Framework (SBAF), this chapter will discuss its use pre- and post-pandemic, and will offer recommendations of how this could be applied to other countries as a preventive policy measure to reduce ELET risk factors by supporting conversion factors both within the field of home and that of school (Hart 2012, 2018), while aiming to increase capabilities. In this case study, the HSCL was analyzed within the Irish context, as opposed to the Maltese educational context that does not have such a preventive programme and has one of the highest rates of ELET within the EU (Ministry for Education 2020). Recommendations will focus on the development of a whole-school approach measure, such as, the HSCL, which targets students experiencing different degrees of poverty and socio-economic marginalization due to disadvantaged family backgrounds, while discussing how it could support conversion factors. The SBAF is therefore innovatively being used not only to evaluate inequalities in relation to ELET within educational contexts, but also to support policy and practice through opportunity development as in the HSCL.

---

[2] Findings as part of a PhD study in Education and Social Justice at Lancaster University supervised by Dr Melis Cin and funded through a scholarship (TESS) awarded by the Ministry for Education, Malta.

The Context following the Outbreak of Covid-19

School closure due to safety protocols has impacted children worldwide during 2020 and 2021 (Downes, Pike and Murphy 2020). Implications of this school closure are still emerging, but a number of intervention measures have been taken across borders (Drane, Vernon and O'Shea 2020; Eivers, Worth and Ghosh 2020). In Malta, during the first closure of March 2020, not all schools were equally equipped for online teaching, thus leading to different educational provision within private, church and state schools (Busuttil and Farrugia 2020; Vassallo et al. 2021). In September, schools were geared up, and when the second school closure occurred, teaching and learning online was more sustainable. However, some parents and students were still not targeted since, for instance, some students found it hard to engage in online learning, particularly those in the early years, those with learning difficulties and others who could not engage due to a lack of resources (Busuttil and Farrugia 2020; Vassallo et al. 2021).

Despite opening school doors in Malta in September 2020, families were free to choose whether to send their children to school or not, depending on what they deemed to be a healthy and safe choice for their child (Busuttil and Farrugia 2020; Vassallo et al. 2021). An online school was set up which, albeit a good initiative, had its limitations such as the ability to accommodate a limited number of students, thus excluding some, like some secondary school students. Due to parents' free choice in sending their children to school, absenteeism increased during the last scholastic year, which can be detrimental to these students' educational journey. As a mitigation measure, a summer programme is being offered in order to target students who were absent from school. This programme is on a voluntary basis, and thus, not all disadvantaged students might attend.

The HSCL programme in Ireland experienced an essential change in its role, but was found to be an essential means of communication during school closure and distance learning. An important component of the HSCL is carrying out home visits in order to build a relationship between the parents and the communities. Nonetheless, these were not possible during school closure because of health mitigation measures (Ross, Kennedy and Devitt 2021). Disadvantaged students were however supported by HSCL coordinators, who monitored these students through phone calls, while targeting their basic needs, such as, ensuring they had food which would usually be provided at school. The provision of basic needs such as food helped to maintain contact with the most vulnerable families. Despite not entering homes, HSCL coordinators dropped off basic needs in front of doors or fixed a drop-off point at school by keeping safe distances. This pivotal change in the role of the HSCL, in spite of being challenging, was found to be an essential factor of support during the pandemic (Ross, Kennedy and Devitt 2021).

Students at risk of ELET, particularly those hailing from disadvantaged families, are more at risk of greater academic disadvantage due to the learning loss experienced during school closure (Downes, Pike and Murphy 2020; Eivers, Worth and Ghosh 2020). Students' well-being, apart from their own agency, depends on the salient adults within their lives, that is, their parents and teachers (Biggeri, Ballet and Comim 2011; Biggeri and Santi 2012). If schools embark on a whole-school approach to learning, their approach would entail collaborating with families and acting timely to support the families' well-being. Teachers however cannot do this alone due to multiple curricular demands and expectations. Therefore, a programme such as the HSCL, despite its limitations, has been essential before and during an unexpected pandemic in order to build a link between school and home, while focusing not only on the students' well-being, but also on that of the families.

The SBAF to Develop Policy Programmes that Target ELET Risk Factors

The Covid-19 pandemic increased the risk factors of ELET and students' well-being (Downes, Pike and Murphy 2020). Families had limited access to support within their communities or the support they usually get from schools or agencies that also had to close down because of health risks. The SBAF (Hart 2012, 2018) provided a solid theoretical lens, serving as a tool to analyze not only students' well-being in relation to ELET risk factors, but also their families' well-being, or lack of it. Bourdieu's notions of 'habitus' and 'capital' (Bourdieu 1997; Bourdieu and Passeron 1977) supported the analysis of family well-being before and after the pandemic, and Sen's capability approach (CA) (1992, 1985) allowed for the analysis and development of opportunity development with regard to supporting conversion factors. The family's lack of financial, cultural and social capital was considered crucial during this study. Following the outbreak of the pandemic, capital loss in multiple areas was experienced by a number of families thereby increasing further this disadvantage and the gap between school and home. For instance, some families that already had limited income lost even this during the pandemic since one or both of the family members lost their job. Loss of social capital was also experienced as most of the community activities were closed, including those at school, such as training programmes provided by the HSCL programme.

Bourdieu's notion of 'field' (Bourdieu 1997; Bourdieu and Passeron 1977) was also crucial and experienced a change before and after the pandemic. While most organized learning happened in the 'field' of school pre-Covid-19, during the pandemic and school closure, organized learning was meant to take place in the 'field' of home (Eivers, Worth and Ghosh 2020). The engagement of learning within this sudden new 'field' of home was consequently marked by the families' 'habitus' and 'capital'. Therefore, if a family had sufficient knowledge, skills, resources and motivation to support their child, the child would engage better in learning, thereby minimizing learning loss. Conversely, if the child did not find support or the necessary resources at home, learning loss was increased, thus augmenting the risk of ELET. The HSCL programme was thus also analyzed under the CA lens to determine whether any functionings or capabilities are increased with this support by empowering students' and salient adults' agency, freedom and well-being. Covid-19 implications within schools result in limited agency, freedom and well-being, thereby affecting academic progression, unless the right support is offered to minimize this negative impact.

Methods

Through a qualitative case study, data were collected during three phases, with the first and second being in Ireland and Malta respectively before the pandemic, and the third in both countries following the start of the pandemic. In total, sixty semi-structured interviews were carried out with parents, policymakers and educators. Four semi-structured observations of training sessions for both parents and teachers were carried out during the first two phases. The participants provided working documents during phases 1 and 2 of the study, which were also analyzed together with two policies on the HSCL in phase 1 and two policies on the context of ELET in phase 2. Following the forty semi-structured interviews in the first two phases, twenty participants from the Irish and Maltese context were interviewed again in phase 3. The participants in the first phase of the analysis were selected from disadvantaged schools within the Irish context. Given that Malta has no schools classified as disadvantaged, the participants in Malta were selected from schools through criteria associated with disadvantage and ELET risk factors, namely, families and teachers of students experiencing low academic scores, students benefiting from resource support due to financial disadvantage and school areas which have a greater number of students from a migrant or minority background.

The HSCL as a Whole-School Approach Measure in Ireland or Lack of It in Malta: Findings before Covid-19

Frequent and chronic absenteeism is one of the greatest markers of ELET. Parents have an active role in deciding whether to take children to school or not and supporting their children's decision in missing school or not, in the case of older students. Amongst many strategies to reduce absenteeism, what is often missing is targeting the real reasons parents do not send their own children to receive a free education. For instance, Cathy is a 25-year-old single parent in Ireland who had a bad experience in school. Adam, her only child, who struggled in his first two years of schooling, is now doing well, and Cathy believes that this happened because of the support she received through Ms Sara, who is an HSCL coordinator. Cathy recalls how she felt scared when the class teacher tried to approach her as she did not know her much, and she knew that Adam was not coping well with schoolwork and homework. She had received some previous notes from the class teacher, but was totally embarrassed as she did not know how to help him nor had the financial means to seek help.

Cathy's own habitus, and hence, her identity in relation to education, were shaped through her own individual negative experience of schooling (Reay 2004). Failing to take this into consideration could have simply led to her own child going through a similar negative schooling experience because, even though children have their own agency (Biggeri, Ballet and Commim 2011; Biggeri and Santi 2012), their own habitus is shaped by individual experiences also brought about by parents, who are salient adults in their lives. Through the HSCL programme, developing absenteeism strategies meant also including Cathy's own experiences, as opposed to a general strategy for all students alike. This implied that the HSCL coordinator worked together with Cathy to identify her own fears and lack of social capital in order to provide support thereby developing Cathy's capabilities, which included the skill of sending her child to school and seeking support if needed. It can be said that, in this case, the HSCL programme increased Cathy's social and cultural capital, which indeed had an impact on her capabilities and functionings.

Julia's mum, Kathleen, is also a young single mum in Malta. Contrary to the Irish context, Kathleen received much judgement and criticism for not sending her child to school. Kathleen had recently broken up with her violent partner, and when eight-year-old Julia told her that she did not have friends at school and they called her names such as 'stupid' or 'idiot', she decided not to send her to school as she did not want her daughter to be upset. Kathleen does not think that Julia can get any better in school, and is not aware of the number of free services that are offered to children experiencing literacy difficulties. Similarly to Cathy, she does not want to face the teacher as she feels that she is going to be judged, especially since she has already received a fine for not sending her child to school and feels that, whenever she takes her to school, teachers do not smile at her. Although it can be debated that Kathleen is refusing to accept support, she is not even aware of it as she is afraid to communicate and is not sending her child to school as she thinks it is the right thing for her at the moment.

Within an SBAF framework, it can be said that Kathleen lacks cultural (educational skills) and social capital (emotional support through family and friends) thereby impacting her capability and functionings (Hart 2018). The HSCL, within the SBAF lens, can therefore be viewed as a tool that identifies ELET indicators within the family unit and works on conversion factors so as to develop agency and well-being of salient adults, thus impacting positively disadvantaged students. Although the HSCL's main aim is to support parents, it was found that it also supports teachers. It can be said that teachers meet students within the field of school, and support is usually targeted at school. Teachers might be aware of students experiencing a disadvantage at home, and try to cater for this in their classrooms. However, during this study, it was evident that this is not sufficient. The HSCL programme can thus be said to target social class inequalities, particularly in the aspect of social and cultural capital, which can have an impact on educational advantage. Lareau and Weininger (2003) maintain that parental and school relationships can be influenced by differences in capital due to social class. Consequently, the HSCL can be seen to target the relationship between school and home as, by providing support to parents within the field of home, it targets conversion factors through identified capital needs thereby impacting not only the parents, but also teachers and, in turn, their students. While both Ms Sue and Ms Charlene discuss the challenging experience of teaching students from a disadvantaged background, Ms Sue recognizes that HSCL coordinators support her in meeting students' needs as she is more aware of the students' background and individual experiences.

Findings within this pre-Covid-19 phase thus demonstrate that the HSCL programme is a useful link between school and home, particularly for students who might be experiencing difficulties due to a disadvantaged background. Lareau et al. (2011) and Ingram (2018) suggest that class can be directly linked to educational disadvantage in a student's life, and that this could create a gap between students hailing from different backgrounds. The lack of such a whole-school approach programme could further increase a gap between school and home due to misinformation, the parents' lack of basic skills and the amount of work already required from teachers. Consequently, inequalities brought about by family disadvantage were minimized through the HSCL as the necessary support was given not only to the student, but also to the family. This increased their agency and well-being, while enabling both students and families to have the freedom to choose the opportunities they really want (Hart 2012, 2018).

The HSCL as a Whole-School Approach Measure or Lack of It: Findings during and after Covid-19

During the pandemic, the HSCL programme experienced two major changes during school closure, namely, the inability to carry out any home visits and organizing any training or face-to-face meetings. These are two essential components of the HSCL, and thus, coordinators were instructed to make regular phone calls. Hannah, an HSCL coordinator for the last three years, explains that their job had a sudden change in providing essential needs before anything else. She however believes that, by providing essential needs such as food, HSCL coordinators have managed to support the students' well-being through the families' well-being. She also speaks of the loss of face-to-face contact which is essential for such a programme. Although most HSCL coordinators believe that there is no substitute for home visits, food delivery or pick-up and other channels such as calls were very useful. While the initial support was to focus on basic needs, when schools resorted to online learning, it was evident that most of the disadvantaged families they were dealing with had either no connectivity, except mobile data bundle, or no digital devices. It was essential for them to liaise with school principals and teachers to be able to not only provide the digital resources needed, but also set up these digital resources for the children to follow any school programmes. Training for parents was continuous, but could not be done face to face, which was very challenging.

It transpired that, although the HSCL was a crucial human resource in Ireland in supporting disadvantaged families and students through basic needs and digital devices, this was not sufficient. Most HSCL coordinators point out the need to work together through a whole-school approach by finding solutions when facing challenging issues, such as, families not being able to use a laptop or connect to the school system. Similarly, in Malta, following school closure and set-up of online learning, a number of digital devices and internet were provided immediately to students who are listed as financially disadvantaged. However, some parents experienced challenges using these devices. Although support was offered, this was very scattered. Some support was offered through individual schools, while others contacted the national IT office. Had there been one person for each school, as was the case with the HSCL coordinators, this could have been more efficient.

It can be said that support following school closure focused on what Sen defines as 'basic capabilities', such as food and housing that is a 'cut-off point for the purpose of assessing poverty and deprivation' (Sen 1987: 109). Nussbaum (2000: 84) defines 'basic capabilities' as 'innate equipment that is necessary for developing the more advanced capabilities'. This implies that support during Covid-19, including that provided by the HSCL, focused on basic needs in order to avoid families that were already classified as disadvantaged experiencing further deprivation. Nussbaum (2000) and Sen (1987) both argue that, in order to develop agency, basic capabilities are needed, but these are not sufficient to develop freedom and agency. This is reminiscent of this study's findings that demonstrate that, although it was an urgent need to focus on basic needs, this has improved well-being; however, this was not the only need that the parents and their children had, thus limiting their agency, well-being and freedom.

Early years students and students with learning difficulties for example often found it very challenging to follow online classes. Some became quite frustrated, thus affecting their parents' well-being. Some parents were also expected to stay with their children all the time while performing their work duties online. Additionally, offering digital devices to those only listed as financially disadvantaged meant excluding those who ended in a disadvantaged situation because of Covid-19 itself; for example, those who suddenly lost their job and had no income. Other parents reported that, even though they had a digital device, having more than two children was a challenge to support them online since they either did not have a digital device for each child, or due to online work that they had to do themselves, or both.

Findings also point out that those students who were disadvantaged through ELET risk factors, particularly those with a difficult family background, learning difficulties, behavioural issues and poor academic achievement (which are main ELET risk factors) struggled even further. This implies that the already existing gap has further increased, and needs to be addressed in order to minimize the widening of this disadvantage. Support systems that were implemented through a whole-school approach were more effective, and helped to minimize the growing gaps. Financial support through digital and essential resources was also essential for well-being, but was not sufficient for academic progression if it was not done holistically.

It can therefore be said that Covid-19 has increased ELET risk factors present prior to the pandemic. In this sense, we can say that conversion factors as defined by Sen (1992) have been strongly affected due to the lack of basic capabilities and lack of capital. Conversion factors have an impact on capabilities and consequently on functionings (Robeyns 2017). For instance, the ability to learn to use a computer system (a capability) offered through online schooling can become a functioning (academic progress). However, if conversion factors are impacted by the resource or service provided – in this case, education being offered online, with different approaches to support services, and a student did not have a device or did not have parents who were digital savvy – the resource of online schooling was found to create further disadvantage. Similarly, although Sen (1985) initially discusses conversion factors in relation to tangible resources, this study has also focused on intangible resources such as the support given through the HSCL that aims to increase financial, cultural and social capital which Sen (1997) later also links to capital that could increase capabilities.

Covid-19 has therefore limited the personal, social and environmental conversion factors not only for students, but also for parents and teachers alike. This has affected students' well-being and agency, and has limited their freedom to convert resources and support into a functioning. In relation to Bourdieu's (1977) notions, disadvantaged families' personal conversion factors were limited because of their deficiency in cultural, social and financial capital. For example, parents may have found it hard to support their child's school progress as they did not have sufficient skills to log onto school online portals or did not have the funds to buy another digital device. Social conversion factors impacted disadvantaged families as, because of Covid-19, people could not get the support they usually get; for instance, families who usually got support through the home visits of the HSCL could not get the same level of support. Those living in poor conditions before the pandemic were also affected badly with regard to environmental conversion factors through long lockdowns. For instance, findings point out that if a family of four during Covid-19 lockdown lived in limited space, this impacted their well-being and freedom more than those living in a bigger space. For example, having an adult working online and two children engaging in online schooling in the same room might limit conversion factors, as opposed to having a room each. Findings following the outbreak of Covid-19 therefore indicate that, through a whole-school approach measure, such as the HSCL, conversion factors can be better targeted so as to increase capabilities and functionings.

Applying the SBAF in Relation to Conversion Factors and Real Opportunities to Develop a System-Wide Programme for Students at Risk of ELET

Hart (2012, 2018) has developed the SBAF as a tool to evaluate injustices in educational systems. In this study, Bourdieu's notions and Sen's CA have however not only supported the evaluation of educational contexts in relation to disadvantaged families, but were also used to analyze a practical policy measure, that is, the HSCL, and how this could be applied within the ELET context to support conversion factors in order to increase capabilities and functionings. Hart (2018: 257) recommends that 'educational policy must go hand in hand with practice developments'. Therefore, Figure 6.1 summarizes what I define as 'opportunity development' within an SBAF (Hart 2012, 2018).

Figure 6.1 further explains how, through the SBAF, ELET risk factors (lack of capital that impacts conversion factors) can be analyzed within two different fields, namely, school and home. Opportunity development therefore implies that a practical policy measure needs to be set up in educational contexts in order to develop agency within both fields. In this study, the HSCL was found to be an opportunity development for disadvantaged families, impacting capabilities and functionings of salient adults in students' lives. In turn, this whole-school approach measure affected students' agency and well-being.

A whole-school approach on the other hand implies that ELET is addressed not only by the class teacher, but also by a number of other stakeholders, including parents, other educators, school heads, the psycho-social team and the community (Carrington et al. 2021). The SBAF applied within the context of ELET and the case of the HSCL suggest that risk indicators and conversion factors both at school and at home need to be addressed. Eliminating barriers in

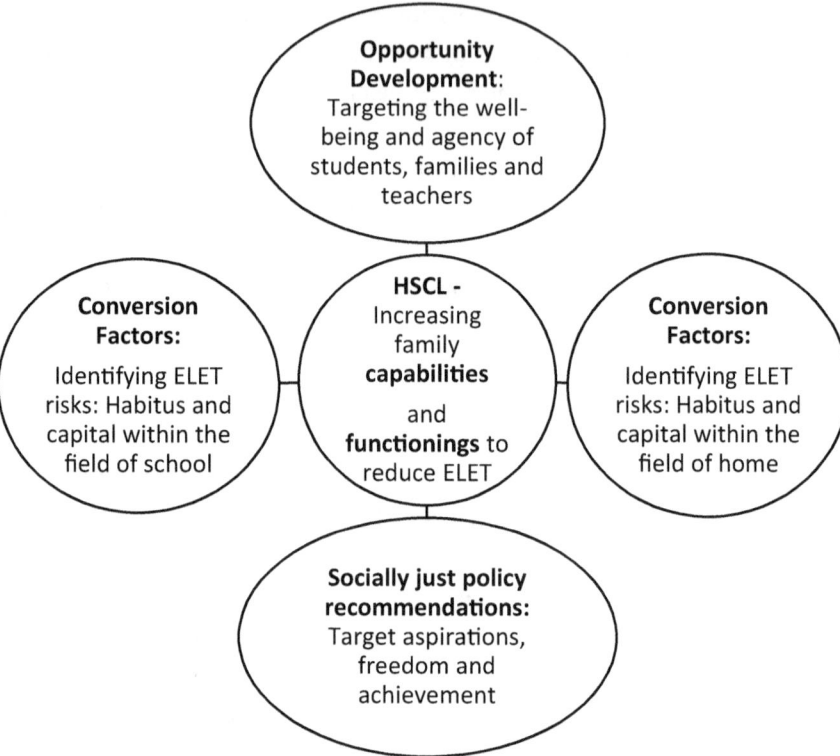

Figure 6.1 The HSCL as an opportunity development programme to reduce ELET risk factors by increasing capabilities and functionings (adapted from Hart 2018: 589–91).

schools is not sufficient. Therefore, taking into consideration Bourdieu's notion of field and habitus, it can be said that home is also a place where students learn, or do not learn, thus increasing the inequality gap.

During Covid-19, all students' learning shifted online, thus highlighting several equity gaps that exist within the home as a learning place (Eivers, Worth and Ghosh 2020). Parents' financial, social and cultural capital impacted students' conversion factors of online learning. Findings indicate that gaps include not only financial ones, but also several others, such as, digital literacy skills among many parents (cultural). Therefore, a whole-school approach programme needs to cater for the individual needs of students by targeting their home background and supporting their families. The community within the school needs to be involved too in order to provide psycho-social and financial support for disadvantaged families. This challenges Bourdieu's pessimistic criticism of structures such as schools that continue to increase the social class and capital gap (Hart 2018). Sen however focuses on the individual and their choices and freedom to live the life they think is best for them (Robeyns 2017), hence explaining why analyzing the HSCL from the SBAF not only allows an identification of ELET risk factors, but also acts upon them. Findings demonstrate that having a system such as the HSCL that supports conversion factors within both the school field and home field ensures a more effective implementation of a whole-school approach, and creates an opportunity for students to develop capabilities and functionings. While teachers in Malta emphasize the difficulty in supporting students at risk of ELET, mainly those who exhibit risk factors such as chronic absenteeism, poor academic achievement and a disadvantaged background, teachers in Ireland who work in disadvantaged schools and can liaise with the HSCL coordinator find that it is essential to both identify any other issues (mainly within the home) and address these issues in a timely manner.

Hart (2018: 594) maintains that:

> The Sen–Bourdieu Analytical Framework deepens understanding of the dynamic social (and psychological) processes involved in the development of an individual's capabilities and the possible roles of educational systems and processes in helping as well as constraining human flourishing. In synthesising the thinking of Sen and Bourdieu, an argument has been made for the importance of developing capabilities as well as considering the distribution of resources, encouraging policy makers and practitioners to strive to ensure that, as far as possible, individuals are free to choose a life they have reason to value.

This implies that, in order for individuals to flourish at school, educational inequalities at home also need to be minimized. Findings indicate that giving uncoordinated support in schools is not sufficient. Coordinated support within the home environment in conjunction with school support could develop further opportunities that reduce ELET risks and increase capabilities. Using the SBAF in this study has also challenged the notion that ELET is measured solely through achievement, where oftentimes, such research is limited to secondary or post compulsory education (Van Praag et al. 2018). This study has therefore challenged the notion of evaluating the risk of ELET at secondary level, and suggests that prevention through SBAF analysis and opportunity development policy programmes should start in the early years of schooling. This would increase students' agency and freedom because any limits in their conversion factors such as social, financial or cultural capital could be catered for in order to ensure their well-being. Downes, Pike and Murphy (2020) similarly suggest that, while the HSCL is an efficient measure to target disadvantaged students, a number of changes need to be made, such as, catering for student well-being, which was drastically impacted during Covid-19 since they possibly endured further disadvantage within their home environment. Therefore, it is imperative to evaluate ELET through the SBAF since it allows policy and practice to create opportunities that develop 'capabilities as well as considering the distribution of resources, encouraging policy makers and practitioners to strive to ensure that, as far as possible, individuals are free to choose a life they have reason to value' (Hart 2018: 154).

Conclusions

This study aims to develop recommendations for a structure that develops opportunities in supporting disadvantaged students, particularly those who exhibit ELET risk factors. Findings emerge from a case study of the HSCL programme in Ireland, which has a low rate of ELET, and Malta's educational context, which has a high rate of ELET, but does not have a whole-school approach programme like the HSCL. This study was underpinned by the SBAF (Hart 2018) in order to not only identify ELET factors, through Bourdieu's notions, but also develop opportunities through Sen's CA. This study's findings indicate that giving support to classroom teachers and parents by developing a policy measure to further opportunities for disadvantaged students such as the HSCL programme could minimize ELET risk factors. The HSCL could be developed as an opportunity model to reduce ELET by developing capabilities and functionings through socially just policy recommendations that target not only the developing agency of students, but also that of salient adults in the students' lives. Recommendations include the development of a whole-school approach measure that identifies ELET risk indicators and acts upon any limiting conversion factors both at school and at home. The SBAF can therefore be used as a framework to develop a system-wide HSCL programme to increase opportunities for students at risk of ELET. This would be done by developing their families' and their teachers' capabilities and functionings which would affect conversion factors and the students' well-being and agency. Socially just policies that seek to minimize the widening gap caused by Covid-19 need to take into consideration opportunities that target freedom by acting on conversion factors, such as, the lack of financial, social and cultural capital both at school and at home.

References

Bayrakdar, S., and Guveli, A. (2020), *Inequalities in Home Learning and Schools' Provision of Distance Teaching during School Closure of COVID-19 Lockdown in the UK* (No. 2020-09), ISER Working Paper Series.

Biggeri, M., Ballet, J., and Comim, F. (2011), *Children and the Capability Approach*. New York: Palgrave Macmillan US.

Biggeri, M., and Santi, M. (2012), 'The Missing Dimensions of Children's Well-Being and Well-Becoming in Education Systems: Capabilities and Philosophy for Children', *Journal of Human Development and Capabilities*, 13(3): 373–95.

Bourdieu, P. (1997), 'The Forms of Capital', in A. Halsey, H. Lauder, and A. Stuart Wells (eds), *Education: Culture, Economy and Society*, 46–58. New York: Oxford University Press.

Bourdieu, P., and Passeron, J.-C. (1977), *Reproduction in Education, Society and Culture*. London: SAGE Publications Ltd.

Busuttil, L., and Farrugia, R. C. (2020), *Teachers' Response to the Sudden Shift to Online Learning during COVID-19 Pandemic: Implications for Policy and Practice*, Malta Review of Educational Research, 14(2): 211–41.

Carrington, S. B., Saggers, B. R., Shochet, I. M., Orr, J. A., Wurfl, A. M., Vanelli, J., and Nickerson, J. (2021), 'Researching a Whole School Approach to School Connectedness', *International Journal of Inclusive Education*, 25: 1–18.

Department of Education and Skills. (2019), *Home, School, and Community Liaison Scheme: Information Booklet for Schools Participating in the Home, School, Community Liaison Scheme*. Available at: https://www.education.ie/en/schools-colleges/information/home-school-community-liaison-hscl-scheme/information-booklet-for-deis-schools-participating-in-the-home-school-community-liaison-scheme.pdf (accessed 1 November 2021).

Donlevy, V., Day, L., Andriescu, M., and Downes, P. (2019), *Assessment of the Implementation of the 2011 Council Recommendation on Policies to Reduce Early School Leaving*. Commissioned Research Report across 35 countries for EU Commission, Directorate General, Education, Sport, Youth and Culture. Luxembourg: Publications Office of the European Union.

Downes, P., Pike, S., and Murphy, S. (2020), 'Marginalised Students in Primary and Post-Primary DEIS Schools and Other Settings: System Gaps in Policy and Practice and the Priority Issues for Consideration, with Reference to the Impact of Covid 19'. Available at: https://www.dcu.ie/sites/default/files/inline-files/submissiondecember2020.pdf (accessed 1 November 2021).

Drane, C. F., Vernon, L., and O'Shea, S. (2020), 'Vulnerable Learners in the Age of COVID-19: A Scoping Review', *The Australian Educational Researcher*, 48: 1–20.

Eivers, E., Worth, J., and Ghosh, A. (2020), *Home Learning during COVID-19: Findings from the Understanding Society Longitudinal Study*. London: National Foundation for Educational Research.

Engzell, P., Frey, A., and Verhagen, M. D. (2021), 'Learning Loss due to School Closures during the COVID-19 Pandemic', *Proceedings of the National Academy of Sciences*, 118(17): 1–7.

European Commission. Education and Training. Thematic Working Group on Early School Leaving. (2013), *Reducing Early School Leaving: Key Messages and Policy Support: Final Report of the Thematic Group on Early School Leaving*, European Union.

Gonzalez-Rodriguez, D., Vieira, M. J., and Vidal, J. (2019), 'Factors that Influence Early School Leaving: A Comprehensive Model', *Educational Research*, 61(2): 214–30.

Hart, C. S. (2012), *Aspirations, Education and Social Justice: Applying Sen and Bourdieu*. London: Bloomsbury.

Hart, C. S. (2018), 'Education, Inequality and Social Justice: A Critical Analysis Applying the Sen–Bourdieu Analytical Framework', *Policy Futures in Education*, 17(5): 582–98.

Ingram, N. (2018), *Working-Class Boys and Educational Success*. London: Palgrave Macmillan.

Kallip, K., and Heidmets, M. (2017), 'Early Leaving from Education and Training: Trends, Factors and Measures in Estonia', *Eesti Haridusteaduste Ajakiri. Estonian Journal of Education*, 5(2): 155–82.

Lareau, A., and Weininger, E. B. (2003), 'Cultural Capital in Educational Research: A Critical Assessment', *Theory and Society*, 32: 567–606.

Lareau, A., Elliot, B. W., Dalton, C., and Velez, M. (2011), 'Unequal Childhoods in Context: Results from a Quantitative Analysis', in A. Lareau (ed.), *Unequal Childhoods: Class, Race, and Family Life*, 333–41. University of California Press.

Ministry for Education. (2020), 'ELET SYMPOSIUM, Early Leaving from Education and Training: The Way Forward and Conference Proceedings, Malta'. Available at: https://epale.ec.europa.eu/en/resource-centre/content/elet-symposium-early-leaving-education-and-training-conference-proceedings (accessed 1 November 2021).

Masonbrink, A. R., and Hurley, E. (2020), 'Advocating for Children during the COVID-19 School Closures', *Pediatrics*, 146(3): 1–4.

Nussbaum, M. (2000), *Women and Human Development: The Capabilities Approach*. Cambridge: Cambridge University Press.

Popovici, M. (2019), 'Research on the Factors Leading to Early School Leaving', *Educația Plus*, 23(SP IS): 147–51.

Reay, D. (2004), '"It's All Becoming a Habitus": Beyond the Habitual Use of Habitus in Educational Research', *British Journal of Sociology of Education*, 25(4): 431–44.

Robeyns, I. (2017), *Wellbeing, Freedom and Social Justice: The Capability Approach Re-examined*. Cambridge, UK: Open Book Publishers.

Ross, C., Kennedy, M., and Devitt, A. (2021), 'Home School Community Liaison Coordinators (HSCL) Perspectives on Supporting Family Wellbeing and Learning during the Covid-19 School Closures: Critical Needs and Lessons Learned', *Irish Educational Studies*, 40(21): 1–8.

Sen, A. (1985), 'Well-Being, Agency and Freedom: The Dewey Lectures 1984', *The Journal of Philosophy*, 82(4): 169–221.

Sen, A. (1987), *The Standard of Living: The Tanner Lectures on Human Values*. Cambridge: Cambridge University Press.

Sen, A. (1992), *Inequality Re-examined*. Oxford: Clarendon Press.

Sen, A. (1997), 'Editorial: Human Capital and Human Capability', *World Development*, 25(12): 1959–61.

Tarabini, A., Curran, M., Montes, A., and Parcerisa, L. (2019), 'Can Educational Engagement Prevent Early School Leaving? Unpacking the School's Effect on Educational Success', *Educational Studies*, 45(2): 226–41.

Van Praag, L., Nouwen, W., Van Caudenberg, R., Clycq, N., and Timmerman, C. (eds) (2018), *Comparative Perspectives on Early School Leaving in the European Union*. London: Routledge.

Vassallo, J., Doublet Meagher, G. L., Zammit, N., Grech, L., Refalo, E., German, J., and Grech, L. (2021), 'Students' and Parents' Perspectives on Emergency E-learning in Kindergarten and Compulsory Education', *Malta Journal of Education*, Institute for Education, 2(1): 167–96.

7

Establishing the Medium- to Long-Term Impact of Covid-19 Constraints on the Socio-Emotional Well-Being of Impoverished Children and Young People (and Those Who Are Otherwise Disadvantaged) during, and in the Aftermath of, Covid-19

Joan G. Mowat

This literature-based chapter draws on a range of insights derived from a synthesis of the literature – empirical studies, journal articles, reports, viewpoints and commentaries, from global to national (Scottish), embracing social and clinical sciences. Some literature is prospective in nature[1] (particularly that published in the earlier stages of the pandemic) and some is retrospective. The purpose of the chapter is to reflect on the medium- to long-term impact of Covid-19 constraints on the socio-emotional well-being of children and young people (from this point onwards referred to as children) living in poverty, and those who are otherwise disadvantaged, to identify key imperatives to inform future public policy and practice. The chapter concludes with directions for future research. Please note that references to parents are inclusive of all carers.

The Nature of the Problem

Global Impact of Covid-19 on Children

According to UNICEF, by 30 April 2020, around 1,383 million children worldwide had been affected by school closures, impacting on progress towards

---

[1] For this reason, some of the discussion is expressed in terms of 'may' and tenses may vary.

achieving the United Nations Sustainable Development Goal 4 on education (UNICEF Office of Research 2020b). By mid-April 2020, 60 per cent of children in primary schools and 86 per cent in low-HDI countries were unable to access education. Yet, in the early stages of the pandemic, as reflected in this statement by Professor Devi Sridhar, University of Edinburgh, it was considered that it would have minimal impact on children and young people: 'The main narrative I hear is that children and young people will be fine' (UNICEF Office of Research 2020a). The impact of lockdown, school closures and restrictions in population movement had halted and reversed much of the progress made in child health globally over the past two decades, heightening inequalities and disrupting social functioning for children (Editor 2020b). In the earlier stages of the pandemic, the United Nations highlighted the devastating impact on children, with the poorest and already disadvantaged bearing the brunt (UNICEF Office of Research 2020b).

Eleven months into the pandemic, the situation had not alleviated with at least three quarters of classroom instruction missed from the pre-primary to secondary sectors. The duration of school closures varied significantly across the world (United Nations Children's Fund 2021). In the period July–October 2020, those children living in low-income countries were more than twice as likely to be affected by school closures than those in high-income countries (United Nations Children's Fund and UN Women and Plan International 2020).

A State of Precarity

A health crisis was becoming a social and a psychological crisis, leading to higher levels of anxiety and stress in society in general (UNICEF Office of Research 2020b). Families, who in normal circumstances would not consider themselves impoverished, through the unique set of circumstances brought about by Covid-19 (job losses, reductions in salary and reduced hours) found themselves on the breadline (Editor 2020c; Save the Children 2021), bringing into question understandings of marginalized and vulnerable populations.[2] For those families already living in precarious financial circumstances, it was a tipping point, with parents using a variety of strategies to cope – cutting back on, or going without, essentials or getting into debt (Save the Children 2021).

---

[2] For a discussion of marginalization see Mowat, J. G. (2015), 'Towards a New Conceptualisation of Marginalisation', *European Educational Research Journal*, 14(5): 454–76. DOI: 10.1177/1474904115589864.

The effects of Covid-19 had served to magnify some of the factors associated with growing up in poverty for children (Child Poverty Action Group 2020). Many families were financially insecure, having less than three months' earnings to support the family. Single parents faced compounded challenges relating to loss of income and lack of childcare and family support. The supports that families in these circumstances would normally draw upon (such as food banks and advice teams) were curtailed (Barnard 2020). In Scotland, the combination of financial worries, along with anxieties about health, caring for children, social isolation and lack of access to support systems, left many parents feeling abandoned: 'I just felt so alone. It literally felt like you were dropped in a cave and it felt like, that's it' (Save the Children 2021: 24, drawing on the account of Keira, a mother).

Displaced and disabled children were also amongst those greatest at risk with the former group less likely to be able to access support systems put in place by governments (UNICEF Office of Research 2020b). The plight of disabled families was showcased in research carried out by the BBC – in particular, the case of Josselin, a young person with a rare genetic condition (with resultant hearing loss, vision impairment and inability to walk, talk or eat normally) who had no access to physiotherapy, speech and language and occupational therapy and respite care from March 2020 onwards (Clegg 2021).

Impact of Covid-19 on the Socio-Emotional and Psychological Development of Children

Amidst the increasing concerns about the mental health and well-being of children in general, and that of adolescents and teenage girls in particular (Mowat 2019, 2020; Patalay and Fitzsimons 2018; World Health Organisation 2016), the impact of social distancing and school closures (Lee 2020; OECD 2020; UK Government 2020) on the socio-emotional and psychological development of this demographic is likely to be significant (Wang et al. 2020). This is compounded by family stressors, including bereavement (UNICEF Office of Research 2020a) and separation from close family (Liu et al. 2020). No opportunity presented to prepare children for the unprecedented changes in their lives and the loss of the rites of passage associated with them (Orben, Tomova and Blakemore 2020), the lack of which may lead to a sense of loss.

UK Context The Oxford Co-Space Longitudinal survey in the UK, initiated in March 2020, established a correlation between periods of the highest levels of behavioural, emotional and attentional difficulties in children and periods when restrictions were greatest, with a sharp decrease in symptoms among both primary and secondary children when restrictions were eased in February 2021. The exception was children with *Special Educational Needs and Disabilities* (SEND) and those from low-income families who continued to show elevated health symptoms (Shum et al. 2021).

Scottish Context A report published in October 2020 by the Scottish government, but drawing from data across the UK, found that standardized measures of mental health and well-being for children were not significantly changed from pre-pandemic levels. However, this disguised the impact on specific groups (Scottish Government 2020a). The findings relating to adolescent girls, low-income families, children identified as having SEND/*Additional Support Needs* (ASN) (Scotland) and those with English as a second language are consistent with those of other studies, including the Oxford University Co-Space study.

The charity, Save the Children, found that the degree to which parents felt that the well-being of their children was well supported by the school or nursery during lockdown varied to a considerable extent with some considering that the support offered was not sufficiently tailored to the needs of their children (Save the Children 2021). What is revealing, however, is that, irrespective of income, the greatest concern of parents and children was not solely around learning but around the emotional support which would be offered to children on return to school: 'they are equally concerned with the longer-term effects of increased social isolation and household stress' (Save the Children 2021: 2–3).

The Importance of Physical Social Interaction

It has been argued that for the development of key social skills and emotional resilience (Music 2017) and the promotion of psychological well-being, companionship, play and peer interaction are essential (Liu et al. 2020; OECD 2020; UNICEF Office of Research 2020a). Parents were concerned that younger children were missing out on key developmental stages essential for socialization, such as interacting with extended family and friends, with limited opportunities for play and reduced access to outdoor spaces (Save the Children 2021). Even when lockdown restrictions were lifted in the summer of 2020 some children did not return to normal levels of play and regular peer interaction, with the effect on younger children being greater (Scottish Government 2020a). Children living in homes where a family member was shielding were particularly affected and children who themselves were shielding felt abandoned as the messaging for this group was often directed at the elderly (Scottish Government 2020a). It was considered that school closures, and the isolation associated with it, could potentially impact on children's capacity to self-regulate, increasing their vulnerability (Burns and Gottschalk 2019; OECD 2020).

For many children, it is not just the loss of learning imposed by lockdown measures (and the periods of time when schools close due to outbreaks of infection or classes or year groups are sent home to self-isolate) that has impacted, but it is also the loss of the social contact associated with school – interaction with friends and teachers (Scottish Government 2021). In England, on 1 July 2021, 8.5 per cent of children in English schools (adjusted for those pupils who were off-site for legitimate reasons) were not in attendance at school for Covid-related reasons, excluding those who were shielding for health reasons (UK Government 2021).

The Impact on Adolescence It is recognized that the peer group takes on a particular significance during adolescence for both sexes as young people grow in independence (Editor 2020a; Orben, Tomova and Blakemore 2020). It is a sensitive period for social development, identity formation and mental health when there is a heightened sensitivity to social stimuli and a greater need for social interaction. Adolescents, in comparison to younger children, spend greater time in interaction with their peer group than their family and are increasingly influenced by them. They are more sensitive to peer rejection, acceptance and approval (Orben, Tomova and Blakemore 2020). The lack of opportunities for physical social interaction, arising from school closures, social distancing and isolation, disrupts networks of support, impacting on psychological well-being (Editor 2020a; Orben, Tomova and Blakemore 2020), with the potential to extend beyond the period of social distancing itself (Orben, Tomova and Blakemore 2020).

Family-Related and Environmental Stressors

While for some children spending increased time with family members may be beneficial, for others, home confinement and the conditions associated with it may put them at greater risk of abuse and neglect (Lee 2020; OECD 2020; Scottish Government 2020a; UNICEF Office of Research 2020a,b; Usher, Bhullar, Durkin et al. 2020). For children living in poverty (Van Lancker and Parolin 2020) who may be living in damp, over-crowded homes (Behbod 2015; UNICEF Office of Research 2020b) and who are unable to access the outdoors and leisure facilities, difficulties may have been compounded with socio-economic differences exacerbated, health risks accentuated (Editor 2020c) and home schooling compromised (Armitage and Nellums 2020; Barnard 2020; UK Government 2020; UNICEF Office of Research 2020b; Van Lancker and Parolin 2020).

'A Perfect Storm' – Child Protection Issues

For children living in abusive homes, perhaps witness to family violence, and for whom school served as a safe haven, home confinement poses particular risks (OECD 2020), with family stressors amplified (Lee 2020). For Usher and colleagues, the combination of isolation, accompanied by the psychological and financial stressors associated with social distancing (particularly if accompanied by excessive alcohol consumption), create 'a perfect storm' which is an ideal breeding ground for family violence, posing greater risks for children (Usher et al. 2020). Beyond those most obviously at risk of abuse and neglect, around eight in ten children aged 1–14 years globally had experienced some form of psychological aggression or physical punishment within the home environment in a one-month period during lockdown, as was the case for three quarters of 2–4-year-olds (UNICEF Office of Research 2020b).

The impact of family bereavement, illness or separation on the capacity to care for children, coupled with the above family stressors and increased care-giving responsibilities arising from the pandemic, places many children at increased risk of abuse or neglect at a time when family supports (such as the support offered by extended family) are reduced (United Nations Children's Fund 2020; Weiner et al. 2020).

This is further compounded by the disruption in child protection services and the lack of contact with school staff who would normally be the first line of defence in picking up signs of child abuse and neglect (Armitage and Nellums 2020; Lee 2020), leading to a reduction in referrals (United Nations Children's Fund 2020; Weiner et al. 2020).

The pandemic had led to widespread disruption to the services that normally support families and children, such as welfare services (United Nations Children's Fund 2020). Further, children may have had less access to key adult supports and services that have a child protection function (Armitage and Nellums 2020; Lee 2020; UNICEF Office of Research 2020a,b; Usher et al. 2020). This is particularly of the essence for children who have experienced *Adverse Childhood Experiences* (ACEs) as it has been established that for these children the support of a key adult can make all the difference in building emotional resilience (Public Health Scotland 2017; Smith 2018).

An Over-Stretched System – Access to Mental Health Services

The loss of familiar routines associated with school – a coping mechanism for many children with mental health issues and on the autistic spectrum – creates anxiety and distress (Lee 2020; Scottish Government 2020a). This is compounded by a lack of access to mental health supports in schools and mental health services (Armitage and Nellums 2020) which, in Scotland, were under strain and inadequate even prior to the pandemic (Mowat 2019, 2020; Murphy 2016). Services such as CAMHS (Child and Adolescent Mental Health Services) in the UK were overwhelmed, with too many referrals rejected due to a lack of resource (Audit Scotland 2018; Office of the Children's Commissioner for England 2019). An audit of referrals to CAMHS in Scotland found that there had been a steep decline during the initial lockdown in the UK (spring 2020), with referrals reducing by a third, but with some recovery during periods when restrictions had eased (Public Health Scotland 2021).

In the UK, a survey conducted by the charity Young Minds identified that 83 per cent of participants consider that the pandemic had had a worsening effect on their mental health with around a quarter being unable to access services (Lee 2020). The OECD (2020) cautions that the long-term effects on children may range from anxiety-related disorders to post-traumatic stress. The newly formed UK Trauma Council found the key issues to be the increased risk of exposure to trauma during the pandemic; the likelihood that those who have previously been exposed to trauma will experience particular difficulties, struggling to adapt to the lockdown environment with less recourse to normal supports; and the disruption to services which would normally support children who have experienced or are experiencing trauma (UK Trauma Council 2020).

A Social Crisis in the Making

Food insecurity, brought about by disruption to school meals (Van Lancker and Parolin 2020) and programmes of international support (Editor 2020c) impact disproportionally on the already disadvantaged, as does lack of access to universal health care (Editor 2020c). Van Lancker and Parolin (2020) speculate that a range of non-school factors (such as the home environment and the degree to which it supports learning) are likely to impact to a much greater extent the physical and mental well-being of children living in poverty than other children. According to the authors, a substantial minority of children in Europe have no suitable place to do homework; lack access to the internet; are living in homes that are poorly heated; have no access to outdoor leisure facilities; and have no access to age-appropriate books in the family home which, coupled with the financial stressors to which reference has previously been made, 'create a social crisis in the making'.

Digital Technologies Serving a Social and Spiritual Function Much attention has been devoted in the literature to the impact of digital technologies on learning and the 'digital divide' that has emerged, exacerbating inequalities (Armitage and Nellums 2020; United Nations Children's Fund 2021). However, the digital divide impacts not only on learning but also on the capacity of schools to maintain contact with families and children at times of disruption to schooling: 'Teachers also play a vital role as relationship builders and connectors' (Fullan et al. 2020: 6). In a study of the digital divide on Catholic schools in Scotland, it was found that digital exclusion, associated with poverty, had led to exclusion from religious education, the religious life, community and pastoral and spiritual aspects of the school (McKinney 2020).

The Importance of the Family Unit and Networks of Extended Support

Whilst the above paints a very distressing and hopeless picture of the impact of the pandemic on the well-being of families and children globally and at a national level, a key lesson to be learned is that not all families and children had the same experience. Save the Children found that some parents enjoyed the additional time that they were able to spend with their children and the insight gained into their children's learning, considering that family relationships had improved. Despite the many trials endured, it has been reported that some families and children were remarkably resilient in the face of the challenges presented. The family unit itself was the greatest source of support as was the lifeline of social media during periods of lockdown (Save the Children 2021).

These findings are consistent with the findings from a literature-based study focusing on the relationship between poverty, attainment and mental health and well-being in which the *nature, quality and strength of networks of support around communities, families and schools*, related, but not restricted, to social capital emerged as a key mediating variable (see Figure 7.1) (Mowat 2019, 2020).

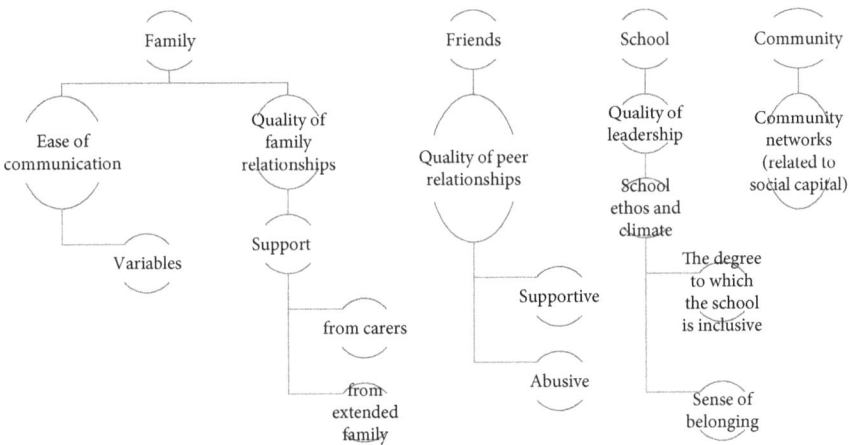

Figure 7.1 Illustration of key theme 'the nature, quality and strength of networks of support around communities, families and schools'.

Implications for Policy and Practice: Key Imperatives

In reflecting on the discussion to this point, in terms of both addressing the immediate imperatives of nations as they seek to tackle the medium- to long-term impacts of Covid-19 and ensuring greater preparedness to meet future challenges, the following insights emerge: firstly, a recognition that no preparation whether at the macro or micro level could ever sufficiently prepare the system or the workforce to meet the challenges posed. What is remarkable is the degree to which systems and people, from all walks of life, have adapted and changed rapidly in a swiftly changing landscape. At the macro level, there needs to be a convergence of public policy globally and nationally and a will to address inequalities in society – health, social, economic and educational – in order to *build resilient communities*. In order to achieve this goal, there needs to be a focus at the local level on *building networks of support* around communities, families, schools and children. Schools need to be not only *inclusive places of learning* but also *places of belonging, caring, compassion, community, relatedness and connection* where the health and well-being of all of the school community lies at the heart of its endeavours, and where all members of that community are given a voice. In order to achieve this, we need to *invest in the workforce* and the professional development of teachers, freeing them from the shackles of overly controlling régimes, creating a body of *critical practitioners* who are given the freedom and autonomy to be creative and to develop a sense of agency. This requires *emotionally intelligent leaders*

(Crawford 2009) and *collaborative and shared forms of leadership* at all levels of the system. Covid-19 presents us with an opportunity to stand back from our 'dearly held assumptions' (Brookfield 1995) about the world and to re-imagine a better future for all children.

To this point, much of the focus globally has been on how schools can address the interruptions to the learning of children but it is too early to ascertain the degree to which such approaches have been, and will be efficacious. There has been much less attention devoted to supporting the emotional and psychological well-being of children, yet, this is crucial as it underpins effective learning. Therefore, the focus must rest on identifying where attention should be devoted with regard to the direction of future research. The final discussion will focus on this aspect.

Directions for Future Research

Gaps within the Literature

The response to the UK parliament's call for experts to share their concerns relating to the impact of Covid-19 highlighted a range of issues pertaining to the mental health and well-being of children, key amongst which is the isolation from peers during critical stages of development, increasing the likelihood of the development of mental health conditions during and after the pandemic (Birmingham 2020).

In the UK, the Economic and Social Research Council (ESRC) identified that there are significant gaps in the literature pertaining to the impacts of social isolation among disadvantaged and vulnerable groups during public health crises, including the positive and negative impacts of social media and digital technologies. Likewise, there is a lack of an evidence base as to the efficacy of social practices and interventions to mitigate the impacts of Covid-19 constraints (Gayer-Anderson et al. 2020). While many of these concerns relate to the adult population, studies such as Growing Up in Scotland have identified a clear relationship between precarity, adult stress (particularly that of the mother), parenting and the mental health and well-being and development of children, leading to significant health and educational inequalities which widen over time (Bradshaw, Knudsen and Mabelis 2015; Marryat and Frank 2019; Marryat et al. 2015; Marryat et al. 2017; Parkes, Sweeting and Wight 2014; Parkes, Sweeting and Wight 2016).

Intersectionality

There is a need to recognize that children living in poverty are not a homogenous group and that, in keeping with the recommendations from the ESRC (Gayer-Anderson et al. 2020), childhood poverty may intersect with other variables, such as coming from a Black or ethnic minority background; being disabled or from a family where a carer is disabled; living in a large family and/or with a sole parent (Child Poverty Action Group 2020); and being displaced (UNICEF Office of Research 2020b), amongst other groups. As such, intersectionality needs to be a key consideration in the design of a research study (Gayer-Anderson et al. 2020).

Research Design

There is a need to conduct longitudinal, cross-sectoral and multidisciplinary study which not only gathers data at a population level to establish key variables, relationships and trends in the medium to long term, but which also examines holistically the lived experience of children as they traverse the many obstacles and significant transitions in their lives brought about by Covid-19. This calls for a range of approaches to be deployed, including mixed methods and ethnographic studies, drawing on expertise across a range of academic disciplines.

Creating Resilient Communities

In order to be able to inform future responses to this and other pandemics, research needs to not only establish the impact of Covid-19 constraints on children but also the mechanisms and inner supports that they have drawn upon both during and in the aftermath of the pandemic. It needs to explore and evaluate the approaches and interventions which have been put in place to support children by agencies such as schools, mental health services, the third sector and children's services in order to establish their efficacy and to identify those aspects which promote resilience (protective factors) not only at the individual level, but also at the social and wider community levels, in keeping with socio-ecological understandings of the concept (Olsson et al. 2003; Rutter 2012; Ungar 2012a,b; Ungar, Mehdi and Jörg 2013). There is also a need to examine the constraints to the delivery of such services, as identified in a survey conducted by the Cross-Party Group for Children and Young People in Scotland (Scottish Parliament, 2022). There may be a danger of an over-reliance on approaches to support children which focus on building resilience within the individual, failing to acknowledge sufficiently the interaction of protective and risk factors external to the individual, which create the conditions under which a child or young person may be able to develop and demonstrate the behaviours which might be construed as resilient within a given context.

A Focus on Adolescence

Whilst we need to address the needs of all children arising from the constraints posed by Covid-19, I concur with the call of Orben and others (Orben, Tomova and Blakemore 2020) that urgent research is required to understand the impact of social deprivation and physical distancing, reduced physical contact and the possibilities posed by digital communication on the development and mental health of adolescents.

Children's Rights as Central

As advocated by the *Lancet* editorial, 'Prioritising Children's Rights in the Covid-19 response' (Editor 2020b), the tumultuous impact of Covid-19 on the lives of children provides an opportunity to stand back and reflect on societal norms and values and, rather than unthinkingly moving towards the 'new normal', give proper consideration to the nature of the world we want to create for the current and future generations of children. As posed by UNESCO, 'What will be the impact on human rights, inclusion and values we hold dear? What values do we want to take into the new world?' (UNESCO 2020) and, arising from the above, what are the implications of these for the actions that we should take collectively and individually? As argued in the *Lancet* editorial (Editor 2020b), 'Children's rights must be central in the recovery phase and in future planning, to regain lost ground and to accelerate progress towards a more equitable, resilient, and sustainable world for all' (p. 479). Covid-19 presents not only as a threat but also as an opportunity.

A Call to Action: Breaking Down Silos

The above calls for researchers, academics and professionals to move out of their silos to collaborate together to co-construct the design of research studies, breaking down barriers to communication and building shared understandings; for clinical and social science researchers to be working side by side; and, for professionals across a range of fields to share their insights, as it is only in so doing that the complexity of what we are dealing with can be understood and the way forward established.

Consideration of Social and Cultural Context

Finally, just as this chapter commenced with the words of Professor Sridhar, it ends with her advocacy to 'build trust with populations', taking account of people's social and cultural contexts in creating interventions to address need (UNICEF Office of Research 2020a). It is important that whichever approaches are adopted, we work respectfully with people, taking them with us on the journey, listening to the voices of children and those with responsibility for their well-being, not just as objects of research but as collaborators also as we build towards and beyond a 'new normal'.

References

Armitage, R., and Nellums, L. B. (2020), 'Considering Inequalities in the School Closure Response to COVID-19 (Correspondence)', *The Lancet Global Health* 2020, 8(5): 644.

Audit Scotland. (2018), *Children and Young People's Mental Health*. Edinburgh: The Accounts Commission.

Barnard, H. (2020), 'Coronavirus: What Does It Mean for People Restricted by Poverty?' Available at: https://www.rethinkingpoverty.org.uk/rethinking-poverty/what-does-covid-19-mean-for-people-restricted-by-poverty/ (accessed 25 May 2022).

Behbod, B. B., Sordillo, J. E., Hoffman, E. B., Datta, S., Webb, T. E., Kwan, D. L., and Kamel, J. A. (2015). 'Asthma and Allergy Development: Contrasting Influences of Yeasts and Other Fungal Exposures'. *Clinical and Experimental Allergy*, 45, 154–63.

Birmingham, R. (2020), 'Public Health and COVID-19: What Are Experts Concerned about?' Education, UK Parliament Post. Available at: https://post.parliament.uk/education-and-covid-19-what-are-experts-concerned-about/ (accessed 25 May 2022).

Bradshaw, P., Knudsen, L., and Mabelis, J. (2015), *Growing Up in Scotland: The Circumstances and Experiences of 3 Year Old Children Living in Scotland in 2007/09 and 2013*. Available at: https://growingupinscotland.org.uk/new-findings-the-circumstances-and-experiences-of-3-year-olds-living-in-scotland-in-200708-and-2013/ (accessed 25 May 2022).

Brookfield, S. D. (1995), *Becoming a Critically Refective Teacher*. San Fransisco: Jossey-Bass.

Burns, T., and Gottschalk, F. (2019), *Educating 21st Century Children: Emotional Well-Being in the Digital Age*. Paris: OECD.

Child Poverty Action Group. (2020), 'The Cost of Learning In Lockdown: Family Experiences of School Closures in Scotland. Available at: https://cpag.org.uk/policy-and-campaigns/report/cost-learning-lockdown-family-experiences-school-closures (accessed 25 May 2022).

Clegg, R. (2021, July 30), 'Disabled People Forgotten during Covid, BBC Research Reveals'. Available at: https://www.bbc.co.uk/news/uk-57652173 (accessed 25 May 2022).

Crawford, M. (2009), *Getting to the Heart of Leadership: Emotion and Educational Leadership*. London: SAGE.

Editor. (2020a), 'Pandemic School Closures: Risks and Opportunities (Editorial)', *The Lancet Child and Adolescent Health*, 4(5): 341.

Editor. (2020b), 'Prioritising Children's Rights in the COVID-19 Response', *The Lancet Child and Adolescent Health*, 4(7): 479.

Editor. (2020c), 'Redefining Vulnerability in the Era of COVID-19 (Editorial)', *The Lancet Global Health 2020*, 395(10230): 1089.

Fullan, M., Quinn, J., Drummy, M. and Gardner, M. (2020), 'Education Reimagined: The Future of Learning. A Collaborative Position Paper between New Pedagogies for Deep Learning and Microsoft Education'. Available at: https://edudownloads.azureedge.net/msdownloads/Microsoft-EducationReimagined-Paper.pdf (accessed 25 May 2022).

Gayer-Anderson, C., Latham, R., Zerbi, C. E., Gayer-Anderson, C., Latham, R., Zerbi, C. E., Strang, L., Hall, V. M., Knowles, G., Marlow, S., Avendano, M., Manning, N., Das-Munshi, J., Fisher, H., Rose, D., Arseneault, L., Kienzler, H., Rose, N., Hatch, S., Woodhead, C., Morgan, C., and Wilkinson, B. (2020), 'Impacts of Social Isolation among Disadvantaged and Vulnerable Groups during Public Health Crises', ESRC, Centre for Society and Mental Health, Kings College London. Available at: https://www.careknowledge.com/media/47410/3563-social-isolation-2-cs-v3.pdf (accessed 25 May 2022).

Lee, J. (2020), 'Mental Health Effects of School Closures during COVID-19', *The Lancet Child and Adolescent Health*, 4(6): 421. DOI: 10.1016/S2352-4642(20)30109-7.

Liu, J. J., Bao, Y., Huang, X., et al. (2020), 'Mental Health Considerations for Children Quarantined because of COVID-19 (Comment)', *The Lancet Child and Adolescent Health*, 4(5): 348–9.

Marryat, L., and Frank, J. (2019), 'Factors Associated with Adverse Childhood Experiences in Scottish Children: A Prospective Cohort Study', *BMJ Paediatrics Open*, 3(1): e000340. DOI: 10.1136/bmjpo-2018-000340.

Marryat, L., Thompson, L., Minnis, H., et al. (2015), 'Exploring the Social, Emotional and Behavioural Development of Preschool Children: Is Glasgow Different?' *International Journal for Equity in Health*, 14(3): 1–16. DOI: 10.1186/s12939-014-0129-8.

Marryat, L., Thompson, L., Minnis, H., et al. (2017), 'Primary Schools and the Amplification of Social Differences in Child Mental Health: A Population-Based Cohort Study', *Journal of Epidemiology & Community Health Education Journal*, 72(1): 1–7. DOI: 10.1136/jech-2017-208995.

McKinney, S. (2020), 'Covid-19: Food Insecurity, Digital Exclusion and Catholic Schools', *Journal of Religious Education*, 68: 319–30.

Mowat, J. G. (2015), 'Towards a New Conceptualisation of Marginalisation', *European Educational Research Journal*, 14(5): 454–76. DOI: 10.1177/1474904115589864.

Mowat, J. G. (2019), 'Exploring the Impact of Social Inequality and Poverty on the Mental Health and Wellbeing and Attainment of Children and Young People in Scotland', *Improving Schools*, 22(3): 204–23. DOI: 10.1177/1365480219835323.

Mowat, J. G. (2020), 'Interrogating the Relationship between Poverty, Attainment and Mental Health and Wellbeing: The Importance of Social Networks and Support – A Scottish Case Study', *Cambridge Journal of Education*, 50(3): 345–70. DOI: 10.1080/0305764X.2019.1702624.

Murphy, R. (2016), 'Child and Adolescent Mental Health –Trends and Key Issues' SPICe Briefing. Available at: https://archive2021.parliament.scot/ResearchBriefingsAndFactsheets/S5/SB_16-76_Child_and_Adolescent_Mental_Health_Trends_and_Key_Issues.pdf (accessed 25 May 2022).

Music, G. (2017), *Nurturing Natures: Attachment and Children's Emotional, Sociocultural and Brain Development* (2nd edn). London: Routledge.

OECD. (2020), *Trends Shaping Education: Spotlight 21. Coronavirus Special Edition: Back to School*. Paris: OECD.

Office of the Children's Commissioner for England. (2019), 'Early Access to Mental Health Support'. Available at: https://www.childrenscommissioner.gov.uk/report/early-access-to-mental-health-support/ (accessed 25 May 2022).

Olsson, C. A., Bond, L., Burns, J. M., et al. (2003), 'Adolescent Resilience: A Concept Analysis', *Journal of Adolescence*, 26(1): 1–11.

Orben, A., Tomova, L., and Blakemore, S.-J. (2020), 'The Effects of Social Deprivation on Adolescent Development and Mental Health', *The Lancet: Child and Adolescent Mental Health*, 4(8): 634–40.

Parkes, A., Sweeting, H., and Wight, D. (2014), 'Growing Up in Scotland: Family and School Influences on Children's Social and Emotional Well-Being', Edinburgh: Scottish Government. Available at: https://dera.ioe.ac.uk/20296/1/00452548_Redacted.pdf (accessed 25 May 2022).

Parkes, A., Sweeting, H., and Wight, D. (2016), 'What Shapes 7-Year-Olds' Subjective Well-Being? Prospective Analysis of Early Childhood and Parenting Using the Growing Up in Scotland Study', *Social Psychiatry and Psychiatric Epidemiology*, 51(10): 1417–28.

Patalay, P., and Fitzsimons, E. (2018), *Mental Ill-Health and Wellbeing at Age 14 – Initial Findings from the Millennium Cohort Study Age 14 Survey*. London: Centre for Longitudinal Studies.

Public Health Scotland. (2017), 'Tackling the Attainment Gap by Preventing and Responding to Adverse Childhood Experiences (ACEs)'. Available at: http://www.healthscotland.scot/publications/tackling-the-attainment-gap-by-preventing-and-responding-to-adverse-childhood-experiences (accessed 25 May 2022).

Public Health Scotland. (2021), 'Child and Adolescent Mental Health Services in Scotland: Waiting Times'. Available at: https://www.isdscotland.org/Health-topics/Waiting-Times/Child-and-Adolescent-Mental-Health/(accessed 6 July 2021).

Rutter, M. (2012), 'Resilience: Causal Pathways and Social Ecology', in M. Ungar (ed.), *The Social Ecology of Resilience: A Handbook of Theory and Practice*, 33–42. New York: Springer.

Save the Children. (2021), '"Dropped into a Cave": How Families with Young Children Experienced Lockdown'. Available at: https://www.savethechildren.org.uk/content/dam/gb/reports/dropped-into-a-cave-compressed.pdf (accessed 25 May 2022).

Scottish Government. (2020a), 'Coronavirus (COVID-19): Impact on Children, Young People and Families – Evidence Summary October 2020', Director-General Education and Justice, Learning Directory. Available at: https://www.gov.scot/publications/report-covid-19-children-young-people-families-october-2020-evidence-summary/ (accessed 25 May 2022).

Scottish Government. (2021), 'Equity Audit'. Available at: https://www.gov.scot/binaries/content/documents/govscot/publications/impact-assessment/2021/01/equity-audit-deepening-understanding-impact-covid-19-school-building-closures-children-socio-economically-disadvantaged-backgrounds-setting-clear-areas-focus-accelerating-recovery/documents/equity-audit/equity-audit/govscot%3Adocument/equity-audit.pdf (accessed 25 May 2022).

Scottish Parliament. (2022). 'Cross Party Group on Children and Young People', Pandemic Impact Survey 2022. Available at: https://childreninscotland.org.uk/covid-impact-risking-future-of-vital-services-for-young-people-across-scotland-survey-finds/ (accessed 20 September 2022).

Shum, A., Skripkauskaite, S., Pearcey, S., et al. (2021), 'Report 10: Children and Adolescents' Mental Health: One Year in the Pandemic', in *Co-Space Study: Covid-19: Supporting Parents, Adolescents and Children during Epidemics* (vol. 10). Oxford: Oxford University Press.

Smith, M. (2018), 'Capability and Adversity: Reframing the "causes of the causes" for Mental Health', *Palgrave Communications*, 4(13): 1–5.

UK Government. (2020), 'Coronavirus and the Social Impacts on Great Britain'. Available at: https://www.ons.gov.uk/peoplepopulationandcommunity/healthandsocialcare/healthandwellbeing/bulletins/coronavirusandthesocialimpactsongreatbritain/previousReleases (accessed 25 May 2022).

UK Government. (2021), 'Attendance in Education and Early Years Settings during the Coronavirus (COVID-19) Outbreak'. Available at: https://explore-education-statistics.service.gov.uk/find-statistics/attendance-in-education-and-early-years-settings-during-the-coronavirus-covid-19-outbreak (accessed 6 July 2021).

UK Trauma Council. (2020), 'Beyond the Pandemic: Strategic Priorities for Responding to Childhood Trauma: A Coronavirus Pandemic Policy Briefing'. Available at: https://uktraumacouncil.org/wp-content/uploads/2020/09/Coronavirus-CYP-and-Trauma-UKTC-Policy-Briefing-Sept-2020.pdf (accessed 25 May 2022).

UNESCO. (2020), 'Imagining the World to Come: Governance and Solidarity: Covid-19 & beyond. From May 2020'. Available at: https://en.unesco.org/sites/default/files/unesco_world_to_come_flyer.pdf (accessed 25 May 2022).

Ungar, M. (2012a), 'Social Ecologies and Their Contribution to Resilience', in M. Ungar (ed.), *The Social Ecology of Resilience: A Handbook of Theory and Practice*, 13–32. New York: Springer.

Ungar, M. (ed.) (2012b), *The Social Ecology of Resilience: A Handbook of Theory and Practice*. New York: Springer.

Ungar, M., Mehdi, G., and Jörg, R. (2013), 'Annual Research Review: What Is Resilience within the Social Ecology of Human Development?', *Journal of Child Psychology and Psychiatry*, 54(4): 348–66.

UNICEF Office of Research. (2020a), 'COVID-19, Global Governance and the Impact on Children: In Conversation with Public Health Expert Devi Sridhar'. Available at: https://www.unicef.org/globalinsight/stories/covid-19-global-governance-and-impact-children (accessed 25 May 2022).

UNICEF Office of Research. (2020b), *How COVID-19 Is Changing the World: A Statistical Perspective (Vol. 1)*. Paris: CCSA.

United Nations Children's Fund. (2020), *Protecting Children from Violence in the Time of COVID-19: Disruptions in Prevention and Response Services*. New York: UNICEF.

United Nations Children's Fund. (2021), *COVID-19 and School Closures: One Year of Education Disruption*. New York: UNICEF.

United Nations Children's Fund, and UN Women and Plan International. (2020), *A New Era for Girls: Taking Stock of 25 Years of Progress*. New York: UNICEF.

Usher, K., Bhullar, N., Durkin, J., et al. (2020), 'Family Violence and COVID-19: Increased Vulnerability and Reduced Options for Support', *International Journal of Mental Health Nursing*, 29(4): 549–52.

Van Lancker, W. V., and Parolin, Z. (2020), 'COVID-19, School Closures, and Child Poverty: A Social Crisis in the Making (Comment)', *The Lancet Public Health 2020*, 5(5): 243–4.

Wang, G., Zhang, Y., Zhao, J., et al. (2020), 'Mitigate the Effects of Home Confinement on Children during the COVID-19 Outbreak (Correspondence)', *The Lancet*, 395(March 21, 2020): 945–6.

Weiner, D., Heaton, L., Stiehl, M., Chor, B., Kim, K., Heisler, K., Foltz, K., and Farrell, A. (2020), *Chapin Hall Issue Brief: COVID-19 and Child Welfare: Using Data to Understand Trends in Maltreatment and Response*. Chicago, IL: Chapin Hall at the University of Chicago.

World Health Organisation. (2016), *Growing Up Unequal: Gender and Socioeconomic Differences in Young People's Health and Well-Being: Health Behaviour in School-Aged Children (HBSC) Study: International Report from the 2013/2014 Survey* (Vol. Health Policy for Children and Adolescents, no. 7). Denmark: World Health Organisation.

8

Possible Contributions of the School in Preventing the Maintenance of Poverty in the Case of Some Romanian Disadvantaged Children and the Context of the Pandemic

Ruxandra Folostina and Loredana Adriana Patrascoiu*

'Every Child Matters' Agenda

Education is an important tool for promoting equal opportunities – the Incheon Declaration summarizes the progression towards the objectives defined by Education for All (EFA) reasserting the transformative and universal role of education as a development engine ('Our vision is to transform lives through education.') (World Education Forum, 2015). Through the lessons learnt, it is urgent to engage ourselves in developing educational services that look at children and the societies they belong to in a holistic manner. These services should focus on access, equity and inclusion, on the quality of education and on results, in a lifelong learning paradigm. This is a quintessential endeavour for peace, tolerance, human fulfilment and durable development, as education is considered the key to eradication of poverty.

An education system is fair if it ensures the same learning opportunities and outcomes, regardless of the students' socio-economic or cultural background. The actual context of the pandemic revealed flagrant inequities. Poverty is a phenomenon that affects more than a third of Romania's children, and a significant number come from rural areas where the institution of the support teacher is almost non-existent. This situation exists due to the fact that in the category of special educational needs disadvantaged students are not included, as provided by the OECD definition.

---

* Both authors had an equal contribution to the chapter.

According to the 2020 reports of EUROSTAT, Romania ranks first in the EU in terms of the risk of poverty/social exclusion. Children are even worse at risk than adults, poverty being about 6 per cent higher among children (41.5%) than in the general population (35.8%). This correlates with the reduced ability of the family to generate income, with the level of parental education, as well as with the family structure (the higher the number of children, the lower the chances that parents have steady jobs).

As the *Report on the Observance of Children's Rights in Romania* (Onu et al. 2019) shows, 54 per cent of the country's population lives in urban areas. The report shows that poverty is much higher in rural areas (45.5%) than in urban areas. The high proportion of persons who are not in education, employment or training (14.5%), the low impact of social transfers (16.07% as compared to EU average of 33.98%), and the very low income of the young employees amplify the need to study the phenomenon of poverty and all its implications.

The Right to Education for the SEN Children in Romania in the Context of COVID-19, Equal Opportunities

Today, maybe more than ever, there is a need for school to become a focal point in each person's existence, because the education system must find solutions to the problems of today and tomorrow. Hence the concept of inclusive school (School for all) which is also a challenge for twenty-first century education, was amplified by the pandemic context. Inclusion transfers the functions of special education to mainstream schooling by assuming education for every individual student. The concept of 'inclusion' was widely debated in the pre-pandemic period, and its different understandings often led to various practices.

Regular schools, with an inclusive orientation, are considered the best means to combat discrimination and build an inclusive society. The 'Pending Issues on the EFA Agenda' (Declaration from Incheon 2015) requires an approach from the perspective of quality education and improving learning outcomes, focused support in terms of resources, process and evaluation of outcomes and the implementation of mechanisms to measure progress.

This picture of inequality of opportunity became even more vivid during the pandemic. Inequality of opportunity has become a sore problem of the system, perceived as such by the majority of the population.

Our focused literature review noticed the paucity of studies conducted in Romania, the lack of public reports on the impact of the Covid-19 pandemic on children with special needs, especially those who were at a disadvantage. Even the data were systematically collected by the Ministry of Education through the county inspectorates. Press articles, discussions with specialists, UNICEF's Rapid Assessment (RA; UNICEF, 2020) of the situation of children and their families, with a focus on vulnerable groups, in the context of the Covid-19 led us to the next big picture. The Covid-19 pandemic shut the schools down, which led to a series of serious problems in the continuity of educational services. The school shifted to a totally different context that required adjustments on the go. Online communication (digital educational platforms and materials) has been approached differently by schools and communities. For students with special needs in Romania, the lack of equipment and digital skills resulted in digital exclusion. Many teachers did not have the necessary skills to suddenly switch to online teaching and learning and, like many other professionals, had to learn and retrain. There have also been serious international concerns about increasing child poverty (UNESCO, Eurostat, The World Bank) during the pandemic.

Such situations, as well as many others, are quite complex. They substantially mark not only the student's school paths, but also their social ones. The problem of equality in education is not only reduced to the access to the system, but also to the educational and social achievements.

It is obvious that school alone cannot fully compensate for the disadvantageous effects that unbalanced social structures can have on any effort to promote an education under the sign of quality and equity. Moreover, the idea that education has nothing to do with underfunding or a precarious economic system cannot be justified either. Even if there were no clear support measures for unforeseen situations, especially against the background of a pre-pandemic precarious existence, equal opportunities are a duty of both the education system and society as a whole; it is not just a problem of the disadvantaged individual.

Research Methodology

This study analyzes how school contributes to preventing or maintaining poverty in their communities. A focused literature review was conducted in order to provide the policy and legislative context for the support available to vulnerable and disadvantaged children in Romania.

Case study interviews: ten parents and ten experts/school principals were selected from the communities marked as marginalized rural areas (Teşliuc, Grigoraş and Stănculescu 2016) in the southern part of the country – Muntenia, Oltenia and Bucuresti-Ilfov regions – and from some disadvantaged urban areas. While the rural principals are in charge of integrating SEN children in regular classes, the urban sample included principals who specialized in integrating SEN children and worked in schools that integrated SEN children from a wide geographical area. We considered such experts to have a clear view of the general situation of the SEN education services. The parents were selected from the same urban space as these principals so we could make a valid comparison between their perspectives.

An important aim is related to identifying the main difficulties regarding: the level of effective participation in peri-pandemic educational activities, access to technology, use of online education technologies and the level of school/teachers' receptivity to support the students' needs during the peri-pandemic period (curricular adaptations).

Scenario method is a method of analysis of strategic type, which has the role of configuring the future educational solutions starting from a set of data. Often, in education, decisions are made in a hurry, on short term, in order to capitalize on momentary opportunities. The OECD recommends this method of strategic thinking as an important working tool that opens up perspectives, anticipates change and helps those who apply it to face the challenges of the unknown. In our case, the defined scenarios represent solutions for the school to access the resources available in the community to meet the needs of SEN students.

As Jonas Svava Iversn (2006) points out, it is very important that the scenario (developed as a set of choices) relates both to a goal and to the processes involved. The nature of the scenario is exploratory and requires informational material from a multitude of sources – it requires description, observation, inductions, deductions, prioritization, quantitative and qualitative data and a creative mix of ideas generated by a stimulus in a participatory context. The 'mapping' of the scenario can be done through documentation, interviews or logical trees. The scenario technique helps us to find solutions of institutional development for educational intervention during and post Covid-19.

Results as Clusters for Development

Through the semi-structured interviews, we aimed to record the opinions of parents and experts/school principals about:

1. Peri-pandemic educational services – main difficulties regarding the level of effective participation in educational activities organized before and during the pandemic.
2. Social vulnerabilities at the level of the educational and social community from the perspective of parents from disadvantaged groups and school principals.

In each interview we listed a maximum of ten problems, and the respective solutions, which they ranked in order of importance. Thus, the most important problem/solution ranked 1 received 10 points, and progressively lower rankings reflected an incremental decrease in importance by 1 point.

Through the content analysis of the open answers, we identified the problems listed by each category of stakeholders (parents and experts/school principals). We considered as outliers all the problems which had the mean scoring under 1 point.

Educational experts identified twenty-four problems regarding pandemic impact on educational services (five of them being under 1 point were removed from statistics). We list them below, placing them by content analysis in specific categories (for descriptive statistics, please consult Table 8.1).

Socialization:

Lack of interactions with other children, typical or with SEN, social isolation;

Lack of access to play; of recreation and socialization activities;

Sedentary lifestyle;

Accentuation of anxiety and nervousness, but also of exhaustion, unmotivated sadness.

Teaching, curriculum adaptation:

Lack of adapted means and methods, teachers do not know how to include students with SEN in online classroom activities from mainstream education;

Leaving the school's educational environment routine generates learning difficulties, especially harmful for children with ASD;

The parents could not manage an efficient program of educational-therapeutic intervention from home, parents become teachers.

Technologies:

The discrepancy between schools with a digital infrastructure, which adapted more easily to the new context, and schools that were taken by surprise by the changes, from all points of view;

The long time spent in front of the screen that led to the faster installation of fatigue;

Most children from rural areas do not have access to the internet and specific devices – their families do not own devices for each and every child, do not have a room for each child, and as such, students could not successfully attend the educational activities.

The material condition of the children:

Regardless of the age, the children with SEN, during this period, can hardly bear the separation from their colleagues, from the school environment,

both from an emotional point of view, and from a financial and material point of view (school meals and snacks are very important for many of these children).

Increasing of social inequities;

Students lagged behind when they lacked the additional support during the pandemic;

Lack of materials needed to work at home on various tasks.

Qualified support:

Limitation/lack of individual support needed for the child with SEN;

In this online learning context, the SEN students' socio-emotional development suffered more than that of the 'typical' students;

Support teachers additionally load the child's schedule, sending homework for them;

The need for recorded lessons in order to return to the information for further processing;

Lack of psychological support for students with SEN and their families;

Exposure of students as a result of chaotic measures taken at the ministry level;

The use of different teaching methods for the SEN students, teachers lack digital competencies, as well as specific educational resources.

Parents overwhelmed by the situation of becoming children's therapists, family members (especially those in a state of social vulnerability) failed to successfully replace the teacher.

Parents identified sixteen problems described below. The descriptive statistics can be found in Table 8.2.

Social isolation, limiting activities in the community with other children;

Detachment of the child from the daily routine of the educational activity, lack of motivation for the educational activity;

Table 8.1 Descriptive statistics for problems identified by experts

Problems identified by experts	Minimum	Maximum	Mean	Standard deviation
Problem_E_1	0	10	**8.10**	3.071
Problem_E_2	7	10	**8.70**	1.160
Problem_E_3	0	10	**7.00**	2.828
Problem_E_4	0	9	**5.50**	3.375
Problem_E_5	6	10	**7.50**	1.354
Problem_E_6	0	7	2.10	2.807
Problem_E_7	0	4	.50	1.269
Problem_E_8	0	5	1.00	1.700
Problem_E_9	0	4	1.00	1.491
Problem_E_10	0	3	1.10	1.287
Problem_E_11	0	3	1.00	1.333
Problem_E_12	0	6	1.50	2.014
Problem_E_13	0	4	.50	1.269
Problem_E_14	0	5	.70	1.636
Problem_E_15	0	6	.80	1.874
Problem_E_16	0	5	1.10	1.912
Problem_E_17	0	7	1.70	2.541
Problem_E_18	0	10	3.00	3.559
Problem_E_19	0	5	.80	1.751
Valid N (listwise)				

Access to IT equipment (no assistive technology or access technology), which made it difficult for children with SEN to attend online classes; limited intervention options.

Lack of adapted educational materials and resources accessible to children with SEN;

Social distancing and transfer of all activities to homeschooling left their mark on children's development and well-being;

The need for additional information and support from specialists;

The need to find availability and understanding from school teachers;

Insufficient knowledge and skills to support the child in solving problems related to educational activity at home;

The management of daily activities, juggling daily duties, child care and homeschooling;

Material problems – job loss;

Access to materials necessary for daily hygiene, knowledge and practices necessary for disease prevention;

Social, medical and educational support;

Uncertainty, ambiguity, overwhelming feeling of helplessness;

Insufficient involvement of the school in solving the discontinuity of educational services;

The need for educational and social assistance at home, mediation, socialization, support for parents,

Lack of social perspectives for the development of the child as a self-sustaining adult.

Table 8.3 shows, in hierarchical order of gravity, the first five problems identified by school specialists compared to the five problems identified by parents regarding the educational services and the needs of children with SEN during the pandemic.

Even from the exploratory stage (identifying the problems/issues), we noticed differences between the parents' and the experts' perceptions. Although predictable issues did come up (such as educational practices and access to technology), they were regarded from different perspectives. For example, the decaying financial situation of the students' families is not a priority for schools (ranking 4/16 for parents, it is only on the 17/23 position for the experts).

The educational experts identified thirty solutions (see Table 8.4), while parents only identified eight (see Table 8.5). This suggests that parents do not trust that authorities (local councils/municipalities) will solve their social-economic problems. School is invested with social and even medical functions, when it comes to managing the socio-economic and social dimensions of family/community crises.

Out of the thirty solutions identified by experts/principals, we only keep eighteen in descriptive statistics (the rest being considered outliers). As in the case of problems, only five solutions met an average score of over 5 points.

Parents identified only eight solutions, which indicates a lack of confidence in services and authorities, but also in their own ability to find solutions. Only four solutions scored over 5 points. The fifth solution presented in the comparative table below scored 4.5.

Table 8.2 Descriptive statistics for problems identified by parents

Problems identified by parents	Minimum	Maximum	Mean	Standard deviation
Problem_P_1	0	10	7.30	2.946
Problem_P_2	0	10	8.30	3.020
Problem_P_3	0	8	1.70	2.710
Problem_P_4	0	7	3.50	3.240
Problem_P_5	0	10	6.40	3.658
Problem_P_6	0	9	5.40	3.098
Problem_P_7	0	6	2.40	2.591
Problem_P_8	0	3	.70	1.059
Problem_P_9	0	5	1.10	1.912
Problem_P_10	0	6	2.80	2.300
Problem_P_11	0	10	7.50	3.028
Problem_P_12	0	3	.80	1.229
Problem_P_13	0	7	3.20	2.530
Problem_P_14	0	3	1.40	1.265
Problem_P_15	0	4	1.30	1.418
Problem_P_16	0	6	1.30	1.947
Valid N (listwise)				

We notice the high scores for standard deviation that the main solutions have – this fact indicates the oscillating importance that the problem/solution received in the manifestation of opinions. These problems/solutions had different ranks of importance.

We detail in Table 8.6, in hierarchical order, the five solutions identified at the level of school specialists compared to the five solutions identified by parents regarding the educational services and the needs of children with SEN during the pandemic. We have to notice the school investment with social and even medical functions, when it comes to managing the socio-economic and social dimensions of family/community crises.

We notice the same difference in perspective among the interviewed categories. But we can define four major areas of intervention:

Table 8.3 Ranking problems parents and experts identified during the Covid-19 pandemic

Ranking	Problems as identified by experts	Problems as identified by parents
1	The discrepancy between schools with a digital infrastructure, which adapted more easily to the new context, and schools that were taken by surprise by the changes, from all points of view.	Access to IT equipment (no assistive technology or access technology), which made it difficult for children with SEN to attend online classes. Limited intervention options.
2	Most children from rural areas don't have access to the internet and specific devices – their families do not own devices for each and every child, do not have a room for each child and as such, students could not successfully attend the educational activities.	Social distancing and transfer of all activities to homeschooling left their mark on children's development and well-being.
3	In this online learning context, the SEN students' socio-emotional development suffered more than that of the 'typical' students.	The management of daily activities, juggling daily duties, child care and homeschooling.
4	The use of different teaching methods for the SEN students, teachers lack digital competencies, as well as specific educational resources.	Material problems – job loss.
5	Students lagged behind when they lacked the additional support during the pandemic.	Insufficient involvement of the school in solving the discontinuity of educational services.

1. Access to technology and digital skills;
2. The school's sensitivity to social issues and the students' educational, social and emotional vulnerability;
3. Developing the school as a resource centre in order to alleviate the students' educational, social and emotional vulnerability;
4. Student well-being considered holistically: their quality of life in its physical, material, emotional and social aspects.

Through the scenario method we have developed an approach to transpose the needs of the beneficiaries identified as a result of consulting the two major categories of stakeholders in institutional development solutions for the education of disadvantaged children in the peri-pandemic period.

Table 8.4 Descriptive statistics for solutions identified by experts/principals

Solutions identified by experts/principals	Minimum	Maximum	Mean	Standard deviation
Solution_E_1	1	10	6.70	3.268
Solution_E_2	0	10	5.90	3.381
Solution_E_3	0	9	5.10	3.446
Solution_E_4	0	9	5.00	3.801
Solution_E_5	0	10	5.70	4.373
Solution_E_6	0	7	2.60	3.406
Solution_E_7	0	10	4.50	4.378
Solution_E_8	0	8	3.70	3.302
Solution_E_9	0	5	1.20	1.874
Solution_E_10	0	4	.50	1.269
Solution_E_11	0	4	.50	1.269
Solution_E_12	0	3	.90	1.101
Solution_E_13	0	6	.90	1.912
Solution_E_14	0	5	1.90	2.183
Solution_E_15	0	9	1.40	2.875
Solution_E_16	0	10	3.50	3.440
Solution_E_17	0	8	3.30	2.908
Solution_E_18	0	7	2.00	2.582
Valid N (listwise)				

Jonas Svava Iversn (2006) presents scenarios as involving four phases: (1) mapping and delineation of the subject matter; (2) identification of critical issues and trends; (3) creating scenarios as a process of identification of drivers, consolidation and prioritization of trends and identification of scenario axes. The fourth phase is an active one for applying scenarios and observing the effects on the school and the community. This phase is the object of future research.

The Affinity matrix was used by the authors as a support technique for developing scenarios, entering the area of mental maps. The problems (support needs) identified by the previous method were connected and (re-)grouped into specific clusters.

Table 8.5 Descriptive statistics for solutions of parents

Solutions of parents	Minimum	Maximum	Mean	Standard deviation
Solution_P_1	0	10	5.50	4.790
Solution_P_2	0	10	8.40	3.026
Solution_P_3	0	9	4.60	4.006
Solution_P_4	0	10	7.10	3.872
Solution_P_5	0	7	.70	2.214
Solution_P_6	0	10	5.80	3.293
Solution_P_7	0	9	1.60	3.406
Solution_P_8	0	7	3.00	3.197
Valid N (listwise)				

As our stakeholders mention, the Covid-19 pandemic brought inequities in education for students with SEN. Online schooling has widened the gap between schools with a digital infrastructure, and those without one. Since the development of scenarios for social-educational services offers a better response to these peri-pandemic challenges, it is outlined based on the identified solutions. We list below by clustering solutions identified by experts and parents (see Table 8.7). We notice that this clustering indicates the dimensions of institutional development of the school, giving the possibility to develop new educational scenarios/approaches.

A brief diagnosis of what happened to the education system during the pandemic indicates two major risks, with consequences that can be dramatic in both medium and long term. One is related to the quality of teacher training in digitized teaching methods, and the second to the widening inequalities in the system. Inequalities are natural, and school success is generally determined, in any society, especially by the characteristics of the student's family. The main problem of the school is that, the way it was originally designed to function increases these inequalities, and teachers are key factors in this phenomenon. Ensuring competent and motivated teaching staff should become a priority in the future, given that school performance depends to a large extent on the professional quality of the teacher body. Teachers should participate in training courses in innovative teaching methods. At the same time, teacher evaluation must take into account performance, not only in what concerns gifted children, but also related to the progress of students from disadvantaged groups.

Table 8.6 Ranking solutions parents and experts identified during the Covid-19 pandemic

Ranking	Solutions as identified by experts	Solutions as identified by parents
1	Providing assistive/access technology; creating online resources which SEN students can access easily, according to the curricular needs.	Access to IT equipment necessary to attend online classes according to their specific needs and preparing children to cope with such activities.
2	Training for parents aiming to teach them how to operate the devices (basic notions on platforms, apps, etc.).	Creating a resource centre at school and ensuring intervention from qualified personnel.
3	Adapting teaching methods – the educational content should be reduced for all students (not just SEN), and focus on quality, key concepts and practical tasks rather than theory-based activities; handbooks in accessible format.	Help from other families or volunteers to manage the educational activities.
4	Adapting classes and necessary therapies in order to reduce the level of anxiety and other emotional responses generated by the pandemic (including the novelty of using technologies for school purposes).	Counselling for SEN students on personal development in order to reduce the negative socio-emotional state.
5	Counselling parents in order to reduce/ manage their fear or ignorance related to the health risks. Meeting with parents and specialized medical personnel that would teach them how to manage their pandemic-related fears, in order not to pass their anxieties on to their children.	Involving local councils/ municipalities and schools in assisting families in difficulty (socio-economical cases), especially since schools are viewed as more accessible than the townhall.

Conclusions

Among the results of this study it was most gratifying for the authors to notice that the impact of the pandemic on the school life in vulnerable communities highlighted the importance of quality of life of beneficiaries. The concern was noticed at the level of the primary stakeholders of the school – teachers, parents and principals – but we could not identify this concern in any of the policies developed during this period by the Romanian authorities.

Our findings obtained in this study by the scenario method will be related to the matrix of recommendations indicated in the World Bank Group study *'Pivoting to Inclusion: Leveraging Lessons from the COVID-19 Crisis for Learners with Disabilities* (2020). The World Bank matrix includes recommendations for six key thematic areas:

1. Rethinking education with an inclusive lens for learning;
2. Preparing and supporting resilient, inclusive teachers;
3. Disability-inclusive social protections;
4. Family and community supports;
5. Inclusive nutrition and water, sanitation and hygiene;
6. Disability-inclusive financing.

Through the scenario method we identified three major areas of intervention:

1. Curriculum changes for digital readiness and children's well-being;
2. Relationship between school and parents (for family empowerment);
3. Relationships within community for improving the school's receptivity to social issues and even the development of the school as a resource center focused to solve students' social vulnerability.

We were mindful that our respondents living for many years in these vulnerable communities are looking for local solutions and show little confidence in the ability of the authorities to respond effectively to their problems.

They find it more feasible to expand the facilitating role of the school through inter-institutional collaborations than the infusion of empowerment by funding these services at the central level. Obviously, disability-inclusive financing is an appropriate solution, but for Romanian schools it is not a known custom, even in the context of social vulnerability.

The pandemic imposed forced digitalization of education in many schools, given that teachers are not sufficiently prepared for e-learning or motivated to

Table 8.7 Clustering solutions identified by experts and parents

Cluster: Changes in the curricular approach specific to the child with SEN in the online educational context, focusing on educational resources.	Cluster: Changes in the curricular approach, focusing the educational and therapeutic process on the personal development and well-being of the student in school.	Cluster: School–family relationship improvement.	Cluster: Inter-institutional collaboration, expanding the role of the school as a facilitator in solving social problems of the beneficiaries.
o Adapting teaching methods. As all students (SEN or non-SEN) are going through a stressful period at the moment, the content should focus on key concepts, it should also be less theoretical and more practical. Also, textbooks should be in accessible formats.	o Maintaining social relationships with colleagues online. Organizing online social clubs where students can play fun social games.	o Family support; parenting courses; counselling parents on how to manage their fear or ignorance about the health risks. Parent meetings with doctors on how to manage their concerns so as to not pass these anxieties on to the children as well.	o State support via municipalities. A mechanism of collaboration with child protection institutions, local authorities and NGOs designed to solve the various problems that arise when working with visually impaired students across the country.
o Access to appropriate tools. Information should be presented mainly visually in online education. Students should receive support in learning how to use hardware and software.	o Setting a good rapport for behavioural therapy or play therapy. Reopening an office for the management of daily life skills. Creating a system of extracurricular and social activities.	o Supporting parents in learning how to use hardware and software.	o Non-invasive Covid-19 tests in schools to prevent transmission; hygiene supplies and the fun activities in which hand washing and compliance with rules of personal hygiene become interesting and motivating.

(continued)

Table 8.7 (continued)

Cluster: Changes in the curricular approach specific to the child with SEN in the online educational context, focusing on educational resources.	Cluster: Changes in the curricular approach, focusing the educational and therapeutic process on the personal development and well-being of the student in school.	Cluster: School–family relationship improvement.	Cluster: Inter-institutional collaboration, expanding the role of the school as a facilitator in solving social problems of the beneficiaries.
o Ensuring the necessary technology; easily accessible online resources (including tutorials) for children with SEN that are in line with the content taught in class. Thus, when the child has a difficulty, the parent or another person (e.g. the therapist) can explain that concept again.	o Adapting the assessment: at the end of the day or weekly, individual meetings could be organized with SEN students where the student and/or the parent will present the challenges and receive suggestions. Diversification of evaluation methods (projects, essays, drawings, etc.).	o Each teacher should make sure that parents use parental control on the internet.	o Finding sponsors for teaching and learning materials (both for teachers and children).
o Additional time allocated by teachers for each student. o An Educational Resource Centre.	o Adapting the necessary therapies. Using fun applications (puzzle, colouring, drawing) and posting the children's results	o Models of lessons that the parent can do with the child (teacher recordings).	o Online counselling.

Table 8.7 (continued)

Cluster: Changes in the curricular approach specific to the child with SEN in the online educational context, focusing on educational resources.	Cluster: Changes in the curricular approach, focusing the educational and therapeutic process on the personal development and well-being of the student in school.	Cluster: School–family relationship improvement.	Cluster: Inter-institutional collaboration, expanding the role of the school as a facilitator in solving social problems of the beneficiaries.
	on a shared group. The praise they receive will reduce their level of anxiety about the novelty of using technology for educational purposes. o Reorganizing school spaces, indoors and outdoors: relaxation spaces (a garden, a gazebo, a school museum, creation of an orientation and mobility club, etc.).	o School meetings with the parents (weekly or every two weeks), or a report to be distributed to parents, where parents are announced the content to be taught in the next week (or two weeks). o Online counselling.	

organize differentiated teaching if they have students who need educational support. Teachers with poor digital skills are an issue in many schools, not necessarily in disadvantaged communities, which affects all categories of students (i.e. gifted children, SEN, regular, etc.). Teachers also have low expectations of students from disadvantaged groups, since the latter do not have full access to online education, which, along with their often inadequate management of online classes, contributes to a very low level of student motivation and aspirations. The pandemic situation highlighted the fact that the education system still has rigidities that make it difficult to adapt teaching, and especially assessment, to the students' specific learning needs. These deficiencies affected the right of all children to a good education, and, in particular, the right of those who need educational support to an inclusive education.

This situation is critical due to the fact that the SEN category in Romanian educational legislation does not include the disadvantaged students, as provided by the OECD definition. Making this inclusion would greatly help disadvantaged children because they would benefit from a support teacher, an adapted curriculum and personalized intervention programmes.

The 'internal' challenges of many countries, as well as the 'external' ones (i.e. the pandemic), undoubtedly have a special impact on the changes in their education systems. Schools must serve the interests of all learners first in the interests of a changing society.

In the context of online learning, the socio-emotional development of these children was affected to a greater extent than that of typical children. Most children in rural areas do not have access to the internet, the families of these children do not have devices for every one of their children, or separate work rooms at home – and in this situation the students could not successfully participate in school. Differentiation of teaching has been an impediment for many teachers in this context.

This study is a qualitative exercise that, despite specific limitations (survey a specific sample of beneficiaries), illustrates a necessity in solving problems. These locally identified clusters can be the source of new institutional development policies. Thus we can illustrate the need for a scenario whereby the education system does not give up values such as inclusion, but focuses on the curricular changes that online education has made necessary, putting the partnership with the family, with other social service providers in education and with the community under a new light. This exercise also highlights the need for the goals of SEN education to be closely linked to psycho-emotional and social development, with an emphasis on the child's safety and well-being. So the great challenge of the education system in the coming years is to provide conditions for: enhancing personal growth and development, assisting young people in pursuing their goals according to their interests and aspirations, promoting an active and inclusive citizenship and enhancing employability. The outcomes of this study illustrate an increased concern from both parents and experts/principals for the children's well-being and for their mental, social and emotional balance, shifting the focus away from acquisition (knowledge, skills) as it was done prior to the pandemic.

The study of the quality of education implies the recognition (and assumption, we add) of the complex and debatable nature of the cultural, economic, political and even historical factors that mark the educational landscape (Tikly 2011). From this perspective, the school's role is not only to teach a child how to write or read, but also to develop their autonomy and form their personality. Sometimes, however, it is precisely this space that becomes favourable to discrimination and inequality, which defeats its very mission. Therefore, the school must have the necessary resources to prevail upon economic, social and cultural inequities in order to provide equal opportunities in learning and development.

Education, as well as disability, are deeply ingrained in the social map of the community. Schools have their specific ways to respond to the challenges raised by their students' special needs depending on the resources at their disposal. The analysis of each case presented here reveals the importance of the community and the way in which schools choose to use the (not yet) identified resources of the community.

References

EUROSTAT. (2020), *Living Conditions in Europe Report – Poverty and Social Exclusion.* Available at: https://ec.europa.eu/eurostat/statistics-explained/index.php?title=Living_conditions_in_Europe_-_poverty_and_social_exclusion (accessed 20 April 2021).

Iversen, J. S. (2006), 'Futures Thinking Methodologies and Options for Education', in *Think Scenarios, Rethink Education*, Organization for Economic Co-operation and Development. OECD Publishing.

Onu, D., Pop, I., Chiriacescu, D., Preda, F., and Roman, G. (2019), 'Report on the Observance of Children's Rights in Romania', Save the Children Romania. BMI Publishing.

Teşliuc, E., Grigoraş, V., Stănculescu, M. S. (2016). 'The Atlas of Rural Marginalized Areas and of Local Human Development in Romania'. World Bank, Bucharest. © World Bank. https://openknowledge.worldbank.org/handle/10986/24770.

Tikly, L. (2011), 'Towards a Framework for Researching the Quality of Education in Low-Income Countries', *Comparative Education*, 47 (1): 1–23.

UNICEF (2020), 'Rapid Assessment (RA) of the Situation of Children and Their Families, with a Focus on Vulnerable Groups, in the Context of the COVID-19 Outbreak in Romania Report', Bucharest.

World Bank Group (2020), *Pivoting to Inclusion: Leveraging Lessons from the COVID-19 Crisis for Learners with Disabilities.* Washington, DC: World Bank Publications.

World Education Forum. (2015), Incheon Declaration Education 2030: Towards Inclusive and Equitable Quality Education and Lifelong Learning for All'.

Part 4
Including Excluded Individuals and Communities in Times of Crisis

9

Covid-19 and Disadvantaged Roma Communities in Romania

Rosa Drown

Roma communities usually live on the margins of villages or towns. The majority are impoverished, lacking many of the amenities enjoyed by the main population. This chapter focuses not only on how measures taken to combat Covid-19 have affected such communities, but also on a promising pilot project which helps ameliorate educational problems for children and their parents. The project demonstrates how its flexible approach is able to benefit Roma and other marginalized communities suffering from deprivation and alienation, both during and following the pandemic.

The Vulnerability of Roma Communities to Covid-19

Prior to the pandemic, surveys and case studies had shown that Roma in Romania live in extreme poverty with most homes lacking basic amenities, such as being without supply of water and some lacking electricity or going hungry (Ringold, Orenstein and Wilkens 2005; Duminică and Ivasiuc 2010; FRA 2012). Research reports (Save the Children 2001; Voicu 2017) have also concluded that a lack of medical care combined with crowded living conditions has resulted in poverty illnesses such as pneumonia and longstanding chronic conditions. Covid-19 has now increased such poverty (EU 2020).[1]

Roma communities usually rely on an adjacent village or town for their basic amenities, for example, shops, medical centres and, if eligible, collecting

---

[1] I use 'Roma' as an umbrella term, although other nomenclatures might be used, for example, Gypsies, Sinti, or by traditional occupations. In Romania they have been defined in law as a single ethnic group (2008 PRPE 2017). Many, but by all means not all Roma, live in impoverished communities.

money for child and other social benefits. Some families, however, do not qualify for financial assistance or medical care because they do not have correct documentation needed such as birth certificates or valid identity papers. The majority also do not have official jobs, depending instead on unofficial casual labour described to me by a social worker as the 'grey economy'. This includes begging, foraging for scraps in rubbish containers and municipal garbage centre as well as, in a few cases, supplementing this by receiving help from charities. A small minority have been able to supplement their income by travelling to other EU countries to engage in temporary or seasonal work (Toma 2021). Measures taken in order to combat the pandemic have rendered the above ways of making a living almost impossible. Therefore, I contend that almost all those who live in Roma communities satisfy the definition of vulnerability to emergency situations given by the World Health Organisation (WHO):

> The degree to which a population, individual or organization is unable to anticipate, cope with, resist and recover from the impacts of disasters ... malnourished people, and people who are ill or immunocompromised, are particularly vulnerable when a disaster strikes, and take a relatively high share of the disease burden associated with emergencies. Poverty – and its common consequences such as malnutrition, homelessness, poor housing and destitution – is a major contributor to vulnerability. (WHO 2019)

Together with the above attributes, Roma have additional problems of being marginalized, suffering extreme discrimination by the majority population. For all the above reasons, the Council of Europe (CoE) recognized that Covid-19 poses extra challenges for Roma communities, therefore suggesting that the state and local administrations play an important role in mitigating such disadvantages (CoE 2020).

At the beginning of this century, the Romanian government had officially recognized that there was a need to improve the situation of Roma and 'remove stereotypes, prejudices and their practices' as well as to 'prevent institutional and social discrimination against Roma' (MPI 2001). Therefore, they implemented a strategy, enshrined in law, to improve the condition of Roma, also stating that 'improving the quality of education for Roma children is a priority' (MER 2003, 2004). However, it has appeared that the strategy has had little, if any, effect (Drown 2019; EC 2016). Within the educational system, discrimination against Roma still exists at both children's and their parents' levels. In working with Roma children in schools, I heard teachers singling out all Roma children as being stupid or lazy. Parents were also considered to be lazy and uninterested in school education as compared with non-Roma parents. An example of extreme discrimination that occurred in school was when a project worker was in the school washroom helping a Roma child to wash her/his hands explaining that it was necessary in order to clean away viruses and germs that could make her/him ill. The school administrator entered the room and asked what they were doing. When the project worker explained, the administrator spoke directly to the child saying that gypsies are dirty people and it would be better if they all die from viruses so the world would get rid of them. The child, understandably, became very distraught by this. The above example in a school environment demonstrates the extreme discrimination of Roma.

The outbreak of Covid-19 has given more opportunities to discriminate against Roma. There are many examples of newspaper articles published in April 2020.[2] Many similar examples have also been published at different times and in different parts of the country. Comments, referring to the virus, are exemplified by the newspaper article below.

> '[Roma] colonies should not be isolated; they should be closed so that they cannot get out.'
>
> 'Well said: 'colonies. Usually, animals live in colonies. These [Roma] are, in fact, we know that they are [animals].'
>
> 'One solution would be to give them gift tokens to India [then] they are gone.'

Centuries of Discrimination of Roma Adversely Affecting Roma during the Pandemic

Possibly, as early as the eleventh century, Roma migrated westwards from various parts of India (Kalaydjieva et al. 2005; Matras 2002; Moorjani et al. 2013). In a large part of Romania, however, Roma settled and initially were treated as a servile and inferior class, followed by being enslaved until the middle of the nineteenth century. In other parts of today's Romania, attempts were made to 'civilize' Roma by forcing them to live in groups of only two or three families. They were also required to abandon their own language and culture in favour of that of their new locality (Achim 1998; Magocsi 2002). In the twentieth century,

---

[2] Examples of newspaper articles published in April: 2020: https://www.bihon.ro/stirile-judetu lui-bihor/posibile-focare-in-patru-colonii-de-rromi-se-foloseste-testarea-prin-pooling-2139447/ https://www.bihon.ro/stirile-judetului-bihor/rromii-din-vadu-crisului-se-revolta-si-injura-autori tatilor-dupa-ce-au-refuzat-testarea-coronavirus-2144792/ (accessed 24 April 2020).

Roma became victims of the Holocaust or, in some parts of Romania, deported to a barren land resulting in many dying of hunger, cold and disease (Achim 1998; McGarry, 2010). Later, during the communist period, Roma were usually forced to perform unskilled, poorly paid work in factories or huge agricultural establishments (Ringold, Orenstein and Wilkens 2005). In 1983, Romanian communist officials blamed Roma for the lack of success of the government's social integration policy. Using highly discriminatory language, they stated that this was due to 'their backward mentality' and 'negative attitude towards work' (Anăstăsoaie 2003). The experiences of Roma throughout this historical period, I propose, cemented the present-day discrimination or alienation and the comparative poverty of Roma people.

Following the overthrow of communism, state factories and agricultural establishments had to close and the land returned to private ownership (Ringold, Orenstein and Wilkens 2005). A consequence of closing state farms meant that many Roma also lost their homes. According to Guy (2001) it also 'soon turned substantial Roma employment levels into almost universal unemployment'; therefore, Roma were forced to survive on whatever state benefits existed. The need to rely on state benefits not only meant that Roma were amongst the poorest in society, but also led to resentment amongst the non-Roma population, who blamed Roma for being burdens on the state (Guy 2001).

More recently, in 2010, a study of teachers and university students in Romania asked whether or not they agreed with a number of statements regarding national minorities, including Roma. The statements included 'Maybe Hitler was a little extreme, but in general his ideas were good' and 'Some people are less developed than others and should be led by a superior people.' On the question about Hitler's ideas, 15 per cent of teachers and 50 per cent of students agreed with the statement, while for the second statement, 30 per cent of teachers and 40 per cent of students agreed (Chircu and Negreanu, 2010). This exemplifies that such views are still held in the twenty-first century.

The deeply held discrimination of Roma has led to a mistrust between both Roma and non-Roma, which came to the forefront during the pandemic. Recent[3] newspaper articles, referred to above, regarding the testing of a Roma community for Covid-19 illustrate this[4]. In one Roma community in Romania,

---

[3] An example of this was that in a state pig farm that had a throughput of one million pigs per year, Roma were provided with homes within the compound. Here Roma had to work alongside prisoners, guarded by prison officers. Following the overthrow of the communist government, Roma were evicted from their homes, therefore losing both their homes and their livelihoods.

[4] When non-Roma people wish to enter some Roma communities, they must be accompanied either by a Roma from the community, or someone already trusted by them but unknown by the

three people were found to have Covid-19 and had been hospitalized. Therefore, it was decided to test the whole community of approximately five hundred people. Tents for the community were set up so that they could all be tested. It was explained that the test would not hurt and that it was free, but only between twenty and thirty agreed to be tested with others saying that there was no need because they were healthy. Later the community complained to others outside their community that they had been forced to take the test. Consequently, the Romanian authorities decided that if anyone from a Roma community contracted Covid-19, the whole community must be quarantined and guarded by the police so they could not leave. Together with the failure of the Romanian government's strategy to address problems of social and educational inclusion for Roma, the pandemic contributed towards the ongoing situation of discrimination and further heightened the lack of trust of Roma towards the majority population.

Impact of Government Measures on Roma Communities

In March 2020, schools in Romania were closed until mid-September and then again a few weeks later. In addition to having an adverse effect on all children's education, it also covered the period where some children transferred from primary to secondary school. School transition can, even in normal times, be problematic for the educational, psychological, social and cultural aspects of children's lives (Jindal-Shape 2021). When combined with the stress created by the pandemic, the problems with school closure before the end of primary school and the beginning of secondary school were even greater. This was exacerbated in Roma communities where almost all parents had abandoned school prior to transferring to junior secondary school, thus having had no personal experience of school transition.

A lack of school experience was exemplified in research during a 2016 census of educational levels reached by Roma in one community (population 1,043). By 2020, 45 per cent of those aged between twenty and thirty-three years would have had no school education at all, whilst only 21 per cent reached junior secondary school (Toma 2021). Elsewhere, research in two villages showed no mother of

---

community. Once you have been accepted by the community, in my experience, you are always welcome.
 In another example a Roma, who sells his goods outside his community, believes that non-Roma people will pay him less than they would non-Roma people for the same goods. In this way he mistrusts non-Roma people to give him a fair price.

school children had transferred from primary to junior secondary school with others either having had no school experience or else had abandoned school before reaching the end of primary school (Drown 2019). Reay (2006) also found that there were difficulties in schools where parents had less educational knowledge and information about the school system and had a different culture from the majority population.

As a result of the pandemic, Romanian government's order that online schooling was compulsory during school closures (Ordinance 4135/20200422) affected children and parents at all levels of school education. Conforming was impossible for most from Roma communities where households rarely had access to the internet. Also, as illustrated above, some parents had had no school experience with most abandoning school before completing their compulsory education, hence they were unable to help their own children's education. Crowded living conditions and a lack of essential materials such as pens, paper and notebooks further exacerbated this situation. Therefore, getting used to a lifestyle without school and with no means of home education resulted in Roma children being less likely to return to schools once they reopened and would widen the existing gap of inequality in education (EU 2020).

As with many European countries during the pandemic, measures were taken which were relaxed and reintroduced depending on the situation. These included the condition that people must stay indoors except to buy essential supplies, for medical reasons, to exercise, or if they were key workers. At times everyone needed to carry a statement which included their ID, the date and reason for their journey as well as the estimated time they would be outside their homes. This was impossible for those who had no official ID, were illiterate or had no paper and pens to make such statements. Other problems were caused by the need to socially distance, wear masks when outdoors and carry out frequent hand washing. In isolated Roma communities, with no media access, many may not have been aware of the imposed restrictions.

In crowded Roma communities, where many had no indoor facilities, it was essential for them to go outside their homes, for example, for hygienic reasons to collect water, or wood for their fires. For the vast majority, there is no demarcation of outside space between houses and there might only be enough space indoors for the family to sleep, with little room even for a table; therefore they needed to be outside for a large part of the day. For these reasons, complying with the order to isolate and stay indoors was impossible for almost all in the community.

A Study of One Roma Community

The chapter now addresses the experiences of a Roma community that was typical in that it had problems for most of the inhabitants, such as extreme poverty, a lack of basic amenities and crowded conditions, as described above. Less typical was that it had its own segregated primary school. In 2007, the Romanian government legislated that all schools must be integrated; however, exceptions were made if, in theory, a community was too remote for children to reach an integrated school.

Children from this community needed to complete compulsory education by attending three separate schools (primary, junior secondary and secondary) that were in different locations. The primary school is situated within the community because the nearest school is considered to be too far for young children to travel on foot with no other means of travel. The integrated junior secondary school is in a village which could be reached on foot by older children, while the secondary school is in a town, comparatively a long distance away with predominately non-Roma pupils. In order to complete compulsory school education, all pupils need to spend one year in the town's secondary school. Travelling to the town caused problems for many Roma children. There were several[5] reasons for this. Firstly, it was difficult to adjust to a school where the majority of pupils were not Roma; secondly the cost of travel was unaffordable. Thirdly, parents had concerns about their children mixing with others who had a different culture. I had also been told by a parent from another Roma community that the people in town were 'too fine' for Roma, so their children felt intimidated because they were not as well dressed as others nor had any money to spend. As referred to above, transition from primary to secondary schools is made particularly difficult when school closures mean that children missed the end of one school and the beginning of the next. It was also much more difficult when each school had a different culture.

Prior to the onset of the pandemic, a project carried out by two practitioners from the Team Friendship Association (TFA) had focused on young Roma primary school children who found school life particularly difficult and were struggling in their lessons. The project considered not only the children's educational needs, but also the psychological, social and emotional aspects of school life. Later, when schools were closed during and following the pandemic, such aspects were also considered to be important (UNESCO 2020).

---

[5] Primary schools have children up to year four, junior secondary schools from years five to eight and secondary schools from years nine to thirteen. Children must complete ten years of schooling.

During this project TFA had recruited three teenagers from the Roma community, who were literate but not able to continue with their own school education. Following the onset of Covid-19, the TFA practitioners explained to me that:[6] 'Unfortunately, because of the pandemic, schools are forced to close from March until September [and] so because children would be without any school education for at least 6 months, we must find another way.'

The determination to ameliorate the above situation led TVA to take positive action.

The Pilot Project

Together with the three Roma assistants from the previous project and with parental cooperation, TFA was able to provide support for children in order to continue with the activities that helped them in their former school-based project. In order to achieve this, it was essential at least to have online contact with both teenage Roma assistants and the children.

TFA explained to me that: 'It was not always easy but it did work, especially with the help of the teenage assistants who are our hands, we can help the little kids in the primary school. School is not easy for them; the majority were struggling and this stop in lessons is not good for them.'

Initially, the oldest teenage assistant was provided with a laptop computer, printer and SIM card so that the TFA practitioners and assistants could communicate via Zoom as well as send materials which could be printed. TFA practitioners then were able to train the assistants on how to help with the new project. Covid-19, and the precautions needed to avoid its spread, were also discussed with the practitioners as it was necessary not only for it to be explained to the children, but also to as many others in the community as possible. Results of the discussions, videos about Covid-19 and other aspects of the project were also sent to the assistants to help them support children's education both during and after school closures. The assistants were also provided with SIM cards for their mobile phones with TFA paying for the subscriptions. Phones were used so that small groups of two or three children at a time could have online sessions with the practitioners. Using the Zoom application practitioners and children

---

[6] Team Friendship Association was formed by people qualified in education, psychology or both. I am very grateful to Diana Craciun and Lavinia Preluca from this association who devised and executed the pilot project and kept me informed of both its progress and their future plans.

could communicate directly with each other and using Zoom's whiteboard features enabled children's sessions to be as close as possible to normal school activity. Worksheets, exercise books and anything else needed was delivered to the borders of the community by a practitioner and received by an assistant, maintaining a social distance between each other. It was also decided that, provided the Roma assistants were involved in the sessions, TFA would provide them with pocket money.[7]

Each assistant worked with one small group of children at a time, then moved on to the next group. In each session children were not only taught schoolwork in order to improve their reading, writing and number skills, but also read stories and sang songs together with their assistant. After this, the assistants discussed the session with the two or three children and helped them with any set tasks. They then moved to the next group and the sessions were repeated. An extra benefit with personalized online teaching was that parents were able to observe the sessions and how their children reacted to them. Therefore, for the first time they were able see how school teaching could be enjoyable for their children and, at the same time, improve their education. Parents appeared to be delighted with the programme. A further benefit was that the sessions helped the teenage assistants by gaining in confidence in their own abilities as well as reinforcing their own learning. Later it was realized that the screens on mobile phones were too small and that tablet computers would be a big improvement so the whiteboard facilities could be used more efficiently with pictures and worksheets seen more clearly.

Holiday Programme

When it would normally be time for the school holidays, TFA practitioners worked directly with all children ensuring that social distance requirements were met. They were unable to use the school building for this purpose, hence obtained permission to use a church that had been recently renovated and had large clean rooms. The children were arranged in family groups to help maintain the legal social distance. There was also sufficient space for the TFA practitioners as well as the assistants to be present in person. Parents happily let their children go with the Roma assistants to their classes.

---

[7] 'Zoom' is a visual and audio conversational internet application (app) which also includes a 'whiteboard' facility in order that written information or pictures can also be displayed.

At times, children, practitioners and assistants walked to a nearby park and, still maintaining the required social distance from each other, were bought ice cream, as well as having fun activities in a spacious environment. It also had the advantage of the Roma children being able to see the world outside their village, if only from a distance. It was both a valuable and pleasant experience which additionally helped children prepare to see non-Roma people (although from a distance) when they returned to their school environment. Such activities also helped the children's psychological and social well-being.

Towards the end of August, in order to reward the children for working during the holidays, they were taken to a pizza restaurant with outdoor space and within walking distance. To their delight, they had the new experience of eating a pizza and each having an individual bottle of cola with a straw. Other surprise guests were invited to make the event more special. The children put on their best clothes and by placing family groups together, were able to keep the regulatory social distance. As well as working with the children during the time when TFA had a physical presence inside the community, they were able to offer some assistance to adults such as helping them with the statements needed to travel outside together with providing both the necessary materials as well as some face masks.

Reopening of Schools in Mid-September

When schools returned in mid-September, TFA volunteers were unable to use the school or the church rooms. The school director had been given instructions that children must not be kept in the classrooms any longer than necessary and also opined that using the church rooms risked exposure for children who would go to school the next day. Therefore, the only option was to return to online distanced learning. Two families, who had a big room with a large table, agreed that their rooms could be used by TFA. This not only meant that longer sessions with the children could take place but also that routers could be provided for each home by linking the two houses to a Wi Fi system in an adjacent village. This provided a much stronger signal for online communication.

In addition to the usual sessions for younger children, a later session was organized for children who had progressed from primary to junior secondary school during school closure. This helped towards making transfer less problematic especially as there was a significant difference in both teaching methods and culture. Because the school project was received very well by the parents, TFA plan to expand the project by providing a 'second-chance class' for older children and adults. If more assistants would be needed to expand the programme in this or other ways more teenagers would be recruited from the community (a fourth teenager had already offered to help).[8]

TFA practitioners explained to me that: 'Distance-learning was never our first choice to help with [the] education of Roma children, but it does give us options for expanding into new areas … If we need more tablets and volunteers, we will do that as the work already done was liked by the parents.'

The educational project, hosted by parents and with the help of Roma teenagers also 'has brought an unexpected deepening of our relationship in the community. We are truly grateful for that!' (TFA)

Families that hosted the classes not only welcomed the children into their homes but were also impressed by what they could hear and see. They also explained to others in the community how the children were taught and the importance of a school education. As reported above, most people living in Roma communities had abandoned school at an early age while some had never attended, hence they had little or no experience of the school system or how it worked. The project, which started simply as a way of providing online teaching to vulnerable children when schools were closed, became a much wider project, jointly owned by Roma parents, their children, the teenage assistants and with the two non-Roma TFA practitioners who, in normal times, taught within the local school.

The joint project enabled parents to become more confident in engaging with the school and its teachers than they were before the Covid-19 pandemic as well as the practitioners to learn more about the Roma community. The pilot project has helped ensure that vulnerable Roma children were not left behind in their school work once schools become fully functional again and, having had positive educational experience within their own community, would boost their confidence in their own abilities. I propose that all these factors will improve the parent–school interface, lead to a partnership between parents, children and teachers and help to protect the community from Covid-19.

TFA's ability to adapt to the different phases of restrictions as well as to visualize ways of extending activities, in partnership with the Roma community, both during and after Covid-19 demonstrates that lessons learnt will have a long-lasting benefit for this community.

---

[8] 'Second-Chance' provides lessons for those who have left school but need to obtain or improve their basic literacy and numeracy skills.

Conclusions

It is widely accepted that Roma communities live in extreme poverty, are marginalized and, together with centuries of discrimination, are much more affected by Covid-19 than the general Romanian population. A mutual mistrust between Roma and non-Roma has further exacerbated the situation. Unfortunately, the Romanian government's strategy to improve the condition of Roma together with removing prejudice and discrimination has had little or no effect on the vulnerability of Roma to the virus.

Across the world, the effect of the pandemic has also resulted in a greater divide between the 'haves and the have nots' in society. For Roma communities, however, no account was made of their isolation from the most basic facilities, such as access to essential goods, collecting social benefits or other means of providing a living. In addition to this, should a member of the community need to leave their community for a legitimate reason, the legal restriction of providing written statements each time they needed to travel was impossible for most, who either did not have information to prove their identity, materials such as paper and pens or else were not sufficiently literate to understand or write down the essential details. Purchasing masks without leaving the community, as well as not having the funds to buy them, also made it impossible to adhere to this regulation. Such restrictions were monitored by police and so, without either the statements or masks, Roma faced a penalty.

The interruption of education is one of the most significant long-term effects of the virus, especially for those living in poor and marginalized communities. This was greatly magnified when children had no access to the internet to engage in online learning, and were already having difficulties at school when parents, with little or no education themselves, were unable to help. In order to mitigate the situation, in one Roma community, a pilot project devised by TFA aimed to ensure that the most vulnerable children had little or no detrimental effects when their schools were closed. Online two-way contact with children helped greatly to meet their educational needs. Also, through its flexibility, and by working both with and within the community, it had several more long-lasting benefits. Parents and children appeared delighted to have support coming from within their community whilst the self-esteem of the older students, who assisted, was enhanced. Another benefit was that parents understood more about the school system, which was operated by non-Roma teachers with a system designed by the majority culture of the country. This way they felt able to become more involved and confident about their children's education, therefore to engage with schools when they reopened. Following the lifting of restrictions that related to the Covid-19 pandemic, in partnership with the Roma community, TVA has expanded the project to include the needs of children in the first years of Junior schools.

The pilot project had the ability to work with a marginalized community and teachers in devising ways to benefit children's school education, as well as their social and emotional well-being. It also lessened the impact of a widening distance of school achievement which would be caused in the aftermath of the pandemic. This could be extended to other communities. Teachers, who had already established good relationships with a disadvantaged community in their school catchment area or could develop them could work with and within the community using both physical and online contact with equipment provided by the project. Rather than simply inviting or encouraging parents to visit school and talk to teachers in an alien school environment, the project would work within the community, be owned by it jointly with the school. This way a greater understanding of how the school system could work to benefit children's education and therefore their future can be gained. I suggest it would also empower parents to engage more with the school, thus improving the parent–school interface although some teachers may also need to change their attitudes towards parents in order for this to be successful. Project teachers should be able to help with this by discussing their own experiences with the community.

Teenagers or other potential assistants from the community, who are ideally already known by the project teachers, who are literate, and have had some school experience of the country's school culture, for example, would be needed for the project. They would act as role models for children as well as to support their learning. They could also provide greater links to the community as a whole. This way assistants would also reinforce their own education and give them more self-esteem.

The lessons learnt from the pilot project need not only be restricted to Roma communities in Romania during the course of this pandemic. They could also be relevant for communities that have a different culture, possibly a different mother tongue, or are unfamiliar with the school system. This should also include those who have migrated from a different country and culture.

References

Achim, V. (1998), *The Roma in Romanian History*, trans. R. Davies. Budapest: Central European University Press.

Anăstăsoaie, M.-V. (2003), 'Roma/Gypsies in the History of Romania: An Old Challenge for Romanian Historiography', *Romanian Journal of Society and Politics*, 3(1): 262–74.

Chircu, E. S., and Negreanu, M. (2010), 'Intercultural Development in the Romanian School System', *Intercultural Education*, 21(4): 329–39.

CoE (Council of Europe). (2020), 'We Are All Equal When It Comes to Protecting Our Health'. Available at: https://www.coe.int/en/web/portal/COVID-19-roma (accessed 15 September 2020).

Drown R (2019), *Educating Roma Children: Going Beyond Integration*, Cluj Napoca, Cluj University Press

Duminică, G., and Ivasiuc, A. (2010), 'One School for All? Access to Quality Education for Roma Children. Bucharest'. Available at: https://www.unicef.org/romania/One_school_for_all_pt_WEB.pdf. (accessed 12 December 2011).

EC (European Commission). (2016), 'Assessing the Implementation of the EU Framework for National Integration Strategies and Council Recommendation on Effective Roma Integration Measures in the Member States 2016'. Available at: ec.europa.eu/justice/discrimination/files/roma_report_2016_en.pdf (accessed 8 July 2017).

EU (European Union). (2020), 'Overview of the Impact of Coronavirus Measures on the Marginalised Roma Communities in the EU'. Available at: overview-of_corvid19_and-roma_-_impact_-_measures_-_priorities-for-funding_-_23_-_23_04_2020.dox.pdf (accessed 17 October 2020).

FRA. (2012), *The Situation of Roma in 11 EU Member States*. Luxembourg: Publication Office of the European Union.

Guy, W. (2001), 'Romani Identity and Post-Communist Policy', in W. Guy (ed.), *Between Past and Future: The Roma of Central and Eastern Europe*, 3–32. Hatfield: University of Hertfordshire Press.

Jindal-Shape, D. (2021), 'Wellbeing during Multiple and Multi-dimensional Primary–Secondary Transitions', *Research Intelligence*, 146(1): 14–15.

Kalaydjieva, L., Morar, B., Kalaydjieva, L., Morar, B., Chaix, R., and Tang, H. (2005), 'A Newly Discovered Founder Population: The Roma/Gypsies', *BioEssays*, 27(10): 1084–94.

Magocsi, Robert P. (2002), *Historical Atlas of Central Europe: From the Fifteenth Century to the Present*. London: Thames and Hudson.

Matras, Y. (2002), *Romani: A Linguistic Introduction*. Cambridge: Cambridge University Press.

McGarry, A. (2010), *Who Speaks for Roma*. London: Continuum International Publishing.

Ministry of Education and Research (MER). (2003), *Ministry of Education and Research Strategic Directions Regarding Roma Education Between 1998 and 2004*. Available at: http://www.oldsite.edu.ro/index.php?module=uploads&func=download&fileId=2096 (accessed 11 October 2016).

Ministry of Education and Research (MER). (2004), *Notificare 29323/20.04.2004*. Available at: http://www.isjcj.ro/crei/crei/pdfeuri/CES/Twinning%20Light/twinphare5.pdf (accessed 11 October 2016).

Moorjani, P., Patterson, N., Moorjani, P., Patterson, N. Loh, P., Kisfali, P., Melegh, B., Bonin, M., Kadasi, L., Rieb, O., Berder, B., and Reich, D. (2013), 'Reconstructing Roma History from Genome-Wide Data'. Available at: https//doi.org/10.1371/journal.pone.0058633 (accessed 20 August 2016).

MPI (Ministry of Public Information). (2001), 'Strategy of the Government of Romania for Improving the Condition of the Roma. Bucharest'. Available at: http://unpan1.un.org/intradoc/groups/public/documents/UNTC/UNPAN016040.pdf. (accessed 25 January 2009).

PRPE. (2017), 'Romanian National Roma Party'. Available at: http://www.partidaromilor.ro/category/asul-de-trefla/politic/page/9/ (accessed 10 December 2018).

Reay, D. (2006), 'Cultural Reproduction: Mothers' Involvement in Their Children's Primary Schooling', in Grenfell, M., and James, D. (eds), *Bourdieu and Education: Acts of Practical Theory*. London: Taylor and Francis.

Ringold, D., Orenstein, M. A., and Wilkens, E. (2005), *Roma in an Expanding Europe: Breaking the Poverty Cycle*. Washington, DC: The World Bank.

Save the Children. (2001), *Denied a Future? The Right to Education of Roma/Gypsy & Traveller Children in Europe*. London: Save the Children.

Toma, S. (2021), 'Counteracting the Schools' Demon: Local Social Changes and Their Effects on the Participation of Roma Children, in School Education', in Mendes, M. M. M., and Toma, S. (eds), *Social and Economic Vulnerability of Roma People*, 117–33. New York: Springer.

UNESCO. (2020), 'COVID-19 Educational Response: Education Sector Issue Notes'. Available at: http://www.legex.ro/Ordin-1540-19.07.2007-82075.aspx (accessed 17 October 2020).

Voicu, M. (2017). *Nevoi si resurse ijn comunitatile de Romi*. Bucharest: Soros Foundation.

WHO (World Health Organisation). (2019), 'Non-pharmaceutical Public Health Measures for Mitigating the Risk and Impact of Epidemic and Pandemic Influenza'. Available at: https://www.who.int/influenza/publications/public_health_measures/publication/en/ (accessed 17 October 2020).

10

Teachers Supporting Refugee Students in Canada during Covid-19: Greater Equity and a Sense of Belonging

Susan Barber

Introduction

Globally, 1.6 billion children and youth have experienced school interruption or closures due to Covid-19 that began in early 2020 (UNESCO 2021). Refugees, and asylum seekers in general, may be particularly at risk of Covid-19 due to pre-existing physical and/or mental health issues, along with little knowledge of how the virus spreads, the importance of vaccines (if they have access) and the health protocols for staying safe. However, in their resettlement, refugee children and their families may be doubly impacted. One striking example is with recent refugees in Canada. Just as they had achieved some safety and stability, the March 2020 school lockdown not only separated refugee students from their teachers and peers, but also deprived them of the technology and a 'third space' (Bhabha 1994; Engeström 2004) at home in which to learn online. While at the time of writing in November 2022 vaccines appear to be reducing the number of cases in much of the world, public health officials warn that freedom from Covid-19 or its variants will not occur anytime soon. For these reasons, it is imperative that educators identify which learning strategies afford flexible and effective delivery, and also ensure inclusion and engagement of all students, whether it be online or in distanced classrooms.

This chapter explores refugee education from a perspective of teacher agency during Covid-19. In late 2022, barriers to refugee settlement continue, but are now compounded by ongoing isolation, low levels of English language skills, doctors' preference to do physical evaluations and mental health support online and an overall lack of hygiene literacy. Framed by an ethic of care, this research explores the 'best practices' of experienced teachers who adhere to evidence-based research that prioritizes fostering relationships and facilitating pupils' socio-emotional development as a means to improving academic success. Through two case studies, we learn that equity plays a role, but it is teachers who provide safe, consistent and stable learning environments which create strong potential for trust and inclusion, and importantly, a path to the paramount goal of integration: a sense of belonging.

Global Impact of Covid-19 on Refugee Children

As of 1 November 2022, the World Health Organization (WHO) reported over 626 million confirmed Covid-19 cases and 6.6 million deaths internationally. Each country from January to March 2020 had to decide rapidly on a plan of action but by early 2021, there were grave concerns worldwide not only about the economy, but also about students and the outcomes of a prolonged lockdown. At this point in time (November 2022), there have also been 12.8 billion vaccinations and boosters administered, which may seem like progress. However, the United Nations Secretary General Antonio Guterres stated, 'The decisions governments and their partners take now will have lasting impact on millions of young people and on the development prospects of countries for decades to come' (Atkins 2021). Most educators agreed that the longer schools remained closed or restricted, the heavier the consequences would be for children, not just academically, but also in developing social skills and maintaining good mental health (Haigh 2021). Notably, as one parent put it, 'I admit to not realizing exactly how much support, not only academically but also physically and emotionally, schools provided my kids' (Haigh 2021: 1).

When considered through the lens of refugee education, school closure is the worst-case scenario for resettlement in a new country. Still dealing with the consequences of war and their difficult migration journeys, most refugee students have experienced grief, loss of loved ones, shattered lives, forced migration, violence towards themselves and may have witnessed violence or torture of others. The importance of enrolling children and youth in school, following a consistent routine and resuming the behaviours of childhood, namely interacting with peers, play and a return to 'normal', cannot be overstated.

The Canadian Context

When refugees arrive in Canada they are taken to a Welcome Centre where they are interviewed, undergo medical exams, receive treatment if necessary and have their educational abilities assessed. Canada accepts the majority of its refugees through the United Nations High Commission on Refugees (UNHCR) after strict background checks. Government-assisted refugees (GARs) comprise the largest group and, on arrival, receive financial support and other services including temporary housing, language lessons and medical services for the first year (Government of Canada 2019). After accepting 40,000 Syrians in 2015-16, Canada is now focusing more on vulnerable groups, for example, refugees with disabilities, women with children, LGBTQs, humanitarian cases and now Ukrainian refugees (UNHCR 2018). Unlike economic immigrants who tend to be fluent in English, highly educated and affluent, refugees may have little to no literacy even in their own language, a high incidence of disabilities and complications with PTSD, depression and anxiety, not to mention feelings of guilt for having left family members behind. At the same time, they also bring their own set of strengths and skills. With a flat birth rate, a burgeoning need for skilled workers and a possible economic recession due to Covid-19, the Canadian government sees immigrants in general, and refugees in particular, as part of its continued plan for future prosperity. For these reasons, resettling and educating refugee children and youth in the Canadian system is a high priority.

Teachers' Best Practices for Refugee Students

Of primary importance is for teachers to understand the phases refugees pass through in their adjustment to schooling that leads to a sense of belonging. This is not just a matter of connecting with students of the same background, but also with adapting to Canada's multicultural and diverse learning populations. In schools, acculturation is accomplished through prerequisite steps: feeling safe in the classroom and the school overall; receiving consistent positive responses from the teacher; being accustomed to reliable routines in the school day; trusting first the teacher, then other adults and eventually other children; being welcomed and encouraged to participate with others; and experiencing an ethos of inclusion in all classroom activities (AMSSA 2017; Custodio and O'Loughlin 2017). With time, a young refugee may slowly let go of the anxiety of leaving their parents or siblings, and turn their attention to their classmates and surroundings. The refugee can then focus on adding new words daily to their English vocabulary, reading social cues, becoming more at ease and naturally joining in play and social interactions. Some refugee students, however, may have to unlearn the survival strategy of mistrust that they acquired on their migration journey before they can believe that offers of inclusion are genuine. This enormous effort in the refugee's psychosocial adjustment is gradually rewarded with a sense of belonging that includes 'generalized trust' or the type of trust that is extended to many different kinds of people who may have different values and customs, a significant step in any person's development (Uslaner 2002). Here, school communities can do their part to meet refugees halfway, and 'create schools that are responsive to their lives and thus, to the ethical demand that schools are worthy of trust' (Veck and Wharton 2019: 6).

Although definitions vary, a student's sense of belonging is related to their attachment or personal investment in school, their agreement to comply with school rules and teachers' expectations, their willingness to engage in academics and activities and lastly, their belief in the value of an education (Kia-Keating and Ellis 2007). Being positively connected to one's school shapes a refugee's academic, behavioural and psychological outcomes including improved self-confidence, social skills, motivation, self-efficacy and achievement, while reducing depression, anxiety and other social-emotional issues (Anderman 2002). For refugees who suffer from trauma, school may return them to the belief they need most: hope (Suarez-Orozco and Suarez-Orozco 2001). The importance of the social environment in the classroom and the whole school, therefore, cannot be underestimated (Block et al. 2014).

When teachers plan their day with their refugee students in mind, teachers must anticipate transitions will be difficult. Some refugees may feel their safety is threatened when changes happen quickly, and teachers might prepare them by showing them images of common shifts in the day, for example, a photo of a child putting on a jacket or eating lunch (Hurley et al. 2011). Teachers must also foresee what stimuli might be frightening, and anticipate holidays (Remembrance Day or Veterans Day), and books or films that might depict war or violence. Teachers should recognize that behaviour problems are often rooted in trauma and model empathy and sensitivity towards the refugee for the other children (Custodio and O'Loughlin 2017). Boldermo (2020) found that children as young as ages two to four understand the concept of belonging and are already sensitive to social hierarchies, and the power and importance of peer culture and negotiating belonging. There are no differences between children, refugee or not, when it comes to the need to belong (Lejung Egeland 2019). Alternately, the

World Organization of Early Childhood Education (2016) has identified social exclusions as a potentially high-risk situation for refugee children.

For older students, a feeling of being physically safe can also lead to emotional and psychological safety, yet for some, this may be elusive (McIntyre and Neuhaus 2021). Having teachers, educational assistants and multicultural brokers in the schools that speak refugees' languages and look like them can help a great deal, especially in English language classes. Along with translators being available at the beginning, teachers can design learning experiences that encourage refugees to take risks and build trust.

In general, the above stages are also a part of a process leading towards improving well-being which has a direct effect on educational attainment, bolstering strengths and self-esteem while developing resilience (Block et al. 2014), all of which contribute to greater socialization. The ethos of inclusion must be holistic in its implementation within a school, along with a celebration of diversity and acceptance (Pinson and Arnot 2010; Taylor and Siddhu 2012) in order to augment refugees' psychosocial development.

Main Research Questions

Given that teachers' implementation of best practices for supporting refugees prior to Covid-19 was delivered through face-to-face, non-socially distanced interactions and often based on teachers' observations of refugees with other students, it is essential to understand teachers' current strategies in maintaining inclusion of refugees. Having identified the intersectionality of multiple disadvantages during the lockdown and later restrictive social distancing in classrooms, it is crucial to grasp what lessons educators have learned. Research questions, therefore, are:

1. What are the challenges for refugees and their learning during Covid-19?
2. How are refugees particularly in danger of becoming socially vulnerable or culturally marginalized?
3. How have teachers promoted a sense of belonging for their students?

Not all teachers are aware of refugees' backgrounds and the arduous journeys some have endured to reach Canada; other teachers may resent the extra work refugees require or the disruptions that occur in their classrooms (Kovinthan 2016; MacNevin 2012; Stewart 2012; Stewart and Martin 2018). While it may be true that some students require more effort on the part of teachers, the 'easier' alternate scenario of excluding these students from educational activities is much worse. My intention was to find teacher participants who care deeply about their pupils and draw on an ethics of care to inform their practice.

A key approach to understanding the hierarchies of power in the educational system, including the logic and decision-making that goes into policymaking, is through a comparison of how these policies are shaped to influence the media and general public, as opposed to how caring individuals on the ground interpret these policies. An ethic of care has its origins in feminism (Gilligan 1982), and fits well here because it is both a moral philosophy and a political approach, advanced most notably by Noddings ([1984] 2003, 2012). Care is fundamental to human existence, mainly because we cannot survive without relationships, and socially, it implies a human morality. Central to Noddings's (2012) work is the idea of the 'caring relation' which involves a carer and the person who is cared for, where both must contribute to upholding the relationship. A teacher expresses care when they give their full attention, apply their skills and make efforts on behalf of the student. Furthermore, a teacher actively listens to what the student pinpoints as their needs, as opposed to what the teacher determines are their needs. The student then must acknowledge that they have understood what the teacher intends to do in terms of fulfilling their needs. While there are other ethics of care, they tend to be teacher-centred, and not developed through the expressed needs of the other, but more focused on acting in a virtuous manner where the teacher believes they know best what the student needs, even occurring outside of a relation (Noddings 2012). Care ethics might be reconceptualized for each stage of a refugee's development on their way to achieving a sense of belonging, and applied to their many relations, from parents to educators, peers, school, the larger community and even government policymakers.

For these reasons I set out to reconnect with teachers who had participated in an initial questionnaire in May 2020 in order to elicit 'before and after' reflections of how they were now working with vulnerable students in June 2021. Eighteen teachers participated, including three school counsellors and two vice principals, all with more than ten years' teaching experience. To better expose the impact of equity, one secondary school (SS-A) and one elementary school (ES-A) in a middle-class suburban area were chosen to be compared with one secondary school (SS-B) and one elementary school (ES-B) in a low-income urban area with a high population of refugees, both school districts in the Greater Vancouver area. Each participant received a questionnaire through email, and their comments were then coded for themes.

Overall, the educators named increasing progress in terms of stabilizing the school community during these nineteen months of Covid-19 and expressed deep concerns about 20 per cent of the pupils, along with some unexpected problems forming on the horizon.

Findings

In analyzing the data, it quickly became apparent that although participants individually and within grade levels in the same schools were consistent in their answers, there were significant differences between schools in differing socio-economic classes. The following is a breakdown of participant responses to questionnaires (May 2020 and June 2021).

April 2020: Immediate Challenges of School Closure

As for most students and their families globally, there was no time to think; everything changed overnight. In British Columbia, the lockdown occurred during spring break, and after extending the holiday for a couple more weeks, policymakers worked out a plan to coordinate the same platforms for online classes. For refugees, however, their needs were more urgent.

> **NE: Secondary School (SS-B) Vice Principal (VP):** Students had one day to clear out their lockers. Some refugee parents asked the educational assistants (EAs) and administrators to continue the fruit and vegetable program and the government's food program at the school. They were worried about food shortages.
>
> **JA – Elementary School (ES-B) VP:** We organized emergency food hampers to be delivered to refugee and low income homes by educational assistants, childcare workers and school counsellors.

When classes resumed online, all students and their families were forced to find ways to cope; for example, some parents had lost their jobs, and others had to juggle care for small children when daycares had been closed, or try to keep older relatives and those with compromised immunity safe. Meanwhile, other families continued by working from home or guiding their children through online Zoom meetings with their teacher and classmates, with little impact on their lives. Gradually other teachers began to apprehend the enormity of the gap between the haves and have nots, especially through teaching lessons online.

AM –ES-A teacher: 100% of my students have devices and internet access. I am able to do daily Zoom meetings as well as post pre-recorded lessons for my students on my teacher website. My primary goal for my live Zooms is to connect. We have weekly class meetings, daily read alouds and virtual clubs (i.e. Lego™ and art) where we play together over Zoom.

FE – SS-A teacher: Of our approximate 900 students, we gave out almost 200 laptops to support online learning.

WL – ES-A teacher: The biggest problem? Attendance: my [low-income] students are coming online sporadically. Students are falling behind – there is the stress of catching them up. I was only online for one month and only 6 families regularly came on.

JA – ES-B VP: Online learning has been an adjustment and focuses on big picture ideas linked to literacy, numeracy and our core competencies. There is no way that online learning in the elementary years can replace direct instruction for any student.

NE – SS-B VP: Some refugee students sleep until 2 pm – they can only get on a single mobile phone late at night that is shared among the family. Then they need help at 11 pm … The attitude of the school district is 'just get through it' … Our school put out the request in the community to donate – nearly 80 laptops went to refugee and low income students who were sharing a family phone.

A second major indicator of inequity was technology. In Canada only 1.2 per cent of households with children of school age do not have access to the internet, and of the households in the lowest 25 per cent of families in poverty, only 4.2 per cent lack internet (Frenette, Frank and Deng 2020). However, of the households that were connected to wifi, 58.4 per cent had less than one device per household member. The types of devices that are available to students within their homes can also affect the quality of their online learning activities. For instance, mobile devices such as smartphones and tablets are designed to enable independent learning, but these are more for receiving information rather than producing it (Frenette, Frank and Deng 2020).

Although the technology helped, teachers had no idea what was happening in their students' homes. Clearly, some students and their families were struggling and teachers searched for solutions.

AM –ES-A teacher: I have started having daily 1:1 and small group Zoom meetings to read to my most vulnerable students.

- **BD-ES-A teacher of special needs students:** I am able to stay in touch through texts, emails, phone calls, and Face Time. Right now the concern is not at all academic. It's there, and we DO cover it, but my primary concern is their social well-being. 'Classes' is a loose term. As an alternate teacher, I'm not doing set lessons. Just checking in on emotional well-being, trying to have a laugh, assess their state and give opportunities for academics in diverse ways. Some are engaging academically; most are not.
- **FE—SS-A teacher:** Connection is key. Forget about the curriculum competencies until you are sure students are fed, supported and connected to at least one champion [advocate] in the building.
- **MC—SS-A school counsellor:** It really is dependent on how their family is handling the situation, in my opinion. If their big people are ok, they are more likely to be ok.
- **NE—SS-B VP:** Refugee kids are the ones working – they get jobs to support their families because their parents are afraid and feel their children are less likely to get sick. Schools across the district are organizing support for other refugees: food hampers, gift cards from major grocery stores. We have applied for grants to create care packages. Our other programs teach families about safety, hygiene and self care.

Exclusion and Being Socially and/or Culturally Marginalized

- **NE—SS-B VP:** Most refugees do not know what is going on. These kids are English Language Learners [ELLs] who have no resources at home. Sometimes they photocopy books.
- **GD—ES-B teacher:** For refugees, the things most altered by Covid-19 are having less sense of belonging, not feeling safe and dealing with family issues. I would also add that some just didn't understand what was happening or why. Language presented a barrier where many families didn't understand what we were asking of them.

Many of the recently arrived refugees have no contact with non-refugee families. There is a high level of mistrust of authority, and many will not answer their phones or respond to email. Due to social distancing, many of the usual places where they might learn about current events through their cultural networks, for instance, in places of worship, community centres and meeting halls, were now off limits.

A profound emotional investment in one's vulnerable students also takes a toll on teachers.

FS—SS-A teacher: I feel like we've regressed to worksheets and busy work. I feel completely disconnected from my students. A sense of community is so important right now. I feel super isolated and my mental health is not good. I feel like I have a big breakdown coming. Anxiety of the unknown. Yet it's been so heart-warming to see how much love is poured out to teachers from the community at large.

FE—SS-A teacher: We are in the unknown and everyone is looking to someone for guidance. For me, I'm looking to Dr. Bonnie Henry (the Provincial Health officer of BC) and drawing on my strengths and being calm. Also, stating the facts and comforting my students.

HE- SS-A school counsellor: Teachers need to be made aware of the parts of the job that are difficult to teach. Recognising trauma, the importance of relationships and setting healthy boundaries, practicing self care. Understanding the VAST differences many students face in their lives, [like levels of] parent support, socioeconomic issues, religious issues, issues of gender and gender expectations (many teachers still have them!), and sexual orientation (never assume).

JA—ES-B VP: We must all lead and show care and compassion more now than ever. I try to reach out to staff, parents. Let them know we are all in this together and that we care. This is extremely important.

By the Summer of 2020, we had learned a great deal about keeping safe and protecting ourselves, and infection rates dropped. In planning for September 2020, school administrators settled on three options: to offer classroom learning for those who demanded it and to respect those who feared coming into public spaces. A third option offered families to choose on a week by week basis, especially as the second and third Covid-19 waves arrived in Autumn 2020 and went on into 2021. Looking back on the year from June 2021, teachers found themselves responding mainly according to their unique situations.

September 2020 – Back to School: What was working well to keep refugee students connected to school and what was difficult?

GD ES-2 teacher: I think the toughest has been building relationships with refugee students, being able to assess their needs and provide effective support in their learning. What helped was definitely reaching out to refugees one on one, having individual times when we could talk and work on activities together. Also providing group games and learning activities where the students felt like they could take part (even if only to listen and observe). Again, playing games that didn't need a lot of language decoding went a long way in helping students feel connected. We played games like Pictionary and 20 questions, or What's in the Bag. My students felt like they could participate and not have to worry about typing or speaking and making mistakes.

NE SS-B VP: The multicultural workers have been phenomenal. They talk to refugee families [in their own languages] and encourage them. The multicultural workers stay with the same students from elementary to secondary school. When the school counsellors assess refugees, they send me their reports. Other refugees who don't go to the counsellors are quiet, suffering in silence. They are a time bomb. Teachers are really receptive to giving refugees breaks. Adding mini-breaks into the day. Everyone is aware of Covid stress and we all need to lower the stress, especially anxiety.

30 June 2021 – End of school year: All teachers agreed that their best course of action in the new school year (September 2021) should focus on creating a safe environment in the school and classrooms, encouraging social relationships and strengthening a sense of belonging.

Obviously, for refugees arriving just before or during Covid-19, this was not an optimal introduction to their Canadian education, but everyone is affected, especially high-school students. School counsellors are still overwhelmed by students' and their parents' needs, and there are not enough adults in a healthy state of mind willing to support youth, refugee or other. In SS-B, in the non-refugee population, there have been several suicides and also attempts at self harm. The hard truth is that educators must prepare to collaborate with school counsellors to do widespread interventions, no matter if we have moved on from infections next year. Clearly, if vulnerable students are suffering more than others, it is a given that their families are just as vulnerable, and no one is receiving the care they need.

All of the teacher participants in this study disagreed with the statement, 'I feel my school district and the Ministry of Education are doing enough to prioritize learner well-being.' From the perspective of refugees who would normally be moving through phases of adaptation towards feeling a sense of belonging right now, educators are wondering what the additional stressor their Canadian peers' mental health issues will have on refugees' adjustment.

Discussion

This glimpse into refugee children's and adolescents' lives ought to serve as a wake-up call. Even if we escape the grip of Covid-19 and its variants through vaccinations or herd immunity, we should not assure ourselves that students have moved out of danger. Those living in poverty are most affected. As one example, refugees who have large families living in a three-bedroom apartment may grow weary of the day-to-day 'togetherness' that impacts their mental, physical and spiritual health. The kids who are subjected to their parents' depression and anxiety, and frequently, domestic violence, and even sexual abuse in their homes, are the ones who suffer most from not being able to return to a normal school routine with friends and teachers. Prior to the arrival of Covid-19, many refugee students were learning English at a much more rapid pace than their parents and were adapting to the culture due to their immersion in school, which restructured the hierarchies in some families. Teachers are often astounded by thirteen-year-olds being the head of the household and guiding their parents' lives, but there is often no one else who can do it in the isolation many people live in. A priority of the Canadian government, the Ministry of Education, the public health authorities, the teachers, the schools and the media should be to make this comprehensible to the public who believe it is exaggerated and cannot be true.

Instead, as we move through this middle phase of Covid-19, educators need to envision a way back to normalcy, and they can begin by explicitly enacting their caring ethos to a larger group of students, adults and the community. Following an ethic of care (Noddings 2012), schools might begin by asking what is needed most in struggling families. For example, when refugee families requested the food programmes remain available at the school but the schools were in full lockdown, many teachers and educational assistants drove to families' homes and dropped off food items. This does not develop dependence on the schools for basic necessities; rather it builds trust and knowing there is a safety net that will allow families to get through tough times. Teachers can 'show' parents that we are on the same team; we all want what is best for their child (Barber and Ramsay 2020). Later, when teachers were concerned about students' learning materials, laptops were solicited and educators also dropped off 'care packages' which contained school supplies, art materials, hobby kits, games, exercise items such as jump ropes, balls and Frisbees as well as hygiene supplies such as soap and hand sanitizers. Schools were already becoming distribution centres, where, if necessary, parents pick up food for their dinners when they fetch their children. Centres for clothing and household needs are already in place, but the public can also be encouraged to increase their donations. Educators cannot do it all alone.

Care received is often reciprocated as care for others. As the community of caring people enlarges, it can raise awareness and reach more people who need care. It does not take long for people to get to know one another and speak English to share information, learn more about services and access to healthcare and medical needs. Classmates meet other classmates at donation sites and services, and introduce their parents, perhaps bridging their social capital outside of schools and trusting others with whom they have much in common (Pearce 2006; Uslaner 2002). For many refugees, the ability to 'give back' is an effective opportunity to uphold one's dignity which lifts mental health. In fact, having a task to do, and especially being employed, is the strongest predictor of improvement in PTSD over time (Sonne et al. 2016). Just knowing there are people who understand and offer empathy while at the same time are working together for a common cause creates a greater feeling of safety in the school neighbourhood, and people will naturally acknowledge and inquire about each other's well-being when they meet. All in all, it is not impossible to imagine that coming together around Covid-19 could be an ideal opportunity for many refugees who are feeling isolated and to turn things around. Allowing them to play a role and encouraging them to take the lead in distribution of goods might bring together many more like-minded individuals of various backgrounds (Barber 2021). The obvious endpoint in this ideal scenario is the goal for all refugees: achieving a sense of belonging.

Conclusion

This chapter has attempted to highlight the situation of refugee and other vulnerable children who have faced many challenges in continuing their education during Covid-19. Teachers, despite their personal fears about being exposed to the virus or bringing it home to loved ones, have laboured to ensure that refugee students and others will remain attached to their schools, their classmates and nearby caring adults while continuing to promote their pupils' psychosocial development. Teacher agency is at the centre of avoiding a much worse outcome, even at the expense of their own stress and anxiety. Moreover, by taking responsibility for listening to refugees' expressed needs, teachers have earned much more trust in the many lives they have touched. This chapter also contributes to the shift towards a collectivist view that 'we are all in this together' and as a society, we will not allow disadvantaged persons to slip through the cracks when we are easily distracted during a crisis. Although it may take much more time to escape the variations of Covid-19, we can still learn to emphasize care towards one another, and by so doing, ensure that it also reaches into other systems of care, impacts more educational institutions and garners the attention of more government policymakers.

References

AMSSA. (2017), 'Promising Practices of Early Childhood Education for Immigrant and Refugee Children in British Columbia', *Immigration and Refugee Children: The Early Years*, 35(1): 6–7. Available at: https://www.amssa.org/wp-content/uploads/2017/08/CW_EarlyYears-Summer2017.pdf (accessed 17 November 2021).

Anderman, E. M. (2002), 'School Effects on Psychological Outcomes during Adolescence', *Journal of Educational Psychology*, 94(4): 795–809. https://doi.org/10.1037/0022-0663.94.4.795.

Atkins, R. (2021, February 19), '*COVID-19 and the School Crisis*' BBC News. Available at: https://www.youtube.com/watch?v=azkycne7SCI&ab_channel=BBCNews (accessed 17 November 2021).

Barber, S. (2021), 'Achieving Holistic Care for Refugees: The Experiences of Educators and Other Stakeholders in Surrey and Greater Vancouver', *British Educational Research Journal*, 47(4): 959–83. http://doi.org/10.1002/berj.3730.

Barber, S., and Ramsay, L. (2020, September), 'Literally Speechless? Refugees to Canada Overcome Preliteracy and Learn to Communicate through a Literacy of the Heart', *English 4-11*. Available at: https://englishassociation.ac.uk/wp-content/uploads/2019/07/Barber-and-Ramsay-Sept-2020-1.pdf (accessed 17 November 2021).

Bhabha, H. K. (1994), *The Location of Culture*. London: Routledge.

Block, K., Cross, S., Riggs, E., and Gibbs, L. (2014), 'Supporting Schools to Create an Inclusive Environment for Refugee Students', *International Journal of Inclusive Education*, 18(2): 1337–55. DOI: 10.1080/13603116.2014.899636.

Boldermo, S. (2020), 'Fleeting Moments: Young Children's Negotiations of Belonging and Togetherness', *International Journal of Early Years Education*, 28 (2): 136–50. DOI: 10.1080/09669760.2020.1765089.

Custodio, B. K., and O'Loughlin, J. B. (2017), 'Unique Issues of Refugee Children', in B. K. Custodio and J. B. O'Loughlin (eds), *Students with Interrupted Formal Education: Bridging Where They Are and What They Need*, 41–68. Thousand Oaks, CA: Corwin. DOI: 10.4135/9781506359694.n3.

Engeström, Y. (2004), 'New Forms of Learning in Co-configuration Work', *Journal of Workplace Learning*, 16(1/2): 11–21.

Frenette, M., Frank, K., and Deng, Z. (2020, 15 April), 'School Closures and the Online Preparedness of Children during the COVID-19 Pandemic'. Catalogue no. 11-626-X2020001. Statistics Canada. Available at: https://www150.statcan.gc.ca/n1/pub/11-626-x/11-626-x2020001-eng.pdf (accessed 17 November 2021).

Gilligan, C. J. (1982), *In a Different Voice*. Cambridge, MA: Harvard University Press.

Government of Canada (2019), 'Government Assisted Refugee (GAR) Program'. Available at: https://www.canada.ca/en/immigration-refugees-citizenship/corporate/publications-manuals/operational-bulletins-manuals/refugee-protection/resettlement/government-assisted.html (accessed 17 November 2021).

Haigh, J. (2021, 27 March), 'Home-Schooling Around the World: How Have We Coped?' BBC News. Available at: https://www.bbc.com/news/education-56417834 (accessed 17 November 2021).

Hurley, J., Medici, A., Stewart, E., and Colon, Z. (2011), 'Supporting Preschoolers and Their Families Who Are Recently Resettled Refugees', *Multicultural Perspectives*, 13(3): 160–6. DOI: 10.1080/15210960.2011.594400.

Kia-Keating, M., and Ellis, B. H. (2007), 'Belonging and Connection to Schools in Resettlement: Young Refugees, School Belonging and Psychosocial Adjustment', *Clinical Child Psychology and Psychiatry*, 12(1): 29–43. DOI: 10.1177/1359104507071052.

Kovinthan, T. (2016), 'Learning and Teaching with Loss: Meeting the Needs of Refugee Children through Narrative Inquiry', *Diaspora, Indigenous and Minority Education*, 10(3): 141–155.

Lejung Egeland, B. (2019), 'Narratives of Belonging: Migrant Children's Friendship Negotiation', in V. Margrain and A. Löfdahl Hultman (eds), *Challenging Democracy in Early Childhood Education: Engagement in Changing Global Contexts*, 28, 183–96. Singapore: Springer Singapore. DOI: 10.1007/978-981-13-7771-6.

MacNevin, J. (2012), 'Learning the Way: Teaching and Learning with and for Youth from Refugee Backgrounds on PEI', *Canadian Journal of Education*, 35(2): 48–63.

McIntyre, J., and Neuhaus, S. (2021), 'Theorising Policy and Practice in Refugee Education: Conceptualising "Safety", "Belonging", "Success" and "Participatory Parity" in England and Sweden', *British Journal of Educational Research*, 47(4): 796–816. DOI: 10.1002/berj.3701.

Noddings, N. ([1984]2003), *Caring: A Feminine Approach to Ethics and Moral Education* (2nd edition). Berkeley: University of California Press.

Noddings, N. (2012), 'The Caring Relation in Teaching', *Oxford Review of Education*, 38(6): 771–81. Available at: https://doi.org/10.1080/03054985.2012.745047.

Pearce, P. W. J. (2006), 'Bridging, Bonding, and Trusting: The Influence of Social Capital and Trust on Immigrants' Sense of Belonging to Canada', *Atlantic Metropolis Centre – Working Paper Series*, No. 18. Available at :http://community.smu.ca/atlantic/documents/2009.01.06WP18Pearce_000.pdf (accessed 17 November 2021).

Pinson, H., and Arnot, M. (2010), 'Local Conceptualisations of the Education of Asylum-Seeking and Refugee Students: From Hostile to Holistic Models', *International Journal of Inclusive Education*, 14(3): 247–67. DOI: 10.1080/13603110802504523.

Sonne, C., Carlsson, J., Bech, P., Vindbjerg, E., Mortensen, E. L., and Elklit, A. (2016), 'Psychosocial Predictors of Treatment Outcome for Trauma-Affected Refugees', *European Journal of Psychotraumatology*, 7(1): 1–11. DOI: 10.3402/ejpt.v7.30907.

Stewart, J. (2012), 'Transforming Schools and Strengthening Leadership to Support the Educational and Psychosocial Needs of War-Affected Children Living in Canada', *Diaspora, Indigenous, and Minority Education*, 6(3): 172–89. Available at: https://doi.org/10.1080/15595692.2012.691136.

Stewart, J., and Martin, L. (2018), *Bridging Two Worlds: Supporting Newcomer and Refugee Youth*. Toronto: CERIC Books.

Suarez-Orozco, C., and Suarez-Orozco, M. M. (2001), *Children of Immigration*. Cambridge, MA: Harvard University Press.

Taylor, S., and Sidhu, R. K. (2012), 'Supporting Refugee Students in Schools: What Constitutes Inclusive Education?' *International Journal of Inclusive Education*, 16(1): 39–56.

UNESCO. (2021, 22 April), 'One Year into COVID-19: Prioritizing Educational Recovery to Avoid a Generational Catastrophe'. Available at: https://unesdoc.unesco.org/ark:/48223/pf0000376984 (accessed 17 November 2021).

UNHCR (2018) Canada: By the governement of Canada: UNHCR resettlement handbook. Available: https://www.unhcr.org/3c5e55594.pdf (accessed 18 September 2022)

Uslaner, E. M. (2002), *The Moral Foundations of Trust*. Cambridge, MA: Cambridge University Press.

Veck, W., and Wharton, J. (2019), 'Refugee Children, Trust and Inclusive School Cultures', *International Journal of Inclusive Education*, 1–14. DOI: 10.1080/13603116.2019.1707304.

World Health Organization (WHO). (2021, 17 November), 'WHO Coronavirus (COVID-19) Dashboard'. Available at: https://covid19.who.int/ (accessed 1 November 2022).

World Organization of Early Childhood Education. (2016), 'Declaration of the 68th OMEP World Assembly and Conference: Seoul, Korea', *International Journal of Early Childhood*, 48(3): 387–9. DOI: 10.1007/s13158-016-0178-9.

11

Making a Place for Refugee Education: Routes towards Meaningful Inclusion for Refugee Teenagers in 'New-Normal' England

Joanna McIntyre

Introduction

This chapter contributes to debates about reshaping education for teenage refugees and asylum-seekers in a post-pandemic world, arguing that meaningful inclusive models of education for all are vital in any reconceptualization of society. Covid-19 has seen social and material inequalities magnified and inevitably refugee and asylum-seeking children have experienced the effects of this. I draw on a theoretical model for the inclusion of refugees in education which has been shaped by educational practitioners (McIntyre and Abrams, 2021). Kohli's theory of 'resumption of ordinary life' (2011, 2014), and Fraser's 'participatory parity' (2003) underpin the model. Across the globe, 'ordinary life' for refugee teenagers during lockdowns changed, as it did for all young people. Most markedly 'participatory parity' became dependent upon material and human resources that marginalized groups, such as refugees, have limited access to.

In what follows, I draw upon my observations of the ways in which educators and artists work with young new arrivals in an English city. These examples were drawn from a range of research projects during a four-year period in which I took an ethnographically motivated position within the research, moving between the roles of participant, observer and interviewer at different points within the projects.

The chapter describes a bespoke post-16 provision for refugees which operationalized the theorized model, and then discusses how the experiences of the practitioners and young people were affected by life after lockdown in England. I argue for consideration of an approach where young peoples' new contexts, the cities and towns they find themselves in, can be utilized as curriculum through place-making methods. I illustrate ways in which cultural and community spaces offer purposeful educational opportunities which allow new arrivals a sense of safety and the beginnings of social belonging potentially contributing towards present and future inclusion and participation as cultural citizens in their new society.

This feels like the right time to explore more socially just inclusive models of education as we experience our 'new-normal' and what societies value is being reconceptualized. During the pandemic, the cessation of ordinary lives for many might lead to greater empathy for refugee children who, as Kohli observes, at the point of becoming forced migrants and refugees, 'experience the death of everyday life' (2014: 86). Kohli describes how they have given up their past for a future elsewhere and that they seek ways to bring things from their past into these new futures. These can be cultural artefacts or memories of people, places or activities. Whilst the prospect of national citizenship is some way off for new arrivals because of complex and often hostile immigration policies, the notion of cultural citizenship can be a tangible reality (UNESCO 2012).

> As he moves round the art gallery, Sheshy uses his phone to take photographs of the artwork. I notice him moving right up close to the exhibits and taking photographs of aspects of the piece. He also is spending time with the pieces that attract him. He seems to be absorbing them. He is particularly attracted by a time lapse video the artist made of the process of creating drawings. I ask if I can see what he is photographing and as we talk, he shows me photographs of his own drawings on his phone. One is of a young woman which he calls 'The Eritrean girl' explaining she is wearing her hair and jewellery in a typical Eritrean manner. The other is of a mother cradling her child.
>
> As part of the exhibition, people are asked to write on a wall and complete the sentence 'I am ...' Sheshy writes 'I am happy to be here.'

Sheshy, aged sixteen, visited an art gallery in his new city, one of the first 'in person' activities that his educational provider could organize as England moved through the stages of social distancing post lockdown whilst Covid-19 was still pausing ordinary life. This was an important trip for Sheshy and the rest of the group as it marked the resumption of activities to help them connect to and feel part of their new place. But this post-lockdown trip had the by now familiar markers of life during Covid-19: no other visitors to the gallery because of social distancing measures, hand sanitizers on the walls of the exhibition, mask wearing – thus making it difficult for the young people to hear and follow the instructions and explanations of the gallery guide. The mask covered the guide's facial expressions, something which this group of young people with varying skills in English language relied on to aid their understanding of the spoken word. Masks, hand sanitizers, isolated (both in the sense of infrequent, and in the sense of limited social contact) experiences of face-to-face interactions had all become the everyday in the 'new-normal' English landscape.

Throughout this opening I have been using terms which pre-Covid-19 would have had limited usage: 'in-person', 'face to face', 'social distancing', 'new-normal'. Our language evolves to reflect our everyday experiences – our ordinary lives. In what follows I draw on the concept of ordinary life in introducing the theoretical underpinning for the model of inclusive education for refugees and asylum-seekers. This theoretical basis which is described more fully elsewhere (McIntyre and Abrams 2021; McIntyre and Neuhaus 2021) brings two theories together which, when combined, have utility for considering a future-focused inclusive approach to refugee education, more necessary in the new-normal which we are configuring. The first of these is Kohli's 'resumption of ordinary life'. Kohli argues that the reality for many children who have left their homes because of forced migration is that their search for an ordinary existence continues, despite reaching their resettlement context. He conceptualizes their forced migration experiences as transitions through 'safety', 'belonging' and 'success' as the children move within and across spatial, temporal and maturational dimensions of change (2011, 2014). Kohli's theory of resumption of ordinary life informed my earlier empirical work to establish a normative operational basis for judging policies and practices for refugee education (McIntyre and Abrams 2021). In this work, experienced practitioners redefined the concepts of 'safety', 'belonging' and 'success' in relation to education for new arrivals (McIntyre and Abrams 2021). The second theory, Fraser's 'participatory parity' is based on the premise that social conditions need to be achieved so that all members of society can participate and interact as peers (2003). Fraser's three components of recognition, redistribution and representation are lenses through which to identify barriers to equitable access and inclusion for refugee children in education. Fraser establishes a normative moral basis against which policies and practices can be measured. Mobilizing the two theories to work together forms the basis for a model of inclusive education for refugee and asylum-seeking students (McIntyre and Neuhaus 2021).

Key to achieving a sense of safety, belonging and success is engaging newly arrived young people in meaningful activities where they can contribute to society using their strengths and talents (Kohli 2011). In many cases this involves activities that foster a sense of belongingness (Massey 2005), helping the young people feel a greater connection to their new place and the communities within that place. It is through this sense of belongingness and connection that newly arrived young people can begin to engage with others within that place and thus begin to achieve aspects of 'participatory parity' (Fraser 2003).

In the second half of the chapter, I describe how the inclusive model has been enacted in a bespoke educational provision for new arrivals pre-, during and post-lockdown. First, I share Sebhat's story to contextualize the realities for many young new arrivals in England who find it difficult to access full-time post-16 education to showcase the need for the bespoke provision. Then I move to describe how arts and cultural activity can become acts of place-making for new arrivals such as Sebhat.

> Sebhat, a 17-year-old Eritrean, had been waiting ten months for a school or college place, with nothing else to do, he simply stayed in his room in semi-independent accommodation. He had trouble sleeping and suffered with recurring headaches and was later diagnosed with post-traumatic stress disorder (PTSD) linked to experiences he had encountered on his solo journey across Libya before reaching Europe. When Sebhat did leave his room, he went to church, to a local refugee charity's youth group's weekly meeting, and to the local library where he tried to work on his understanding of the English alphabet. Eventually he was offered 7 hours (of ESOL/Employability skills/ICT) a week at college. He was finding it difficult to make connections with the others in the shared house who were much older than him. He said he was feeling lonely and spent much of his time isolated from others. He was hopeful that he would be able to access more hours at college in the next academic year. However, a few months later, he ran away to London to be with two other Eritrean boys he had befriended whilst in the Jungle at Calais. In effect he made himself homeless and extremely vulnerable until a charity in London took care of him. Sebhat's experiences reflect national concerns about both social isolation and a lack of appropriately funded education provision for new arrivals, a particularly vulnerable group of young people, especially those with no family support or network. I maintained contact with him once he moved to London. When the pandemic hit, Sebhat found himself even more isolated and scared.
>
> (Expanded from original text in McIntyre and Abrams 2021: 101)

Sebhat's experiences were echoed in conversations I had with young people who arrived in the city following the increase in forced migration into and across

Europe from 2015. Like Sebhat, many were waiting for a place at a post-16 education provision. For social contact with others, they mainly relied on the support of the Tuesday evening youth group run by a local charity. The youth group depended on short-term funding for the weekly social activities which comprised arts and crafts, pool, table tennis – scenes common to any youth group but here aimed at teenagers from refugee and asylum-seeking backgrounds. Occasionally external bodies received funding for short-term projects with the youth group.

In the next section of the chapter, I describe two short-term, externally funded arts-based projects that involved people from the refugee youth group. My intention is to draw out the potential of place-making for new arrivals through the arts. In so doing, I draw on previous work with Susan Jones where we analysed the ways in which a group of teenagers in a marginalized community engaged in arts-based place-making activities which helped them *connect to* resources around their town and also *to connect* narratives of people and place in collaborative creative making of meanings (Jones and McIntyre 2014).

Place-Making in the City through the Arts

The first activity was a film-making project as part of a wider initiative called Journeys to Justice (https://journeytojustice.org.uk/). Two young local film-makers worked with a small group of teenagers from the refugee youth group. Some of the group had recently arrived and had little spoken English skills – as the group comprised people from all over the world there was little common language to aid communication. The film-makers who were only a few years older than the young participants wanted to help them to get to know parts of the city. They met the young people each day in the city square by one of the statues – a well-established meeting place for teenagers. This immediately inducted the new arrivals into this local habit. From there, they walked to an arts space they had booked for the project. Over the period of the film-making, this became a social space for the young people. The issue of creating dialogue with a limited common language was overcome because the young people shared a love of the TV character Mr Bean and they quickly decided to make silent films. The film-makers walked with the group around the city introducing them to popular places where other teenagers in the city hang out. The young people used these as locations in their films. The resulting short films were shown as part of the *Journeys to Justice* exhibition in an iconic city cultural institution.

The young people were invited to the premier of the showing and mingled with audiences of other films that were on show.

The second project was led by Ruth Lewis-Jones,[1] the educational officer in an art gallery. Ruth was keen to encourage members of refugee communities to feel that they could visit the gallery which had been difficult to access until a tram line from the city centre was built which went around the back of the gallery. Ruth was particularly keen to engage young people at the refugee youth project. She began by inviting the young people into the gallery and inviting them to choose any exhibit which resonated with them and draw whatever came to mind. Some stayed for a good ninety minutes in front of the same painting quietly sketching (Figure 11.1).

Ruth engaged a young artist, again little older than the teenagers themselves, to work with them on a collaborative piece. During a walk around the university lake, they saw some disused rowing boats which they decided to repurpose for an exhibit. They stripped and repainted the boat and turned it into a large planter to attract the attention of the passengers on the tram. The artist taught them spray painting techniques and encouraged them to design their own slogans for the side of the boat to send messages to the commuters. She demonstrated how art could be used to convey political messages showing them the work of Ai Weiwei amongst others, thinking this would interest them. But they individually chose slogans which paid no reference to their identity as refugees but were about humane messages of care for each other and the planet. They voted on their favourite slogan 'Don't stop thinking about our world' which was sprayed on their newly created sail of the boat so that passengers on the tram could see it. Ruth entered them for their Bronze Arts Award, which entailed them exhibiting their work and teaching the arts techniques to members of the public. The project ended with a celebration event where the young people were awarded their certificates – the first formal recognition of their skills since entering the country. Within the English context, recognition of skills and merits within education is manifest in certification. The Arts Award symbolizes a small but significant step towards entry into the normative mode of recognition (and hence beginnings of participatory parity) within the new arrivals' new place.

Pedagogical processes involved in working with arts is well documented. These two projects showcase the affordances of these for engaging creativity, voice and agency of young people – especially in their rejection of representation of their identity as 'refugee' in the Arts Award project. The power of these

---

[1] With the expectation of Ruth all names in this chapter have been changed.

Figure 11.1 Sketching at Lakeside

projects is rooted in their close focus on the young people in a specific place. This pedagogical approach also includes participatory and collaborative practice and the transformative potential of place-based pedagogies (Jones and McIntyre 2014). The creative process of making the artefacts as well as the resultant artefacts themselves have the potential to be place-making (Jones et al. 2013). For

Comber 'the study of place affords complex opportunities for collective meaning making practices' which result in collaborative text production (2016: 101). This, she argues, 'can be a positive site for identity work, community building' (103). This is showcased in the Arts Award project; the young people were involved in a (re)creation of the place of the art gallery – repurposing the disused boat and creating a focal point for commuters to see on their journeys into the city – reminding them to think 'about our [intentionally shared possessive] world'.

The collaborations emerging from the projects led to powerful learning in several ways including opportunities where the young people could demonstrate their capacity to be 'subjects of action and responsibility' (Biesta 2013: 1). This agency was central to the Arts Award project. In their remaking of the boat and reclaiming of the elitist space of the art gallery for the passersby, they did more than connect to the site, they helped others to connect to their message in an act of what Comber (2016: 64) describes as 'reciprocal knowledge building'.

Now as the young people pass these locations for their films and the art gallery, they can see how they fit into a story of their new place. This resonates with Creswell's articulation of place as a 'meaningful location' (Creswell 2004: 5), where meaning is derived from the 'interplay of people and the environment' (11). In the case of the art gallery, they left their imprint, which will be there for some time and represent new possibilities for the future. Through these two projects, the young people gained a greater sense of their new city where they have been able to build emotional attachments to specific places within the city and to value what had previously been 'unknown' spaces (Tuan 2003).

The arts activities were spaces of community, sociability and inclusion (McIntyre 2016). There was a shared sense of purpose – all working together towards a shared outcome for a real audience and every voice was valued and heard. The artists recognized that each member of the group brought individual talents and skills which were equally recognized through the process of making the art and the artefacts themselves.

Place-Making Underpins Belonging at Fern College

Comber and Nixon state that a place-based approach not only allows people to connect with that place and the people within it, but also empowers them as they realize that through these activities they can 'make a positive difference to the world' (2014: 86). The films and boat exhibits, along with the process of creation, also represent new possibilities for the future. They are responsive to what the young people have brought to the process rather than being elitist artefacts and places – the young people have been changed by the places and have changed the places too. Arguably, the projects allowed the young people to connect to spaces in their new city – and in so doing they helped them encounter feelings of not only belonging but also safety and successes.

I now turn to a specific place that was created to cater for young people arriving after the age of sixteen in the same city, referred to by the pseudonym, 'Fern College', in McIntyre and Abrams (2021). I have followed the development of 'Fern' since its inception, observing the young people in their activities and meeting regularly with the teachers. I draw upon focus groups with the latter in what follows.

'Fern' is a unique full-time post-16 education provision for newly arrived young people, initially funded by the English government's two-year controlling migration funding aimed at supporting positive outcomes for unaccompanied asylum-seekers. The manager of Fern had been involved in previous projects with me and was aware of the theoretical framings of Kohli and Fraser; she also had an active role in shaping these into practical realities for an inclusive model for teachers to utilize. She shared my concerns regarding opportunities available in the city to Sebhat and others. In her vision for 'Fern College' she drew on her understanding of the inclusive model and to develop the provision to ensure that as far as possible there was a fair distribution of resource to meet the needs of the young people, that the provision recognized and responded to their specific needs and assets and that it would be guided by representative voices from the refugee community or from those who worked closely with them. In these ways, the provision aimed to fulfil Fraser's tripartite conditions for achieving some sense of participatory parity or 'justice for all' (2003: 94). There was an understanding that there would be a need to design flexible programmes to accommodate young people arriving at any point in the academic year (a challenge for most traditional educational settings). An advisory board comprising expertise from education, children's mental health, refugee law and social care was established.

Thus, the provision was established to offset the barriers that prevent marginalized individuals like Sebhat from participating on a par (Fraser 2007) with others in order to offer an inclusive educational experience for its young people. The full-time holistic provision offered a curriculum for building safety, belonging and succeeding with an academic programme enhanced by planned activities designed to foster relational, cultural and social learning (McIntyre and Abrams 2021: 103–4).

What emerged was a commitment to place-making activities, taking the young people to different community groups and helping them to feel a part of their new city. This involved a range of enrichment activities including trips to key places within the city and its surroundings, guided historical walks around the city, physical activities such as climbing, ice-skating at the Christmas market, archery and trips to the seaside and to forest school camps. The young people also went on work experience to various sites in the city. Additionally, there were activities where the young new arrivals created something, often in collaboration with others in their new place, through allotment gardening, through cooking with community groups, through pottery, through woodcraft, through activities in the city's art galleries, museums and theatres. They designed artwork for the entrance of the provision to welcome visitors, they created poems (including one for Prince Harry when he visited). They were selected for a prestigious award by the local newspaper and 'Fern' and its students became known in the city. As James, one of the teachers observes, 'as we've tried to take them out into the city, we're trying to develop that sense that it is theirs as well. They're not a kind of visitor. It is their city' (McIntyre and Abrams 2021: 109).

By March 2020, the indicators were that the provision was a success in terms of educational outcomes and perhaps more importantly in terms of other indicators of well-being for the young people. The two-year funding was coming to an end and the city's education officers and Fern's advisory board were actively seeking funding streams to allow the provision to continue to operate.

And then the country went into lockdown. The young people were told that they could not attend 'Fern' each day and to return home to their different accommodations dispersed across the city. Like other education providers, the staff immediately worked to move their provision online. The practitioners were concerned about the mental health impact of enforced physical isolation on some students. It became clear that ordinary life had changed for these young people who had become used to daily contact with peers with similar experiences and teachers who were interested in how they were doing both in and out of the educational setting. The pandemic exacerbated already existing social and material inequalities (Ismail et al. 2021). Social justice is felt most keenly when participatory parity is dependent upon material and human resources that marginalized groups, such as the students at Fern, have limited access to (Fraser 2003). The advisory group and teachers sourced laptops as most of the young people could only access a mobile phone. Eventually each student had access to a working computer and teachers began working with them in their virtual classrooms whilst continuing to hand deliver work packs for those with no or limited internet access. Some sense of normalcy resumed – at least as far as the academic curriculum was concerned.

But there was clearly a felt need to work more holistically with the young people. The teachers found creative solutions to ensure that safety, belonging and succeeding resumed for these young people. They phoned them individually each week. They established a WhatsApp group which gradually saw the young people interacting with one another as they overcame their shyness. The teachers celebrated birthdays on the app and the young people followed suit, they posted pictures of meals they had cooked, and the young people began to do the same; they celebrated Eid, they explained Victory in Europe Day celebrations and posted pictures of these on the WhatsApp group. The teachers also made videos of themselves with personalized messages to the group encouraging them to stay positive and promising that they would be together again soon.

One of the things that triggered most responses from the young people was when the teachers started posting photographs from activities the young people had been involved in as part of the enrichment provision before Covid-19, with funny recollections of those place-making activities (cooking, trips to different places, pottery, music, drama, dance and the garden they had been creating). These memories clearly resonated within the group with one post generating over one hundred comments.

In some ways, for those with reliable internet access, the technology helped achieve aspects of the holistic ambition of the safety, belonging and succeeding model. But what was most difficult was connecting beyond 'Fern' – connecting the young people to a wider community which was locked down. For those who arrived shortly before the lockdowns came into force, whilst they were beginning to get a sense of the community of 'Fern', they had no opportunity to get to know their new city. The teachers reflected that those who would have engaged with creative place-making activities found it hard to do so online. Anna, the manager of the provision, tried to link some of the girls to an online community workshop: 'a really lovely art group remotely for women … So I was able to engage some of our young people with that. We had a couple of really arty girls. So that was one way in which we did it, but we weren't as good during that first lockdown in knowing how to do that.' They also tried to move beyond the academic curriculum in their online offer with limited success as Jacob, one of the teachers, observed, 'We were able to offer some extra stuff on Teams like there was a bit of music, a bit of art, but the active engagement wasn't as much.' And as James commented, this meant that the young new arrivals 'still have a strong anchor here (at Fern) but not beyond that'.

After that first period of lockdown, the English government announced a partial relaxation of social distancing measures which meant that educational sites were allowed to open. The young people returned to 'Fern' and elements of their pre-Covid-19 life, especially the academic programmes, resumed. However, staff were keen to prioritize resumption of the enrichment activities even if they couldn't involve locals working alongside the students as they had pre-Covid-19. But reconnecting to the wider community proved difficult; as Anna observed, arriving and living in England during Covid-19 meant that, 'it's very hard for them to get a sense of [city] … at the moment'.

During the period in England between the first and second lockdown there were strict guidelines on social distancing limiting numbers for outdoor gatherings. An exception was activities organized as part of an educational provision. So, in order to rebuild connections with the city, James recalled that they 'did a few walks around the city to start with'. But this was not straightforward, as Anna explained:

> We were very conscious as well of being very visible, because there are so many of us. If we took them out anywhere it was like 'what are people going to think when there are 20 young people walking down the pavement – that is not really what we should be doing'. So, we made a pass, really. Just a very simple pass that said, you know, 'Out on School' business. I am a student at FERN this is the phone number you can phone to check in case anybody gets asked, by the police even.

So, whilst the teachers were keen to refocus on activities which took the young people out into their community, they were having to confront aspects of regulation and surveillance that had for some young people been a regular feature of their pre-migration experiences. But for the teachers at Fern, it was important to help the new arrivals move beyond the disorientation of life in their new city during the pandemic, even if this was problematic.

Thus, as England began to further reopen and people talked of a 'new-normal', the teachers at 'Fern' made a conscious decision to focus on helping their students get a sense of connection and of belonging to their new city and its communities. They did this through taking advantage of opportunities to engage in place-making through sports and physical activity and through engaging with arts and cultural activities within the city – such as the post-lockdown trip to the art gallery described in the opening of this chapter.

Life in Covid-19's New Normal England: Recalibrating Belonging and Ordinariness

Fern college and others working with teenage new arrivals want to explicitly help them feel part of their new place – to begin to experience what it is to belong and feel ordinary. Educational contexts play a pivotal role in engendering a sense of belonging for new arrivals (Gifford, Correa-Velez and Sampson 2009). The complexity of the processes at play in developing belonging (Hiorth 2019) takes time and is underpinned by an individual's webs of connection (Stewart 2011). Kohli observes that new arrivals need to be able to 'use their own talents and capacities to grow webs of belonging that hold them in place' (2011: 318). Teachers, like those at Fern, have a key role to play in helping the development of these webs of belonging. Arguably developing a sense of place and one's relationship to that place is essential to this process, especially:

> For children who may have moved away from family, friends, locations and a sense of entitlement to a home, the need to belong to someone, to somewhere, becomes a conscious goal, and the refurbishment of ordinary life takes on a precedence that is at times vivid and urgent.
>
> (Kohli 2011: 315)

Making space for place-making is even more important as we all make sense of our new normal, as the pandemic leaves societies struggling to resume a sense of ordinariness. For young people newly arrived in locations across Europe at this time, it becomes even more important to consider how social isolation can be lessened and to consider how to help them 'to become full members of the social and cultural fabric of the city' (Pero, Tenegra and Zontini 2008: 62) and to be able to fully participate in society on a par with others in the city (Fraser 2007). For teenage new arrivals, there is a need to consider how to enable them to build connections with their new place such that they can lead lives of meaningful engagement in their city as they become adults in these new places.

Making Place for Refugee Education

At the time of writing, in England, we are gradually approaching resumption of some sense of ordinary life in wider society, and it would be a missed opportunity not to consider how societies and models of schooling could be reshaped rather than assuming a return to what was there before.

As barriers to operationalizing aspects of safety, belonging and succeeding for all students are identified, the lenses of redistribution, recognition and representation shed light on the causes or sources of these barriers (McIntyre and Abrams 2021). Inevitably, localized experiences are shaped by national and global policy contexts. We need to:

Make place for policy: where the concepts of safety, belonging and succeeding are foregrounded in policymaking.

Make place for talking about practice based on:

- an asset-based pedagogy which aims to enable all students to realise their potential contributions to society,

and
- schools should also be encouraged to adapt place-making and culturally responsive pedagogies in recognition of the needs of newly arrived pupils.

(adapted from McIntyre and Abrams 2021: 170–1)

Making a place for refugee education therefore means that we need to find ways to allow young new arrivals to engage in place-making. Considering how arts institutions and arts practices engender a sense of social and cultural citizenship is key to this process. Sheshy on his trip around the art gallery finds in the 'new-normal' ordinariness of a trip to a gallery (Figure 11.2), the process of being in the arts space and engaging with the art work, the very real potential for him to

Figure 11.2 Image taken during visit to New Art Exchange, Phoebe Boswell HERE exhibition

belong, to resume a sense of connection focusing on what he is able to do and what he potentially can contribute to that place.

Consequently, he dissolves into place, he becomes *ordinary* in his love of the exhibition and his connection with the artist. The interactions with the place 'make him' – his identity shifts slightly as he sees himself reflected in the space and they develop a sense of him as a cultural citizen in that space; he 'remakes the place' – as he and his peers join in the artist's invitation to write on the walls, they *participate* as other visitors to the exhibition have done. Sheshy writes with pride 'I am happy to be here.'

References

Biesta, G. (2013). *The Beautiful Risk of Education*. Boulder, CO: Paradigm Publishers.

Comber, B. (2016), *Literacy, Place, and the Pedagogies of Possibility*. London: Routledge.

Comber, B., and Nixon, H. (2014), 'Critical Literacy across the Curriculum: Learning to Read, Question and Rewrite Designs', in J. Pandy and J. Ávila, *Moving Critical Literacies Forward: A New Look at Praxis Across Contexts*, 83–98. New York: Routledge.

Creswell, T. (2004), *Place: A Short Introduction*. Oxford: Blackwell.

Fraser, N. (2003), 'Social Justice in the Age of Identity Politics', in N. Fraser and A. Honneth (eds), *Redistribution or Recognition? A Political-Philosophical Exchange*, 7–109. London: Verso.

Fraser, N. (2007), 'Re-framing Justice in a Globalizing World', Anales de la Catedra Francisco Suarez (2005), 39 89–10. Available at:https://www.semanticscholar.org/paper/Re-framing-justice-in-a-globalizing-world-Fraser/d2170289b4fcbd284dec04b93fb50e5a49145102 (accessed 27 May 2022).

Gifford, S., Correa-Velez, I., and Sampson, R. (2009), *Good Starts for Recently Arrived Youth with Refugee Backgrounds: Promoting Wellbeing in the First Three Years of Settlement in Melbourne, Australia*. Melbourne, Australia: Refugee Health Research Centre & Victorian Foundation for Survivors of Torture.

Hiorth, A. (2019), 'Refugee Student Transitions into Mainstream Australian Schooling: A Case Study Examining the Impact of Policies and Practices on Students' Everyday Realities', in J. L. McBrien (ed.), *Educational Policies and Practices of English-Speaking Refugee Resettlement Countries*, 57–87. Leiden: Brill.

Ismail, S., Tunis, M., Zhao, L., and Quach, C. (2021), 'Navigating Inequities: A Roadmap out of the Pandemic', *BMJ Global Health*, 6: e004087. Available at: http://dx.doi.org/10.1136/bmjgh-2020-004087, Available at SSRN:https://ssrn.com/abstract=3695697 or http://dx.doi.org/10.2139/ssrn.3695697 (accessed 27 May 2022).

Jones, S., and McIntyre, J. (2014), 'It's Not What It Looks Like. I'm Santa': Connecting Community through Film', *Changing English*, 21(4): 322–33.

Jones, S., Hall, C., Thomson, P., Barrett, A., and Hanby, J. (2013), 'Re-presenting the "Forgotten Estate": Participatory Theatre, Place and Community Identity'. *Discourse: Studies in the Cultural Politics of Education*, 34(1): 118–31.

Kohli, R. (2011), Working to Ensure Safety, Belonging and Success for Unaccompanied Asylum-Seeking Children', *Child Abuse Review*, 20: 311–23.

Kohli, R. (2014), 'Protecting Asylum Seeking Children on the Move', *Revue Europeene Des Migrations Internationales*, 30(1): 83–104.

Massey, D. (2005), *For Space*. London: Sage.

McIntyre, J. (2016), 'Riots and a Blank Canvas: Young People Creating Texts, Creating Spaces', *Literacy*, 50(3): 149–57.

McIntyre, J., and Abrams, F. (2021), *Refugee Education: Theorising Practice in Schools*. Abingdon: Routledge.

McIntyre, J., and Neuhaus, S. (2021), 'Theorizing Policy and Practice in Refugee Education: Conceptualising 'Safety', 'Belonging', 'Success' and 'Participatory Parity' in England and Sweden', *British Educational Research Journal*, 47(4), 796–816.

Pero, D., Tenegra, B., and Zontini, E. (2008), *New Migrants in Nottingham: MigrantGrant Cities Final Report*. British Council and IPPR https://ec.europa.eu/migrant-integration/library-document/migrant-cities-research-nottingham-0_en (accessed 27 May 2022).

Stewart, J. (2011), *Supporting Refugee Children: Strategies for Educators*. Ontario: University of Toronto Press.

Tuan, Y. (2003), *Space and Place: The Perspective of Experience Minneapolis*. Minneapolis, MN: University of Minnesota Press.

UNESCO. (2012), 'The Cultural Rucksack and Other Measures Targeting Different Age Groups'. Available at https://en.unesco.org/creativity/policy-monitoring-platform/cultural-rucksack-other-measures (accessed 27 May 2022).

12

Thinking about the Emotional Well-Being of Black Children in a Post-Pandemic World

Siya Mngaza

Introduction

During the first wave of the Covid-19 pandemic in England (from 24 January 2020 to 11 September 2020), data from the Office for National Statistics in the UK illustrated that people from Black and other minoritized ethnic groups had an elevated mortality risk from Covid-19 than the white population. By the time that the second wave started (from 12 September 2020 onwards) further analysis had taken place which adjusted for occupation, housing and pre-existing health conditions. Even taking these factors into account, adults from Black and South Asian heritage remained at elevated risk (ONS 2021). This leads us to the question: How did the children in these communities experience loss and bereavement during the pandemic?

This chapter focuses specifically upon the impact of Covid-19 on Black (children from African and Caribbean backgrounds) school-aged pupils in the UK.

Resiliency factors can arise from experiencing loss or trauma (Fraley and Bonanno 2004; Tedeschi and Calhoun 2004), but research suggests that some children who experience parental bereavement can experience understandable dips in their engagement in school, their achievement and some academic aspirations (Abdelnoor and Hollins 2004; Brent et al. 2012; Oosterhoff, Kaplow and Layne 2018). Within this chapter, Black children are centralized, in their proximity to Covid-19 and their potential elevated risk of experiencing parental bereavement. Specifically, Black children are focused on because of the way that schools have historically been a source of further misunderstanding, a lack of empathy and harsh discipline for Black children. At a time where more love, structure and understanding are needed, what can schools offer to this community?

Black children are perceived as more threatening and less child-like than white children when carrying out an identical action (Goff et al. 2014). Qualitative research indicates that Black British pupils of Caribbean heritage in the UK may receive harsher behavioural sanctions due to being perceived as 'physically larger' (Gazeley and Dunne 2013). In addition, young people from Caribbean backgrounds are three times as likely as their white counterparts to be permanently excluded from school in the UK (DfE 2019), with some researchers finding racism as a causal factor this picture (Demie 2021; Graham et al. 2019a). Models of post trauma coping position 'perceived support' from immediate social contexts (such as schools) as playing an active role in stress management following bereavement (i.e. Joseph, Williams and Yule 1997). The current chapter proposes that it is necessary to consider these psychological frameworks when evaluating how young Black people – given the wider context of their trajectory and experience of schooling – may utilize school environments as a factor within emotional healing.

Black children, both prior to and throughout the pandemic, have experienced a compounded range of health, emotional and social factors that urgently point towards us needing to take good care of their emotional recovery. This chapter will further analyse impact that Covid-19 has had on Black children and families in the UK, followed by a consideration of how children and young people generally experience loss and bereavement. Finally, it will explore universal and specialist forms of support that practitioners can begin to consider in the process of supporting the long-term emotional well-being of their school communities. (It is important to note that the psychological approaches discussed throughout the chapter are not recommended as frameworks for consideration, and the implementation of any psychologically informed approach should be done so with professional guidance.)

The Intergenerational Impact of Covid-19 on Black Children and Families in the UK

Covid-19 has impacted Black children and families in the UK in a disproportionate manner, mirroring other aspects of disproportionate disadvantage. The following section will explore data and statistics that illustrate this picture. Behind each of the following statistics are people, families, mothers, fathers, children, loved ones and community members, and it is crucial that we acknowledge that at the centre of every number is a story which is granted with deep respect and honour.

The link between race, ethnicity and severe Covid-19 is complex, but well established (Saatci et al. 2021). Throughout the pandemic, and especially during the first UK lockdown, there was a vast amount of media coverage which emphasized the Covid-19 disparities between Black and other minoritized people and the white population. Fierce debate surrounding the causes and contributory factors to this picture became a prevalent part of public discourse. Parallel to this, institutions worldwide began paying lip service to their acknowledgement of the entrenched nature of systemic racism across institutions, particularly in the United States and the UK, following the murder of George Floyd. For a brief period in the public imagination, health inequities and structural racism were being given an equal footing to other factors that acted to compound Covid-19 outcomes for Black and minoritized communities. Additionally, this apparent shift in collective consciousness caused many educational providers to explore structural racism, the legacies of colonialism and how their policies and practices had been shaped by this. The longitudinal impact of these momentary acknowledgements of racism are yet to be seen.

During the first wave of the pandemic all minoritized ethnic groups had an increased rate of death in comparison to the white population. Black women had between 1.8 and 2.6 times higher risk than their white counterparts and Black men, between 2.7 and 3.7 times higher risk (ONS 2020). Analysis of the second wave is ongoing, however data suggest that Caribbean adults remained at an elevated risk, although their risk in comparison to white people had reduced (ONS 2021).

This disparity has also been observed among children aged 0–18 in England. In one of the largest studies ($N = 2{,}576{,}353$) (Saatci et al. 2021) to analyse racial disparities in Covid-19 outcomes among children from a range of racial and ethnic backgrounds, they found that:

- Covid-19 testing was inequitable among racial groups, with 17 per cent of the sample of white children having access to tests; 13.6 per cent of the sample of Asian children having access to tests and 8.3 per cent of the sample of Black children having access to tests;
- Among those children who had been tested for Covid-19, the highest number of positive cases were among the non-white populations;

- When admitted to hospital with Covid-19, Black children and those of mixed and other races were more likely to stay in hospital for more than thirty-six hours in comparison to the white children.

Whilst the data may seem to follow an intuitive logic – that is, if there are higher rates amongst older members of the community, there will be higher rates amongst the children – in the context of this overall chapter, Covid-19 impacts Black children in the UK on three different levels – testing, positive cases and hospitalization.

Older adults from Afro-Caribbean and South Asian communities with dementia have also been heavily impacted by the pandemic. In a qualitative study (West et al. 2021), older adults with dementia and their carers were impacted by a lack of access to appropriate services and cultural knowledge. Many of the participants in this study were identified as 'vulnerable' community members, making them eligible for additional food/resources, which participants found were often inappropriate owing to their dietary needs, not accounting for their culture.

This research indicates Covid-19 has had an intergenerational impact on the Black community in the UK. There are a multitude of factors at play in explaining these disparities, including housing, socio-economic status and proximity to the virus based on work status (Sze et al. 2020). Each of these discreet comorbid forms of disadvantage point towards the ways in which structural racism in the healthcare system shapes *who* is impacted by disease (Bailey et al. 2017; Farmer et al. 2020).

Activists and thinkers have been carefully illustrating the legacies of medical racism for decades illustrating the dark history of medical experimentation on Black bodies, mistreatment in healthcare and how these factors are a direct result of anti-Black racism in the West (Washington 2009). Dennis-Heyward and Shah (2021) provide a useful discussion about plausible interventions to unpick these issues at the health level for children. However, the following section will focus more concretely upon pairing this health context with the historical context for Black children in UK schools.

The Context for Black School Children in the UK

The discourse surrounding Black children in UK schools has long been one of concern about disproportionate levels of school exclusion, racial discrimination and 'underachievement' (Gillborn 2001; Gregory, Skiba and Noguera 2010; Harris and Parsons 2001). More recently, researchers have started to 'humanize' Black children and change this discourse, through exploring voices and perspectives of young Black people (Abijah-Liburd 2017; Mclean 2016; Mngaza 2020; Vincent et al. 2012). The current chapter will briefly provide an overview of some of the interacting factors that set the context for Black pupils in UK schools, to ensure we understand how the recovery process may be culturally relevant to their positive inclusion in a post-pandemic education system.

Let us first look at the historical context of education policy in England. Within 'The Education of Immigrants', a policy circular from 1971 from the Department of Education and Science in England – the following stark and sweeping generalizations are made about non-white families:

> For the West Indian child ... the environment is one in which marriage is not always considered important ... the unknown father with which his mother may be living ... Asian mother's tendency to live a withdrawn life. (DES 1971: 4)

Here we can see how policymakers, whilst discussing educational 'deficits', position the culture of Caribbean and Asian as problematic rather than turning the lens inwards. Whilst this may seem like a harmless artefact that exemplifies the era it was written in, psychologists have explored the way that prevailing ideologies set out in legislation and policy can go on to form 'normative' or accepted ideas about cultures (Dovidio, Pearson and Penner 2018). Indeed, these discriminatory ideas were not only observable in policy but also in practice:

During the 1970s, Bernard Coard, a Grenadian teacher, activist and writer, conducted research that explored the ways that UK schools were sending Black pupils to schools for 'the educationally subnormal' (ESN) in disproportionately high numbers (Coard 1971). Part of the mechanism of these children being placed in the ESN schools took place through the assessment of their cognitive abilities by educational psychologists. This included the use of psychological, psychometric or cognitive assessments which were culturally and class biased. These 'gold-standard' assessments emerge from eugenicist world views which attempted to measure innate ability and posited race as a marker of biological difference (Mngaza 2021; Wright 2020).

Within this seminal text, Coard illustrated that in 1967, West Indian (Caribbean) children made up 54 per cent of the population within ordinary schools and 75 per cent of the population within ESN schools in the Inner London Education Authority. He advocated strongly for community action and culturally appropriate and relevant forms of assessment.

Now, Black children are three times as likely to be excluded from school (DfE 2019) and are disproportionately likely to be labelled as having social, emotional and mental health needs (Strand and Lindorff 2018). The Department of Education (DfE) commissioned a review to explore literature and research that would illuminate why some populations are disproportionately excluded. In the case of Black Caribbean boys, the authors stated the following: 'The literature review found much less material on unique factors, apart from racism, which could explain why Black Caribbean boys had such a high risk of exclusion' (Graham et al. 2019a: 96). In a London based study which employed focus groups and case studies to explore the causes behind disproportionate levels of school exclusion they identified that institutional racism, a lack of racial diversity within the professionals interacting with the children, a lack of nuanced training of race and anti-racist education were contributory factors (Demie 2021).

When we discuss 'school recovery' for Black pupils, we are thinking both about the universal provisions required to support them back into school *and* considering the inequitable and racist historical backdrop.

How Children May Experience Loss and Grief

Children in the UK and overseas have experienced a spectrum of loss throughout the pandemic, ranging from the loss of daily routine, breaks in newly formed friendships, loss of connection to their teachers and school communities, to more tangible losses, such as the loss of a parent or loved one. Psychological models of child grieving can support us in thinking about what an appropriate school recovery approach might include.

Children and young people often lack experience with loss and death, so the grieving process can be an alien, overwhelming experience for them (Case, Cheah and Liu 2020). Furthermore, the impact of grief, regardless of the magnitude of loss, can go on to impact into adulthood. Research emanating from attachment psychology (Bowlby 1958) highlights that when parents have experienced grief in childhood that they did not have a chance to process, this can reduce the likelihood that they will go on to form 'secure' bonds with their children (Siegel and Hartzell 2003).

Not all children will have experienced a traumatic loss during the pandemic. Many children will have gained precious time with their parents and a closeness to their family environment that they hadn't experienced before. Emerging research from the Open University shows that Black children have developed interesting hobbies during the pandemic and have shown levels of resilience to the monotony of lockdown life (Boampong et al. 2021).

However, understanding some of the common developmental sequences involved in loss and grief can support us in understanding how to work with children from all backgrounds after the pandemic. Infusing this understanding with a racialized lens can provide even further possibility for the positive inclusion of Black children after the pandemic.

First, we will consider how children impacted directly by death may understand and process this. We will then look at attachment theory and loss to generalize our understanding.

Researchers have identified 5 key 'facts' that form a child's understanding of death:

1. People will all die one day (inevitability)
2. All living things will die (universality)
3. Death is permanent (irreversibility)
4. All mental and physical functions stop with death (Cessation)
5. Death is caused by the body's inability to continue functioning (causality).

(Jaakkola and Slaughter 2002)

Children of different ages understand these stages at different times. For example, five-year-olds have been shown to understand the irreversibility and inevitability of death (Panagiotaki et al. 2015; Panagiotaki, Nobes and Engelhardt 2017). The understandings of universality and cessation can emerge around six and seven years of age (Slaughter and Lyons 2003). Causality is thought to be the most complex process for children to understand and they may understand this in non-human life (i.e. plants) before applying this to human death (Nguyen and Gelman 2002; Patagiotaki et al. 2015).

This chapter emphasizes that although developmental trajectories are useful in mapping and planning for a variety of responses, caution is suggested in 'benchmarking' children based on these frameworks, particularly as we are embracing diversity.

Children's Experiences of Grief: A Cultural Lens

Culture, ethnicity, race and religion can all play a role in both the understanding of loss and in the way loss is experienced. Research amongst children with religious beliefs found that they were slightly more likely to believe that mental functions continue after death, due to their belief in the afterlife (Bering, Blasi and Bjorklund 2005).

Additionally, some researchers have posited that a child's proximity to death and poverty may impact the age at which they come to understand the irreversibility of death (Hopkins 2014). Indeed, a study found that children living in rural areas in Pakistan understood irreversibility earlier than children living in London (Panagiotaki and Nobes 2014).

Another way that culture can influence grief is through end-of-life ceremonies. Funerals can offer families psychological support following a bereavement by providing the opportunity to express respect and love for the deceased (Burrell and Selman 2020). Children who have the chance to participate in the funerary ceremony of a loved one showed lower rates of depressive symptomatology several months post-bereavement (Fristad et al. 2001). Children in the study also expressed feeling an appreciation of the finality signified within the funerary process.

Within some Caribbean cultures, there is an extended period of mourning called a nine-night where the community of a loved person will gather for nine nights after their death to share stories, food, drink, memories and express condolences for the loss (White 2020).

We need further, sensitively conducted, research to explore how Black children interact with nine nights and other cultural end-of-life ceremonies in the UK. However, many cultural gatherings and funeral practices such as the nine-night and Shiva gatherings were carried out online during the pandemic (Burrell and Selman 2020; Schuck, Hens-Piazza and Sadler 2020; White 2020). These factors are of importance when considering the initial and ongoing disruption to ceremonies marking the end of life during the pandemic. Whilst there are currently no legal limits on the number of guests allowed to attend funerals in the UK, during the first wave of the pandemic, a series of restrictions were in place, limiting the numbers of mourners permitted and placing conditions upon the ways that funerals could be conducted. It will be important to consider the needs of children who lost out on the ability to mourn in personal and culturally specific ways during this period.

Supporting Children to Adjust to Change and Loss More Generally

Whilst some children will be directly impacted by bereavement through the pandemic, most children will have experienced some adjustment to their day-to-day life and will have to engage in some degree of change. Children experienced a range of well-being related changes including changes to their learning and productivity which can in turn interact with their sense of belonging, self-efficacy and motivation (Brooks et al. 2020; Kia-Keating and Ellis 2007; Neel and Fuligni 2013). Children and young people initially faced an indefinite 'pause' on their relationships with teachers, school staff and peers during the first lockdown. Other children attended school in small cohorts; for many, this may have been a unique experience of learning in smaller groups, with (potentially) fewer academic and social demands.

The common understanding of bereavement is tied to the tangible loss of a loved one. Incorporating the less concrete changes associated with bereavement – such as changes/endings to relationships and routines – can support us in providing a healthy container to provide support to the full spectrum of experiences children may have faced.

Within adult populations, attachment style (a relational pattern developed in early childhood) has been shown to impact the way people can adapt to loss. There is some intuitive data within this research: adults with a 'fearfully avoidant' attachment style (being afraid of both distance and closeness in interpersonal relationships) find it difficult to adapt to loss. Within the same research, adults identified as having a 'dismissive avoidant' attachment style (being so weary of emotional abandonment that they do not connect to others) showed a pattern of *resilience* to loss (Fraley and Bonanno 2004).

It is too soon to gather reliable longitudinal data about how the different attachment styles of children will support their resilience to changes in schooling in the Covid-19 pandemic. Indeed, it is wise to use caution not to be overly deterministic about labelling children with one 'style' or another, when attachment can be better considered as a relational dynamic. But it is not too soon for professionals to begin considering how the relational histories of children may provide risk or resilience factors when thinking about how they have adjusted to the everyday loss incurred in the pandemic. This research may also encourage us to learn from children who have found it necessary to develop resilience to change prior to the pandemic.

How Can We Think about Supporting the Emotional Well-Being of Pupils in UK Schools after the Covid-19 Pandemic?

Communicating with children and young people about grief and providing information and a space for them to express emotion can help enable the reduction of depressive symptoms in children who have experienced loss (Shapiro, Howell and Kaplow 2014; Weber et al. 2019). These aspects of dealing with grief may be particularly pertinent in the context of children and young people attending schools in the UK, which was heavily affected by the Covid-19 pandemic.

In July 2021, the UK experienced the highest rates of Covid-19 within the European region aside from Cyprus (Our World in Data 2021). Within England, the policy approach to curving the pandemic – and the subsequent impact of this approach on education – has been labelled as 'laissez faire' (Holt and Murray 2022). Holt and Murray (2022) highlight several aspects of the policy approach which led to extended lockdowns in both the first and second waves of the pandemic in the UK, including:

- The adoption of a 'minimal intervention' and herd-immunity approach to the early news of the spread of Covid-19 in the UK;
- Allowing organizations that enable social mixing (schools, colleges, pubs, restaurant and offices) to function whilst cases rose heavily in March 2020;
- Rolling out a series of confusing and 'light-touch' remedies to local outbreaks using a tier system.

The Oxford Covid-19 Government Response Tracker (OxCGRT), which collects data on the policy measures taken in the UK to impact the pandemic, revealed that the UK had one of the longest school lockdowns in Europe (OxCGRT 2021), with school closures lasting up to six months.

Research in the UK demonstrated that children experienced the lockdown in a multitude of ways (Children's Commissioner 2020). Whilst the proximity to parents and home environments was positive for some children, the proximity to mental illness and other forms of disadvantage, usually alleviated by school attendance, was predictably negative for others.

Globally, researchers have identified that lockdowns such as this can further disadvantage children by removing secondary support services normally supplied through school systems (Clemens et al. 2020). Families were also observed to seek less medical support for common ailments resulting from the fear of Covid-19, but attended healthcare institutions when children required more severe intervention (Ciacchini et al. 2020). Furthermore, the prevalence of psychological effects of living through a pandemic including stress and anxiety (Xiang, Zhang and Kuwahara 2020) are not exclusive to adults. Zhou (2020) indicated that children and young people's developing sense of emotional regulation may put them at greater risk of developing symptoms of post-traumatic stress.

Early research in the UK has revealed that many parents already report a significant increase in emotional challenges, as measured by outward behaviour. The Institute for Social and Economic Research used data derived from around 1,900 children, which indicated a 14 per cent increase in negative behaviours and emotional difficulties as measured by the Strengths and Difficulties Questionnaire (SDQ) (Blanden et al. 2020). Although the SDQ has been described as a reliable and valid tool to measure mental well-being in children, it should be noted that the study used reports from the perspective of mothers and not self-reports from the children themselves. In the context of a pandemic which impacts the emotional well-being, perception and emotional climate for families in general, this style of measurement should be treated with some caution. This caveat aside, the ISER study data show that children newly exhibited an emotional difficulty or behaviour 'some of the time'.

This wider context of Covid-19 in the UK education system indicates that children will have been through a vast range of experiences, ranging from immediate experiences of grief and loss, to losses within the school community, to losses within one's neighbourhood or sense of normalcy. In time, there will be a wide enough lens to fully analyse the methods of resilience and strength that families and communities developed to manage and respond to such changes.

The response to these challenges in the past may provide some indication of the general direction of travel, in terms of providing appropriate support through schools. A review of interventions for children who experienced close family loss (parent, sibling or other) indicated a range of therapeutic interventions, including play therapy, cognitive behavioural therapy and art therapy (Chen and Panebianco 2018). Within all of the seventeen reviewed, an element of psycho-education (teaching and learning about how to manage mental well-being) was involved. In an earlier meta-analysis that looked at interventions to support bereaved children highlighted two school based approaches as effective in reducing some of the symptoms of grief. These were:

1. Music therapy and
2. Trauma and grief focused school based psychotherapy.

Indeed, the identification and specialized support of individual children using the psychological approaches above continue to be of paramount importance. Zhou (2020) advocates for the adoption of a systemic approach to the psychological support for children returning to school. Using Bronfenbrenner's (2005) bio-ecological systems theory, Zhou highlights the potential for a cooperative model of support for children through family, school and social systems. At the centre of these intersecting systems sits the child, who requires unconditional support and alleviation of distress from parents, teachers, friends and others in their social system. Importantly, Zhou indicates that what enables these systems to cooperate is a wider context of material and resource support from the government. Without practical and material support, how can schools and other systems effectively provide safe and nurturing environments for staff and children after a pandemic? Inevitably, this prompts us to explore universal and 'whole-system' approaches which can meet the needs of communities of children and is less deficit based that an individual assessment and therapy model. Recently, thinkers in this area have combined this systemic perspective with attachment theory in their attempt to enrich psychological understandings of Black life (Stern, Barbarin and Cassidy 2021). The ecological nature of racism, in the way it exists and manifests within on structural, institutional and interpersonal levels, is depicted seamlessly within Stern, Barbarin and Cassidy's (2021) adaptation of Bronfenbrenner's bio-ecological systems theory. See Figure 12.1 (Stern et al., 2021, p. 12)

Within the UK, the school system (along with other institutions) as described in the previous section presents both a potential form of support and a potential form of oppression for Black children. The following sections of this chapter aim to explore the potential forms of emotional well-being support that can deconstruct the oppressive forces and enhance the potential for schools to be sites of emotional safety for all children.

Universal and Whole School Approaches to Providing Emotional Well-Being Support in Schools

The wide numbers of children experiencing some form of loss indicate a need to look towards ways that whole school systems can provide mechanisms for support. The trauma-informed schools approach provides a useful blueprint that can support whole school communities to understand the process and effects of trauma, including identifying how trauma can show up later and within the classroom. A trauma experienced in childhood that involved harm or the threat of harm can, if personal or violent in nature, cause children to later develop an enhanced identification of potential threats (McLaughlin and Lambert 2017). Whilst Covid-19 has impacted individual families and communities differently, the pandemic has been viewed as an example of a collective trauma, which

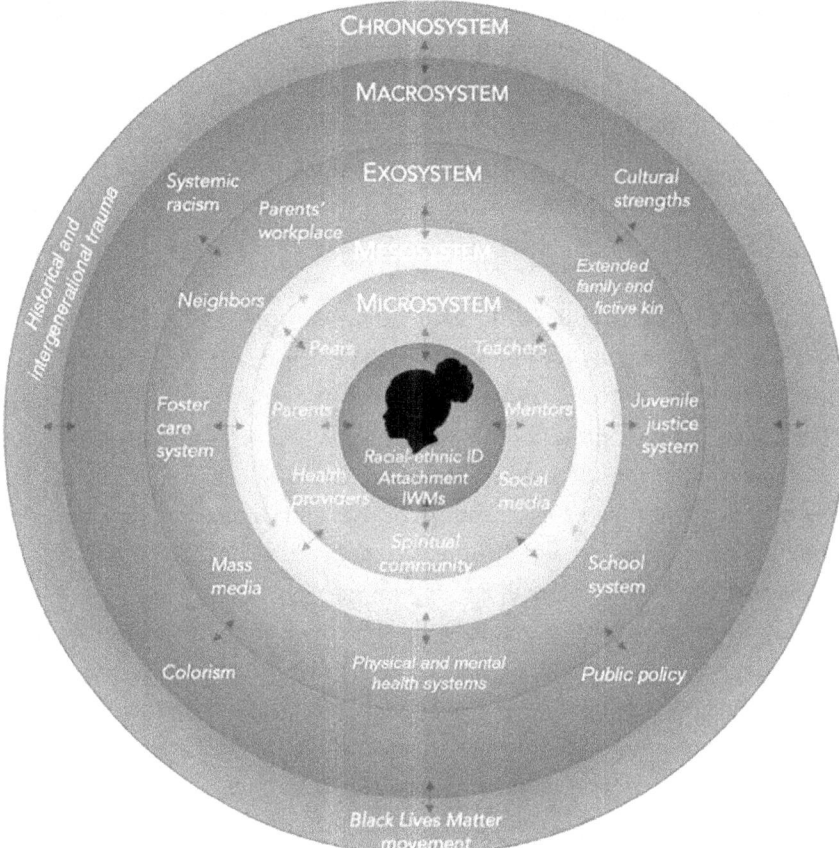

Figure 12.1 Stern, Barbarin and Cassidy's (2021) adaptation of Bronfenbrenner's bio-ecological systems theory

goes on to impact some disproportionately (Youansamouth, Collingwood and Ruston 2020).

As previously mentioned, in the UK, Black communities were disproportionately impacted by the Covid-19 pandemic. Within a trauma-informed approach, the focus shifts away from viewing behaviours as problematic and encourages us to enquire:

- What has happened to you?
- How can we use this knowledge to impact the way we support you?

(Youansamouth, Collingwood and Ruston 2020).

This shift in perspective could be particularly powerful for Black pupils in UK schools as it moves away from the traditional behaviourist approach which uses sanctions to manage behaviour. This sanction based approach may have historically been one which disproportionately impacted Black school pupils, as it decontextualizes what behaviours mean and where they come from.

The trauma-informed approach could – if sensitively combined with an understanding of the historical context for Black pupils in UK schools – extend the possibility that school systems can be a place of culturally relevant psychological support for all children.

The Complex Role of 'Dialogue' and Culturally Sensitive Approaches to Psychological Support in School

Trauma-informed approaches are thought to be a supportive universal mechanism when considering the reintroduction of all children to schools. But how might specific psychological approaches be helpful or harmful in supporting culturally diverse children in returning to school post-Covid-19?

Researchers have cautioned the appropriateness of applying eurocentric/individualistic approaches to culturally diverse clients without adequate critique, consideration and adaptation where necessary (Naidoo, 1996). We also need to consider that Black people have necessarily developed community groups, Saturday schools and large bodies of academic scholarship in reaction to the racist experiences children have had in UK schools. This context must be considered when deciding how to embed support for Black children. Questions including – 'Do the family feel they trust the school? Does the child feel heard and respected within the school? How may these factors impact the way they may respond to support offered through the school system?' – should be a driving force in the coordination of emotional recovery support. The importance of 'extended family' in Afro-Caribbean families who migrated to the United States has been identified as a central aspect of personal identity (Muruthi et al. 2016). As such, enhancing and constructing experiences that evoke collective belonging should be considered as part of the wider tapestry of school recovery following Covid-19. In the case of Black pupils in UK schools, many are second- or third-generation African and Caribbean children who will have sophisticated ways of existing and navigating different worlds; however, their emotional landscape at home may embody some of these aspects of collective identity.

The Tree of Life approach (Ncube 2006) is an example of a therapeutic approach that infuses a sense of collective belonging in the process of healing from grief and loss. This approach provides a structure to the healing process, which avoids re-traumatizing children by encouraging them to engage in uncontained catharsis. Ncazelo Ncube, who worked with bereaved children in South Africa, refined the Tree of Life approach to incorporate elements of narrative therapy, to ensure this was a safe approach to use with children and young people in her professional role. Within her 2006 paper, Ncube explains that prior to engaging with the Tree of Life process, she has encouraged children to engage in group singing and dancing. Following this, the children are introduced to a process of exploring their life and experiences using a structured activity that goes from their history and origins to their hopes, dreams and wishes using the tree as an analogy. Within Ncube's 2006 paper, she explores how this framework moves away from a problem-saturated and overwhelming approach to one which acknowledges pain, but positions this within the wider context of a child's strengths, qualities and community.

The Tree of Life approach aligns with the psychology of post-trauma growth, which prompts us to consider how shifts in subjective meaning can imbue a sense of transformation following a trauma. One way of altering subjective meaning is through reconstructing narratives about potentially negative events (Neimeyer 2004). In this narrative process, individuals can externalize dominant scripts which may be disempowering, leading to profound personal growth (Neimeyer 2004).

It has been argued that this strategy can be used to facilitate post-traumatic growth (PTG), which refers to the positive psychological change that some people experience after a challenging life circumstance (Tedeschi and Calhoun 2004). The original cognitive model of PTG explains that following a traumatic event, people are often thrust into a ruminative state, which can be an opportunity to reconstruct stories about the self and the world. Within PTG, these mechanisms challenge the world view of the individual, causing them to grow in response. Recent work has shown that some populations have experienced PTG throughout the pandemic, including those who have a proximity to the virus (nurses) and may require the reframing more than non-health care professionals (Cui et al., 2021).

Individuals who have experienced PTG report feeling higher levels of self-acceptance and autonomy (Triplett et al. 2012). As mentioned, the pandemic has been positioned as a collective trauma, which may be supported by reconstructing the narrative of the pandemic using safe and professionally supervised approaches.

Research has found that Black students can experience some forms of PTG in response to racism in predominantly white schools (Mngaza 2020). Although this indicates that some Black children may have an increased resilience to traumatic factors impacting school, it also means that Black children require extra consideration and humanization when thinking about the range of emotional journeys they have travelled. Pupils have the right to experience childhood and adolescence without the added pressure of oppressive and racist experiences.

Conclusion

This chapter explored the ways in which Covid-19 has had an intergenerational impact on Black communities in the UK. By exploring targeted and universal approaches to school support, I centred the needs of Black pupils who have not only been disproportionately impacted by Covid-19 but who have also faced a legacy of oppression in the education system. Many Black children have experienced ongoing dehumanization through the education system in the UK, as a direct influence of anti-Black racism that exists in society as a whole (Mngaza 2020). It is crucial to consider both targeted interventions and ongoing attitudinal, relational and policy related changes that can support Black children to thrive post-pandemic and beyond. Trauma-informed approaches to school, the Tree of Life approach and PTG are considered areas of psychology that can inform culturally relevant emotional well-being support in schools. In many ways, the murder of George Floyd caused us to pause and really reflect upon the systemic nature of the racist forces that enable such an act to play out, real time, with the whole world as an audience. As the dust settles, we must take this systemic lens and apply it to the education system.

References

Abdelnoor, A., and Hollins, S. (2004), 'The Effect of Childhood Bereavement on Secondary School Performance', *Educational Psychology in Practice*, 20(1): 43–54.

Abijah-Liburd, M. (2017), '"And Your Future Is Looking … ?" "… Hopeful". Exploring the Experience of School for Young of African-Caribbean Descent: An Interpretative Phenomenological Study'. DAppEdPsy Thesis, University of Nottingham.

Bailey, Z. D., Krieger, N., Agénor, M., Graves, J., Linos, N., and Bassett, M. T. (2017), 'Structural Racism and Health Inequities in the USA: Evidence and Interventions', *The Lancet*, 389(10077): 1453–63.

Bering, J. M., Blasi, C. H., and Bjorklund, D. F. (2005), 'The Development of Afterlife Beliefs in Religiously and Secularly Schooled Children', *British Journal of Developmental Psychology*, 23(4): 587–607.

Blanden, J., Crawford, C., Fumagalli, L., and Rabe,B. (2020), 'School Closures and Children's Emotional and Behavioural Difficulties'. Institute for Social and Economic Research. Available at: https://www.iser.essex.ac.uk/files/projects/school-closures/SDQnote2021_final.pdf (accessed September 2022).

Boampong, M., Choak, C., Gunter, A., Heather, M., and Sondhi, G. (2021), 'The Impact of COVID-19 on Black Children and Young People Living in London'. Available at: https://www.open.edu/openlearn/education-development/childhood-youth-studies/the-impact-covid-19-on-black-children-and-young-people-living-london (accessed September 2022).

Bowlby, J. (1958), *Can I Leave My Baby?* London: National Association for Mental Health.

Brent, D. A., Melhem, N. M., Masten, A. S., Porta, G., and Payne, M. W. (2012), 'Longitudinal Effects of Parental Bereavement on Adolescent Developmental Competence', *Journal of Clinical Child & Adolescent Psychology*, 41(6): 778–91.

Brooks, S. K., Webster, R. K., Smith, L. E., Woodland, L., Wessely, S., Greenberg, N., and Rubin, G. J. (2020), 'The Psychological Impact of Quarantine and How to Reduce It: Rapid Review of the Evidence', *The Lancet*, 395(10227): 912–20.

Brofenbrenner, U. (Ed.). (2005). *Making human beings human: Bioecological perspectives on human development*. Thousand Oaks, CA: Sage Publications.

Burrell, A., and Selman, L. E. (2020), 'How Do Funeral Practices Impact Bereaved Relatives' Mental Health, Grief and Bereavement? A Mixed Methods Review with Implications for COVID-19', *OMEGA – Journal of Death and Dying*, 85(2): 345–83.

Case, D. M., Cheah, W. H., and Liu, M. (2020), '"Mourning with the Morning Bell": An Examination of Secondary Educators' Attitudes and Experiences in Managing the Discourse of Death in the Classroom', *OMEGA – Journal of Death and Dying*, 80(3): 397–419.

Chen, C. Y.-C., and Panebianco, A. (2018), 'Interventions for Young Bereaved Children: A Systematic Review and Implications for School Mental Health Providers', *Child & Youth Care Forum*, 47(2): 151–71.

Children's Commissioner. (2020), 'Lockdown Experiences: What Being in Isolation Is Like for Children'. Available at: https://www.childrenscommissioner.gov.uk/2020/04/21/lockdown-experiences-what-being-in-isolation-has-been-like-forchildren/.

Ciacchini, B., Tonioli, F., Marciano, C., Faticato, M. G., Borali, E., Pini, A., Felici, E. (2020), 'Reluctance to Seek Pediatric Care during the COVID-19 Pandemic and the Risks of Delayed Diagnosis', *Italian Journal of Pediatrics*, 46(1): 87.

Clemens, V., Deschamps, P., Fegert, J. M., Anagnostopoulos, D., Bailey, S., Doyle, M., Eliez, S., Hansen, A. S., Hebebrand, J., Hillegers, M., Jacobs, B., Karwautz, A., Kiss, E., Kotsis, K., Kumperscak, H. G., Pejovic_Milovancevic, M., Råberg Christensen, A. M., Raynaud, J. P., Westerinen, H., and Visnapuu-Bernadt, P. (2020), 'Potential Effects of "Social" Distancing Measures and School Lockdown on Child and Adolescent Mental Health', *European Child & Adolescent Psychiatry*, 29(6):739–42.

Coard, B. (1971). *How the West Indian Child Is Made Educationally Sub-normal in the British School System*. London: New Beacon.

Cui, P. P., Wang, P. P., Wang, K., Ping, Z., Wang, P., and Chen, C. (2021), 'Post-Traumatic Growth and Influencing Factors among Frontline Nurses Fighting against COVID-19', *Occupational and Environmental Medicine*, 78(2): 129–35.

Demie, F. (2021), 'The Experience of Black Caribbean Pupils in School Exclusion in England', *Educational Review*, 73(1): 55–70.

Department for Education (DfE). (2019), *Permanent and Fixed Period Exclusions in England: 2017 to 2018*. London: National Statistics.

Dennis-Heyward, E. A., and Shah, S. N. (2021), Pediatric COVID-19 Disparities and Prioritizing Equity—Children Are Not Spared', *JAMA Pediatrics*, 175: 928–38.

Department for Education and Science (DES). (1971), *The Education of Immigrants*. London: HMSO.

Dovidio, J. F., Pearson, A. R., and Penner, L. A. (2018), 'Aversive Racism, Implicit Bias, and Microaggressions', in G. C. Torino, D. P. Rivera, C. M. Capodilupo, K. L. Nadal and D. W. Sue (eds), *Microaggression Theory: Influence and Implications* 16–31. Hoboken: John Wiley & Sons.

Farmer, N., Wallen, G. R., Baumer, Y., and Powell-Wiley, T. M. (2020), 'COVID-19: Growing Health Disparity Gaps and an Opportunity for Health Behavior Discovery'? *Health Equity*, 4(1): 316–19.

Fraley, R. C., and Bonanno, G. A. (2004), Attachment and Loss: A Test of Three Competing Models on the Association between Attachment-Related Avoidance and Adaptation to Bereavement', *Personality and Social Psychology Bulletin*, 30(7): 878–90.

Fristad, M. A., Cerel, J., Goldman, M., Weller, E. B., and Weller, R. A. (2001), 'The Role of Ritual in Children's Bereavement', *OMEGA – Journal of Death and Dying*, 42(4): 321–39.

Gazeley, L., and Dunne, M. (2013), 'Initial Teacher Education Programmes: Providing a Space to Address the Disproportionate Exclusion of Black Pupils from Schools in England'? *Journal of Education for Teaching*, 39(5): 492–508.

Gillborn, D. (2001), 'Racism, Policy and the (Mis)education of Black Children', in R. Majors (ed.), *Educating Our black Children. New Directions and Radical Approaches*, 27–41. Falmer: Routledge.

Goff, P. A., Jackson, M. C., Di Leone, B. A. L., Culotta, C. M., and DiTomasso, N. A. (2014), 'The Essence of Innocence: Consequences of Dehumanizing Black Children', *Journal of Personality and Social Psychology*, 106(4): 526.

Graham, B., White, C., Edwards, A., Potter, S., and Street, C. (2019a), 'School Exclusion: A Literature Review on the Continued Disproportionate Exclusion of Certain'. Department for Education.

Graham, B., White, C., Edwards, A., Potter, S., and Street, C. (2019a), 'School Exclusion: A Literature Review on the Continued Disproportionate Exclusion of Certain Children'. Retrieved from the Department for Education Website: https://

assets. publishing.service.gov.uk/government/uploads/system/uploads/attachment_data/file/800028/Timpson_review_of_school_exclusion_literature_review.pdf Accessed September 2022.

Gregory, A., Skiba, R., and Noguera, P. (2010), 'The Achievement Gap and the Discipline Gap: Two Sides of the Same Coin'? *Educational Researcher*, 39: 59–68.

Harris, R., and Parsons, C. (2001), 'Black Exclusions in a Moral Vacuum', in R. Majors (ed.), *Educating Our Black Children. New Directions and Radical Approaches*, 142–52. Falmer: Routledge.

Holt, L., and Murray, L. (2022), 'Children and Covid-19 in the UK', *Children's Geographies* (20)4: 487–94.

Hopkins, M. (2014), 'The Development of Children's Understanding of Death'. Doctoral dissertation, University of East Anglia.

Jaakkola, R. O., and Slaughter, V. (2002), 'Children's Body Knowledge: Understanding 'Life'as a Biological Goal', *British Journal of Developmental Psychology*, 20(3): 325–42.

Joseph, S., Williams, R., and Yule, W. (1997), *Understanding Post-Traumatic Stress: A Psychosocial Perspective on PTSD and Treatment*. Chichester, England: Wiley.

Kia-Keating, M., and Ellis, B. H. (2007), 'Belonging and Connection to School in Resettlement: Young Refugees, School Belonging, and Psychosocial Adjustment', *Clinical Child Psychology and Psychiatry*, 1: 29–43.

McLaughlin, K. A., and Lambert, H. K. (2017), 'Child Trauma Exposure and Psychopathology: Mechanisms of Risk and Resilience', *Current Opinion in Psychology*, 14: 29–34.

McLean, A. (2016), 'Power and Racialisation: Exploring the Childhood and Educational Experiences of Four Mixed Young People Using Interpretative Phenomenological Analysis'. Unpublished DEdPsy thesis, University of Sheffield.

Mngaza, S. (2020), 'Racism, Identity and Belonging: How Do These Factors Interact for Young Black People in Predominantly White Settings'? DAppEdPsy thesis, University of Nottingham.

Mngaza, S. (2021). Black Feminist Epistemology: An Opportunity for Educational Psychology Praxis. Educational & Child Psychology, 38(4), 63–75.

Muruthi, B., Bermúdez, J. M., Bush, K. R., McCoy, M., and Stinson, M. A. (2016), 'AfroCaribbean Mothers in the US: An Exploratory Study from a Transnational Feminist Perspective', *Women & Therapy*, 39(3–4): 413–31.

Naidoo, A. V. (1996), 'Challenging the Hegemony of Eurocentric Psychology', *Journal of Community and Health Sciences*, 2(2): 9–16.

Ncube, N. (2006), 'The Tree of Life Project: Using Narrative Ideas in Work with Vulnerable Children in Southern Africa', *International Journal of Narrative Therapy and Community Work*, 1: 3–16.

Neel, C. G. O., and Fuligni, A. (2013), 'A Longitudinal Study of School Belonging and Academic Motivation across High School', *Child Development*, 84(2): 678–92.

Neimeyer, R. A. (2004), 'Fostering Posttraumatic Growth: A Narrative Contribution', *Psychological Inquiry*, 15: 53–9.

Nguyen, S. P., and Gelman, S. A. (2002), 'Four and 6-Year Olds' Biological Concept of Death: The Case of Plants', *British Journal of Developmental Psychology*, 20(4): 495–513.

Office for National Statistics (ONS). (2020), *Updating Ethnic Contrasts in Deaths Involving the Coronavirus (COVID-19), England: 24 January 2020 to 11 September 2020*. London: Office for National Statistics.

Office for National Statistics (ONS). (2021), *Updating Ethnic Contrasts in Deaths Involving the Coronavirus (COVID-19), England: 24 January 2020 to 31 March 2021*. London: Office for National Statistics.

Oosterhoff, B., Kaplow, J. B., and Layne, C. M. (2018), 'Links between Bereavement due to Sudden Death and Academic Functioning: Results from a Nationally Representative Sample of Adolescents', *School Psychology Quarterly*, 33(3): 372.

Our World in Data. (2021), 'United Kingdom: Coronavirus Pandemic Country Profile'. Available at: https://ourworldindata.org/coronavirus/country/united-kingdom (accessed November 2021).

OxCGRT, O. (2021). 'COVID-19 Government Response Tracker, 2021. COVID-19 Government Response Tracker'. Available at: https://www.bsg.ox.ac.uk/research/research-projects/covid-19-governmentresponse-tracker (accessed November 2021).

Panagiotaki, G., and Nobes, G. (2014), 'Cultural Influences on Children's Understanding of the Human Body and the Concept of Life', *British Journal of Developmental Psychology*, 32(3): 276–90.

Panagiotaki, G., Nobes, G., Ashraf, A., and Aubby, H. (2015), 'British and Pakistani Children's Understanding of Death: Cultural and Developmental Influences', *British Journal of Developmental Psychology*, 33(1): 31–44.

Panagiotaki, G., Nobes, G., and Engelhardt, P. E. (2017), 'The Development of Intention-Based Morality: The Influence of Intention Salience and Recency, Negligence, and Outcome on Children's and Adults' Judgments', *Developmental Psychology*, 53(10): 1895–1911.

Tedeschi, R. G., and Calhoun, L. G. (2004), 'Posttraumatic Growth: Conceptual Foundations and Empirical Evidence', *Psychological Inquiry*, 15(1): 1–18.

Saatci, D., Ranger, T. A., Garriga, C., Clift, A. K., Zaccardi, F., San Tan, P., and Hippisley-Cox, J. (2021), 'Association between Race and COVID-19 Outcomes among 2.6 Million Children in England', *JAMA Paediatrics*, 175(9): 928–38.

Schuck, D. A., Hens-Piazza, G., and Sadler, R. (2020), 'Different Faiths, Same Pain: How to Grieve a Death in the Coronavirus Pandemic', *The Conversation*. Available at: https://theconversation.com/different-faiths-same-pain-how-to-grieve-a-death-in-the-coronavirus-pandemic-138185. Accessed 23 Septemeber 2022

Shapiro, D. N., Howell, K. H., and Kaplow, J. B. (2014), 'Associations among Mother–Child Communication Quality, Childhood Maladaptive Grief, and Depressive Symptoms', *Death Studies*, 38(3): 172–8.

Siegel, D. J., and Hartzell, M. (2003), *Parenting from the Inside Out: How a Deeper Self Understanding Can Help You Raise Children Who Thrive*. New York: Tarcher/Putnam.

Slaughter, V., and Lyons, M. (2003), 'Learning about Life and Death in Early Childhood', *Cognitive Psychology*, 46(1): 1–30.

Stern, J. A., Barbarin, O., and Cassidy, J. (2021), Working toward Anti-Racist Perspectives in Attachment Theory, Research, and Practice', *Attachment & Human Development*, 24(3): 1–31.

Strand, S., and Lindorff, A. (2018), *Ethnic Disproportionality in the Identification of Special Educational Needs (SEN) in England: Extent, Causes and Consequences*. Oxford: University of Oxford.

Sze, S., Pan, D., Nevill, C. R., Gray, L. J., Martin, C. A., Nazareth, J., and Pareek, M. (2020), 'Ethnicity and Clinical Outcomes in COVID-19: A Systematic Review and Meta-analysis', *EClinicalMedicine*, 29–30,100630.

Tedeschi, R. G., and Calhoun, L. G. (2004), 'A Clinical Approach to Posttraumatic Growth', in P. A. Linley and S. Joseph (eds), *Positive Psychology in Practice*, 405–19. Hoboken, NJ: Wiley.

Triplett, K. N., Tedeschi, R. G., Cann, A., Calhoun, L. G., and Reeve, C. L. (2012), 'Posttraumatic Growth, Meaning in Life, and Life Satisfaction in Response to Trauma', *Psychological Trauma: Theory, Research, Practice, and Policy*, 4: 400–10.

Vincent, C., Rollock, N., Ball, S., and Gillborn, D. (2012), 'Being Strategic, Being Watchful, Being Determined: Black Middle-Class Parents and Schooling', *British Journal of Sociology of Education*, 33(3): 337–54.

Washington, H. A. (2009), 'Medical Apartheid: The Dark History of Medical Experimentation on Black Americans from Colonial Times to the Present', *International Journal of Applied Psychoanalytic Studies*, 6(4): 353–5.

Weber, M., Alvariza, A., Kreicbergs, U., and Sveen, J. (2019), 'Communication in Families with Minor Children Following the Loss of a Parent to Cancer', *European Journal of Oncology Nursing*, 39: 41–6.

West, E., Nair, P., Barrado-Martin, Y., Walters, K. R., Kupeli, N., Sampson, E. L., and Davies, N. (2021), 'Exploration of the Impact of the COVID-19 Pandemic on People with Dementia and Carers from Black and Minority Ethnic Groups', *BMJ Open*, 11(5): e050066.

White, N. (2020, May 10), 'Inside the Online Caribbean Nine Night Celebrations Paying Tribute to Black Lives Lost', *Huffington Post UK*. Available at: https://www.huffingtonpost.co.uk/ entry/inside-the-online-caribbean-nine-night-celebrations_uk_5eab1d7cc5b62b68ab 546965.Accessed Septmber 23 2022

Wright, R. (2020), 'Navigating Blackness in Educational Psychology: Reflections of a Trainee Educational Psychologist', *Educational Psychology Research and Practice*, 6(1): 1–9

Xiang, M., Zhang, Z., and Kuwahara, K. (2020), 'Impact of COVID-19 Pandemic on Children and Adolescents' Lifestyle Behavior Larger than Expected', *Progress in Cardiovascular Diseases*, 63(20): 531–7.

Youansamouth, L., Collingwood, S., and Ruston, R. (2020), *Post-COVID-19 Trauma Informed Guidance for Schools.* Lancashire: Lancashire Violence Reduction Network.

Zhou, X. (2020), 'Managing Psychological Distress in Children and Adolescents Following the COVID-19 Epidemic: A Cooperative Approach', *Psychological Trauma: Theory, Research, Practice, and Policy*, 12(S1): S76–S78.

Part 5

Disability and Crisis

13

Teach in the Mornings, Cry in the Evenings: The Impact of Covid-19 Remote Schooling on the Mothers of Emergent Bilinguals with Disabilities

María Cioè-Peña

US schools were forced to shift to remote schooling in Spring 2020 due to Covid-19, exacerbating pre-existing educational inequalities. Remote schooling created major challenges for parents, requiring many to adopt roles they were ill-equipped for (Levine 2020), like monitoring academic progress. Elementary- and middle-school-aged emergent bilinguals (EB) and students with disabilities (and their families), were especially affected since services (e.g. speech and language therapy; English as a Second Language) were not always linguistically accessible or remotely adaptable (Daniels 2020; Shapiro and Harris 2020). Most national discourse and programmes aimed at remediating the academic effects of Covid-19 centre students with only one of the aforementioned classifications. This highlights the pre-existing absence of intersectional approaches that resulted in dually classified emergent bilinguals with disabilities (EBwDs) experiencing disruptions in linguistic *and* special education (SpEd) service delivery (Amin 2020; Amin, Zimmerman and Viega 2020). The holistic needs of multiply marginalized students will remain unmet while their absence in research persists (Cioè-Peña 2017c), contributing to sustained opportunity gaps and new deficit-centred labels like 'Long-term English Language Learner'(Brooks 2017).

Before Spring 2020, EBwDs were regularly placed in monolingual settings rather than multilingual ones due to faulty conceptions of language learning, which result in teachers often recommending EBwDs' placement in English-only settings foregrounding their disability-related needs and relegating their linguistic needs into 'extras' (Cioè-Peña 2017a,b,c, 2020a,b; Kangas 2014, 2017).

As such, Covid-19 related interruptions in schooling could not be remedied by Spanish-dominant mothers of children who had been educated solely in English, further marginalizing and systematically excluding these mothers from their children's quotidian, academic experiences. The reason for this is that school agents often make, and present, monolingual English placement decisions as fast tracks to disability remediation for EBwDs (Cioè-Peña 2020a). Many mothers accept these placements because they believe doing so will hasten their children's perceived recovery (i.e. increasing their proximity to 'normal'; Cioè-Peña 2021). However, these placements often result in mothers being relegated to supplementary roles in EBwDs' school-based lives (Cioè-Peña 2021).

Mothers are keenly aware of the cultural, linguistic and communicative divide that exists between them and schools. To counter this exclusion, many mothers utilize family members as linguistic intermediaries and support their children's development of home language through extracurricular activities and academics with supports like tutoring. With social distancing and remote schooling mandates, the divide between school and home language became more palpable, particularly for mothers isolated from their extended networks with limited technology access. EBwDs previously placed in monolingual settings experienced reduced access to supports due to limited availability of resources and services – which, *when offered by the school, were English-only* – thus, widening opportunity gaps. This chapter aims to examine the experiences of Spanish-speaking mothers of EBwDs during remote schooling, placing focus on the impact that language, social distancing and remote schooling had on mothers' well-being and capacity to support their children's academic development, at home.

Relevant Literature

EBwDs are functional bilinguals with complex linguistic practices (Cioè-Peña and Linares 2021). Yet, the majority are placed in monolingual English settings because educators believe that learning disability needs supersede language needs (Kangas 2014). School agents regularly make linguistic placement decisions with minimal input from students or parents (Cummings and Hardin 2017), often resulting in monolingual English placements (de Valenzuela et al. 2016; Kangas 2014). These placements benefit schools (e.g. reduced cost) while negatively impacting EBwDs – typically resulting in declines in home language use and family contact for the child (Algood, Harris and Hong 2013; Brown and Ault 2016; de Valenzuela et al. 2016). These placements reflect deficit-centred biases grounded in racism, linguicism and ableism (Annamma, Ferri and Connor 2018; Blanchett, Klinger and Harry 2009). Subsequently, EBwDs are subject to more restrictive environments than non-EBs, have limited or unequal access to general education and 'are more likely to remain in more restrictive classrooms' for their entire schooling experience (Gonzalez, Tefera and Artiles 2014; Zhang, Katsiyannis and Roberts 2014: 119). Moreover, unable to receive English-bound academic support from their linguistically diverse parents, EBwDs are also susceptible to intellectual and linguistic segregation at home (Gonzalez, Tefera and Artiles 2014). Placement decisions also reflect school resource availability, but during remote schooling the home became the school. It is imperative that we expand the educational lens beyond the classroom to the home to understand the range of educational practices mothers use in supporting their children.

Mothers of EBwDs are central to their children's academic achievement. However, due to their sociocultural position, many have limited opportunities to engage as advocates in similar ways as white middle-class parents (Montelongo 2015; Rodriguez, Blatz and Elbaum 2013). Spanish-speaking mothers of EBwDs face racial and linguistic barriers, are acutely aware of how schools devalue their cultures and/or voices (Ijalba 2015) and feel ill-informed, craving more school support (Aceves 2014; Wolfe and Durán 2013). The linguistic dissonance between families and schools became more consequential as mothers were tasked with managing their children's academic lives during remote schooling. Therefore, it is critically important to understand how mothers bridge this gap in ways that can be supported in schools. This study supplements the dearth of literature focused on EBwDs' language use at home by employing a critical lens that highlights how minoritized mothers support children's educational growth across languages and perceived ability.

Conceptual Framework

Conceptually, this chapter is guided by intersectionality (Crenshaw 1991), Dis/abilities Critical race studies (DisCrit; Annamma, Connor and Ferri 2013), and forms of capital (Bourdieu [1986]2011). Grounded in Black feminist theory, intersectionality acknowledges how inequalities and/or disadvantages compound to create unique forms of oppression not readily understood by conventional narratives of systemic oppression (Crenshaw 1991). Intersectionality demands we understand that the experiences and forms of educational inequity EBwDs and their mothers endure are unique compared to the experiences of able-bodied EBs or culturally and linguistically dominant people with dis/abilities. DisCrit 'aim[s] to more fully account for the ways that racism and ableism are interconnected' (Annamma, Ferri and Connor 2018: 47). Thus, DisCrit presents a distinct perspective with which to understand how remote schooling practices impact mothers of EBwDs differently from parents of disabled white children and able-bodied EBs. With this stance, this study seeks to foreground how *disability*-related restrictions to bilingual education deepen educational inequalities, particularly during crisis situations like Covid-19. Finally, according to Bourdieu (2011), all individuals navigate through various fields, each of which is accessed by three distinct forms of capital: economic, social and cultural. Bourdieu's theory of capital is important because ability and English-language proficiency can be understood to be symbolic forms of capital thus granting and denying access to non-symbolic forms of capital (i.e. economic, social and cultural) to individuals whose linguistic or intellectual/physical practices are not deemed as 'normal' or valuable. As such, EBwDs and their Spanish-speaking mothers are multiply marginalized during remote schooling, which was designed with able-bodied, English monolinguals in mind.

Methods

Using a qualitative design, data were gathered through Spanish-language conversational and narrative interviews. As an Afro-Dominican mother, who immigrated to the United States in 1990, who has a disability and experience with a disabled family member, and who has conducted research with this population, I was able to establish rapport and facilitate interviews. By encouraging mothers to share their narratives, I aimed to uncover how shifting to remote schooling affected them, centring the perceptions of mothers whose experiences are usually ignored by educational authorities. The sub-study shared here was guided by two research questions:

1. How are monolingual Spanish speaking mothers navigating their children's remote schooling experiences?

2. What, if at all, has been the emotional toll of remote schooling for mothers and families?

Sample and Selection

The data shared here arose from a 2020 study that was situated in New York City (NYC). With over 39,000 students, EBwDs are nearly 25 per cent of NYC Department of Education's (NYCDOE) English language learners population (Division of Multilingual Learners 2020). Since more than 75 per cent of this subpopulation lives in a home where Spanish is the primary language, this study centres Spanish-speaking families. Specifically, the study focuses on thirty mothers (including the mothers from the 2016-17 study) who supported their children during remote schooling in Spring 2020. Mothers whose (1) identified home language is Spanish and (2) child was in grades 2–8 with an IEP and an English language learner classification qualified. Participants were recruited through faith- and community-based organizations, social media and referrals. After screening for inclusion criteria, interested participants were interviewed on a rolling basis until the cap was reached. Due to the urgent need to document mothers' educational practices, data collection began in June 2020 with a university-based seed grant. I seek funding for data analysis and findings dissemination. See Table 13.1.

Data Sources

Conversational interviews (Currivan 2008) followed a uniform protocol developed from existing surveys, including the NYCDOE's survey on remote schooling, and from interview questions used in the 2016–17 study. Using Qualtrics, this interview gathered demographic and contextual information: participant background, child's classification, family language use, technology access and school satisfaction before and during Covid-19. This format facilitated understandings of language and disability-related needs during remote schooling, including supports. Narrative interviews (Acevedo 2001) focused on mothers' personal experiences: their circumstances, how they coped with remote schooling, unique issues that emerged and consequences of remote schooling. The second, loosely structured interview elicited personal narratives. A third interview was conducted in Fall 2020, which focused on changes encountered between remote schooling during Spring 2020 and Fall 2020.

Table 13.1 Participant and qualifying child demographics

Total Sample Size, n = 30

Country of birth/origin	Education level	Time in the United States	Number of children	Number of Children with IEPs	Qualifying child pronoun	Disability classification[1]	Spring 2020 grade level	School type	Class type
Mexico = 13 Ecuador = 5 Dominican Republic = 5 Peru = 3 Venezuela = 1 Puerto Rico = 1 Continental USA = 1	Some or all of… Elementary school = 4 Middle school = 3 HS/GED = 12 College or above = 9 Undisclosed = 1	0–5 yrs = 3 6–10 yrs = 4 11–15 yrs = 11 15+ yrs = 12	1 child = 7 2 to 3 children = 19 4 to 5 children = 4	1 child with an IEP = 15 2–3 children with IEPs = 15	He, Him, His = 18 She/Her/Hers = 11 Undisclosed = 1	Autism = 18 Speech and language impairment = 8 Specific learning disability = 4 Intellectual disability = 2 Emotional/behavioural disturbance = 2 Multiple disabilities = 1	Second = 5 children Third = 8 children Fourth = 5 children Fifth = 4 children Sixth = 3 children Seventh = 1 children	Community school = 18 District 75[2] = 9 Charter = 1 Private special education school paid with public funds[3] = 2	General education = 2 students Self-contained special education class = 21 students Integrated Co-Teaching (ICT) Class = 6 students Dual language ICT = 1 student

[1] Six of the participating children had co-occurrent classifications like Autism and ID or SLI and LD.

[2] According to Edutopia: District 75 is an archipelago of 61 schools serving only children with special needs in New York City. While most of the city's 223,000 students with disabilities are educated within their neighbourhood schools, 24,000 of them have such severe needs – behavioural, emotional, neurological, physical or cognitive – that they must be educated in schools with other students like them. They are served by 6,050 teachers and 8,700 paraprofessionals who have some of the toughest jobs in education. (McKenna 2019, para. 5–6)

[3] According to NYCDOE officials '4,431 students with disabilities attended private schools paid for by the education department in fiscal year 2017 … a third more than in 2014' (Zimmerman 2019). This growth is viewed by some as recognition that the NYCDOE can't provide an adequate education to students with disabilities within traditional public schools.' (Zimmerman 2019)

Data Collection

As part of this institutional review board approved project, data (audio recordings, Qualtrics report and fieldnotes) were collected from June to December. Audio-recorded interviews were offered in three sessions: conversational interview first, then two narrative interviews. Interview format was based on recommended public health guidelines. Audio recordings were transcribed by a third party and translated as needed. Participants provided written or oral consent for all forms of data collection. Oral consent was used in addition to written consent to allow for the inclusion of participants with diverse literacy and technological capacities/access. All data were collected and stored as anonymized data using pseudonyms selected by the participants.

Data Analysis

Guided by the research questions and conceptual framework, multiple forms of analysis were employed. For this chapter, data from conversational interviews were analysed and reported using descriptive statistics, medians and interquartile ranges using Qualtrics.

Findings

This chapter is rooted in two findings: (1) The impact of language and technology access on mother's stress levels. (2) The emotional impact of the isolation that resulted from Covid-19 on mothers and children. The findings stem primarily from data collected during the conversational interviews. As such, the data being shared are primarily quantitative and shared in an effort to showcase the collective experiences of the participants; wherever appropriate, numerical data are presented in tables.

Teach in the Mornings: The Impact of Language and Technology Access on Mothers

At the onset of the first interview mothers were asked how they were feeling today. The most commonly used words were: 'stressed', 'worried' and 'tired', in

Table 13.2 Participant responses to question: Did your child receive a device from NYCDOE and/or school?

Response	Percentage	Count
Yes	70.00%	21
No, I did not request one	16.67%	5
I did not know this was an option	10.00%	3
No, I wanted one but did not receive it	3.33%	1
Total	100%	30

that order. Much of the 'stress', 'worry' and 'exhaustion' mothers encountered stemmed from their experiences with remote schooling.

A Hectic Shift: The Race to Provide Children with Materials

Initially, when the pandemic lockdowns first started many parents were concerned with ensuring that their children had the material resources needed to transition to remote learning. Many of the mothers in this study ensured that their children had the technological hardware necessary to attend school remotely. Some procured devices, some repurposed household devices and others sought out loaner devices from the NYCDOE, see Table 13.2.

Still, devices were not sufficient, particularly given the inequity in Wi-Fi access that is true not only in the rural parts of the United States but also in urban communities that experience income inequality. As such, once a device had been secured many of the mothers then had to sort out how to provide their children with internet access. Some sought out devices from the NYCDOE, but the overwhelming majority would tether their children's designated devices to their smartphones, with over 80 percent of the participants reporting that they used cell phone data to access the internet at home; some half, most or all of the time; see Table 13.3.

This personal encounter with the digital gap would often push mothers' personal stress levels but would also put pressure on a family's limited financial resources given that nineteen participants (63%) lost their jobs as a result of the lockdown. While some experienced unemployment resulting from loss or lack of work, the overwhelming majority had to quit their jobs in order to care for their children. Facing this tangible loss of income, many mothers expressed a desire to install Wi-Fi in their homes but named the financial impact of the pandemic as an

Table 13.3 Participant responses to question: How often do you use cell phone data to access the internet at home?

Answer	Percentage	Count
Always	30.00%	9
Most of the time	23.33%	7
About half the time	16.67%	5
Sometimes	10.00%	3
Never	20.00%	6
Total	100%	30

unsurmountable limitation, a feeling that would also arise whenever schools would ask parents to print materials based on assumptions that families had the material and economic resources with which to support those requests. Still, once secured, devices and internet access were small stressors compared to the actual learning practices that mothers encountered.

Starting from Behind: Pre-existing Inequities

Many of the social and educational inequities that surfaced during the Covid-19 pandemic related to pre-existing social issues related to the stratification of society along racial, socio-economic, linguistic and gendered lines. However, the magnitude of these inequities changed drastically during the pandemic related lockdowns and the implementation of remote schooling. Remote schooling was implemented as a safety measure in order to protect vulnerable populations and save lives; however, this safety of life did not come without a cost – both to children and to families. This was particularly evident when mothers were asked to discuss their academic experiences during the 2019–20 academic year with a specific request to compare their experiences prior to, and after, March 2020. When asked about their level of satisfaction with their children's learning experience before and during the Covid-19 related pandemic lockdowns, nearly 65 percent of mothers replied that they felt somewhat or extremely unsatisfied (see Table 13.4) with remote schooling compared to 33.67 percent mothers who were unsatisfied before remote schooling (see Table 13.5).

Mothers shared multiple reasons for this shift in satisfaction; however, the most frequently named were language of instruction, limited technical and content area expertise and poor communication from schools. All these factors

Table 13.4 Participant responses to question: How satisfied were you with your child's school experience before Covid-19 remote schooling?

Answer	Percentage	Count
Extremely satisfied	33.34%	10
Somewhat satisfied	30%	9
Neither satisfied nor unsatisfied	3.33%	1
Somewhat unsatisfied	20%	6
Extremely unsatisfied	13.33%	4
Total	100%	30

Table 13.5 Participant responses to question: How satisfied are you with your child's current school experience during Covid-19 remote schooling?

Answer	Percentage	Count
Extremely satisfied	16.67%	5
Somewhat satisfied	20%	6
Neither satisfied nor unsatisfied	0%	0
Somewhat unsatisfied	23.33%	7
Extremely Unsatisfied	40%	12
Total	100%	30

had already been identified in literature as barriers to parental engagement pre-pandemic, but their impact increased during the enactment of remote schooling, a time when parental engagement was critical to student success. Although many of the factors that caused mothers stress related to their children's academic experience, the pandemic also brought with it new, or at least, unexpected hardships which are discussed in the next section.

Cry in the Evenings: The Impact of Covid-19 Pandemic Related Lockdowns on Mothers

The Covid-19 pandemic is primarily identified as a public health crisis; however, the pandemic also had major impacts on the financial and emotional prosperity of individuals and family units (Gautam and Hens 2020). Additionally, the pandemic has resulted in increases in racial wealth gap (Williams 2017) and health disparities (Institute of Medicine (US) Committee on Understanding and Eliminating Racial and Ethnic Disparities in Health Care 2003) further marginalizing many already marginalized populations and communities.

Things That Go Boo in the Night: Financial Stress in the Lives of Mothers

The study shared in this chapter focused primarily on the impact of remote schooling brought on by the Covid-19 pandemic. However, given the complex ways in which Covid-19 impacted all aspects of living (Kantamneni 2020), participants were also asked about other ways that the Covid-19 pandemic has impacted them (see Table 13.6).

Many of the hardships experienced by the mothers, especially the ones that kept them up at night, related to the economic impact of the pandemic. As a result of the pandemic, mothers experienced financial hardships, which then results in changes to living conditions with at least seven mothers noting that they were either evicted from their homes, had to take in family members or were months behind on rent as a result of the pandemic. This also meant that families were forced to combine households, increasing the number of individuals in the home and the chances of a Covid-19 outbreak within the home while also decreasing space and privacy. These combined factors can often increase interpersonal conflict and, as a result, impact a mother's capacity to support her child during remote instruction.

The economic impact of the pandemic on the study participants was significant with nearly 80 percent identifying a loss of income stemming from the pandemic which impacted other parts of their lives like their ability to pay their bills with almost 65 percent of the participants citing this as a strain. This economic strain made the shift to remote school even more burdensome because, as previously mentioned, many families did not have the necessary hardware, software or internet access needed to successfully transition to a fully remote experience nor did they have the wealth privilege that would make it possible to procure these items at short notice without a significant impact on the overall stability of the family unit. At the same time, mothers were also struggling with accessing food, groceries, toiletries and hygiene products for themselves and their children indicating the hopelessness of wanting to support your child's learning while simultaneously managing the realities of food insecurity. In other

Table 13.6 Participant responses to question: Since the Covid-19 pandemic started, have you experienced any of the following? Please select all that apply:

Answer	Percentage	Count
Adverse discrimination from people unknown to you	13.33%	4
Difficulties due to changes in your living condition, including eviction	23.33%	7
Difficulties working, including loss of employment for yourself or a family member	76.67%	23
Difficulty paying bills	63.33%	19
Difficulty accessing healthcare	50.00%	15
Difficulty accessing food or groceries	40.00%	12
Difficulty accessing toiletries or hygiene products, for yourself or your children	50.00%	15
Death or illness of a family member as a result of Covid-19 complications	26.67%	8
Fear of deportation, for you or a family member	33.33%	10

Note: Totals are not provided in this section as participants were able to select multiple options. As such the percentage presented indicates the prevalence of the issue within this participant pool.

words, it is hard to rationalize or even allocate money to purchase a computer, tablet or even ink and paper for your child when one's ability to provide food and care for themselves and/or their children is already limited due to financial hardship. Furthermore, economic stress has been shown to result in other forms of stress (Anakwenze and Zuberi 2013) – this is evident in this study when we look at other Covid-19 related factors that impacted mothers' well-being.

Tossing, Turning and Mourning: Covid-19 Related Isolation, Illness and Death

The unfortunate and most devastating aspect of the Covid-19 pandemic is the ways in which it impacted people in so many dimensions: economically, emotionally, physically and socially. Enduring a loss in any one of these areas can bring intense stress and hardship in a family. However, many of these women were experiencing losses in all realms. Many of the participants had felt ill during the lockdowns but at least fifteen encountered difficulties in accessing healthcare. Since this study took place during the earlier part of the pandemic, the Trump administration was still in charge resulting in ten participants reporting that they feared deportation for themselves or someone close to them. At least eight participants had experienced the death of a family member due to Covid-19. One participant reported having lost ten people close to her, including the principal at her children's school, who had died in late March due to complications of Covid-19. The fear of illness, death and even deportation coupled with the burden of economic loss, food and shelter insecurity and the stress of remote schooling led many to feel both physically *and* socially isolated.

Mothers shared experiences of poor sleep, emotional dysregulation, changes to weight and even hair loss as manifestations of their stress. When asked what, if anything at all, they did for self-care, two said they went on walks, one stated speaking with a therapist whom she had a pre-existing relationship with due to a diagnosis of PTSD, but for the most part these mothers had no outlet. Perhaps it is for this reason that at least thirteen mothers were heard crying during the first interview session alone. However, the mothers were less concerned about their emotional well-being than that of their children. When asked how worried they were about their children's social or emotional well-being during pandemic related remote schooling only one mother stated that she had no concern, four mothers were slightly concerned, three were somewhat concerned and twenty-two were quite or extremely concerned. Overwhelmingly, mothers were worried that their children, many of whom were diagnosed with autism (Table 13.1), would regress socially, impacting their ability to reintegrate into society after the lockdown is lifted. As such, mothers were not just worried about their children's present-day emotional well-being but also the long-term implications of social isolation on their children. Mothers were just as concerned about their children's well-being as they were about their children's academic development (see Table 13.7).

These mothers were carrying with them a heavy burden bust; still each day, they rallied, got up and took on the challenge of supporting their children's academic development in a language and in a medium they found challenging. This is indicative of how vested mothers were in ensuring their children were safe, cared for and educated during the Covid-19 pandemic related lockdown and the subsequent remote schooling mandates.

Mothers had little input in how remote schooling programmes were developed and/or implemented, and few opportunities to seek support. And yet they continued to show up and support their children as learners and in many ways to support the physical demands of their children's teachers' and service providers' plans. In the years after the pandemic, there will be many talks of

Table 13.7 Concern over academics versus socio-emotional concerns during Covid-19 pandemic related remote schooling

Participant responses to question: How concerned are you about your child's learning while their school building is closed?			Participant responses to question: How concerned are you about your child's social or emotional well-being while their school building is closed?		
Answer	Percentage	Count	Answer	Percentage	Count
Extremely concerned	36%	11	Extremely concerned	16.67%	5
Quite concerned	36%	11	Quite concerned	56%	17
Somewhat concerned	10%	3	Somewhat concerned	10%	3
Slightly concerned	13.33%	4	Slightly concerned	13.33%	4
Not concerned at all	3.33%	1	Not concerned at all	3.33%	1
Total	100%	30	**Total**	100%	30

'learning loss' but we should also make sure to talk about the learning resiliency, the communal and familial efforts that were undertaken to minimize that loss, often to the detriment to the family's economic position and caretakers', but particularly mothers', mental health.

Implications and Conclusion

It is unrealistic and unproductive to talk about the ways in which schools could have better managed remote schooling, better supported families, better included parents in their planning considerations and so on. It is much more critical to talk about the ways in which parents, particularly mothers and those who are linguistically minoritized, must be included not only during crisis planning but also during all curricular development. Western forms of parental engagement are an expectation in most Western schools including those that educate large populations of linguistically and culturally diverse students. However, it is important to recognize that much of those expectations centre and privilege forms of capital accessible to, and reflective of, white, middle-class, heteronormative, English monolingual families, simultaneously limiting and devaluing the forms of capital available to the culturally and linguistically diverse (CLD) families of EBwDs. EBwDs are being supported and co-educated by intergenerational, racially, ethnically, economically, CLD families with different, but no less valuable, ways of being and caring. As such, moving forward, educators must consider the ways in which they explicitly and implicitly alienate CLD families' forms of capital, especially those of EBwDs whom we must legally partner with. Because as was shown in this chapter, our education decisions not only impact students but also families and, in many cases, they cause these families harm by introducing economic and emotional stress. Future crisis management must not only be expeditious and attentive to students' intersectional needs but also to those of their families. We must consider the ways in which we can maximize home support while reducing the parental burden.

Finally, as a society we need to take an intersectional approach to social nets and foreground the mental health needs of mothers and caretakers of colour, particularly those who are caring for EBwDs, during crisis. Very few mothers in this study had access to mental health support prior to, during or after the Covid-19 pandemic related lockdowns. As a society, we must recognize the emotional toll that care work has on caretakers particularly when they are tasked with managing the care of multiple people at the same time, in mediums that they may not be familiar with and in languages that they cannot readily access. We must keep in mind the mental anxiety that is created when communication breaks down between the home and the school while simultaneously expecting parents to manage the physical components of their children's remote learning experience (e.g. procure materials, provide technical support, time management, etc.). We must also understand the perplexing contradiction of hosting a food bank at school, knowing that families in the school experience food insecurity, yet asking those very same families to print materials at home. Once again schools are not attending to the different forms of capital that their communities possess and lack, thus limiting their capacity to maximize communal partnership. We must remember that the overwhelming majority of educators continue to lead lives of greater economic and social privilege (Garcia and Cook 2017) than most of their culturally and linguistically diverse students (Tarasawa and Waggoner 2015). Thus, educators must consider their students' positionality in their planning and in their interactions with parents, particularly those of EBwDs. This is not an invitation to be reductionary and/or view these families from deficit perspectives. Rather, this is an invitation to take up a DisCrit approach to curriculum planning, to find new ways of partnering with caretakers that shift away from traditional forms of capital, and towards a more holistic lens for including and relating to CLD families' funds of knowledge (Gonzalez, Moll and Amanti 2006; Moll et al. 1992; Oughton 2010) and cultural capital (Trainor 2010; Yosso 2005). This is an invitation to position parents, especially CLD mothers of EBwDs, as child-centred experts rather than teacher-focused supporters, and to consider their contributions to their child's and the classroom's cultural, academic, and socio-emotional development. This is an invitation to build a collaborative school–home relationship that won't get lost amid a crisis, but rather that will see the children, families and whole school community through the crisis feeling, at the bare minimum, academically and socio-emotionally supported and united.

References

Acevedo, L. del A. (ed.). (2001), *Telling to Live: Latina Feminist Testimonios*. Durham, NC: Duke University Press.

Aceves, T. C. (2014), 'Supporting Latino Families in Special Education through Community Agency–School Partnerships', *Multicultural Education*, 21(3/4): 45–50. Available at: http://search.proquest.com.ezproxy.gc.cuny.edu/socscicoll/docview/1648093615/abstract/AC9AFCD9AC064A02PQ/4.

Algood, C. L., Harris, C., and Hong, J. S. (2013), 'Parenting Success and Challenges for Families of Children with Disabilities: An Ecological Systems Analysis', *Journal of Human Behavior in the Social Environment*, 23(2): 126–36. Available at: https://doi.org/10.1080/10911359.2012.747408.

Amin, R. (2020, April 30), 'Many of NYC's Bilingual Special Education Students Don't Get the Right Services. Remote Learning Has Made It Even Harder'. *Chalkbeat: New York*. Available at: https://ny.chalkbeat.org/2020/4/30/21242991/many-of-nycs-bilingual-special-education-students-dont-get-the-right-services (accessed 2 May 2020).

Amin, R., Zimmerman, A., and Veiga, C. (2020, March 22), 'Many NYC Public School Students Still Without Computers as Remote Classes Start'. *The City*. Available at: http://thecity.nyc/2020/03/many-nyc-students-without-computers-as-remote-classes-start.html.

Anakwenze, U., and Zuberi, D. (2013), 'Mental Health and Poverty in the Inner City', *Health & Social Work*, 38(3): 147–57. Available at: https://doi.org/10.1093/hsw/hlt013.

Annamma, S. A., Connor, D., and Ferri, B. (2013), 'Dis/ability Critical Race Studies (DisCrit): Theorizing at the Intersections of Race and Dis/ability', *Race Ethnicity and Education*, 16(1): 1–31. Available at: https://doi.org/10.1080/13613324.2012.730511.

Annamma, S. A., Ferri, B. A., and Connor, D. J. (2018), 'Disability Critical Race Theory: Exploring the Intersectional Lineage, Emergence, and Potential Futures of DisCrit in Education', *Review of Research in Education*, 42(1): 46–71. Available at: https://doi.org/10.3102/0091732X18759041.

Blanchett, W. J., Klingner, J. K., and Harry, B. (2009), 'The Intersection of Race, Culture, Language, and Disability Implications for Urban Education', *Urban Education*, 44(4): 389–409. Available at: https://doi.org/10.1177/0042085909338686.

Bourdieu, P. ([1986]2011). 'The Forms of Capital, in I. Szeman and T. Kaposy (eds), *Cultural Theory: An Anthology*, 81–93. Oxford, UK: John Wiley & Sons.

Brooks, M. D. (2017), '"She Doesn't Have the Basic Understanding of a Language": Using Spelling Research to Challenge Deficit Conceptualizations of Adolescent Bilinguals', *Journal of Literacy Research*, 49(3): 342–70. Available at: https://doi.org/10.1177/1086296X17714016.

Brown, J., and Ault, P. C. (2016), 'Disentangling Language Differences from Disability: A Case Study of District-Preservice Collaboration', *Journal of Multilingual Education Research*, 6(1): 111–36. Available at: http://fordham.bepress.com/jmer/vol6/iss1/7.

Cioè-Peña, M. (2017a), Disability, Bilingualism and What It Means to Be Normal', *Journal of Bilingual Education Research & Instruction*, 19(1): 138–60.

Cioè-Peña, M. (2017b), 'Who Is Excluded From Inclusion? Points of Union and Division in Bilingual and Special Education', *Theory, Research, and Action in Urban Education*, V(1). Available at: https://blmtraue.commons.gc.cuny.edu/2017/02/24/who-is-excluded-from-inclusion-points-of-union-and-division-in-bilingual-and-special-education/.

Cioè-Peña, M. (2017c), 'The Intersectional Gap: How Bilingual Students in the United States Are Excluded from Inclusion', *International Journal of Inclusive Education*, 21(9): 906–19. Available at: https://doi.org/10.1080/13603116.2017.1296032.

Cioè-Peña, M. (2020a), 'Raciolinguistics and the Education of Emergent Bilinguals Labeled as Disabled', *The Urban Review*. Available at: https://doi.org/10.1007/s11256-020-00581-z.

Cioè-Peña, M. (2020b), 'Bilingualism for Students with Disabilities, Deficit or Advantage?: Perspectives of Latinx Mothers', *Bilingual Research Journal*, 0(0): 1–14. Available at: https://doi.org/10.1080/15235882.2020.1799884. DOI: 10.1080/15235882.2020.1799884.

Cioè-Peña, M. (2021), *(M)othering Labeled Children: Bilingualism and Disability in the Lives of Latinx Mothers*. Bristol: Multilingual Matters.

Crenshaw, K. (1991), 'Mapping the Margins: Intersectionality, Identity Politics, and Violence against Women of Color', *Stanford Law Review*, 43(6): 1241–99. Available at: https://doi.org/10.2307/1229039.

Cummings, K. P., and Hardin, B. J. (2017), 'Navigating Disability and Related Services: Stories of Immigrant Families', *Early Child Development and Care*, 187(1), 115–27, DOI: 10.1080/03004430.2016.1152962.

Currivan, D. B. (2008), 'Conversational Interviewing', in P. J. Lavrakas (ed.), *Encyclopedia of Survey Research Methods*, 152–2. London: Sage. Available at: https://doi.org/10.4135/9781412963947.

Daniels, N. (2020, April 24), 'Lesson of the Day: "Imagine Online School in a Language You Don't Understand"', *The New York Times*. Available at: https://www.nytimes.com/2020/04/24/learning/lesson-of-the-day-imagine-online-school-in-a-language-you-dont-understand.html.

de Valenzuela, J. S., Bird, E. K.-R., Parkington, K., Mirenda, P., Cain, K., MacLeod, A. A. N., and Segers, E. (2016), 'Access to Opportunities for Bilingualism for Individuals with Developmental Disabilities: Key Informant Interviews', *Journal of Communication Disorders*, 63: 32–46. Available at: https://doi.org/10.1016/j.jcomdis.2016.05.005.

Division of Multilingual Learners. (2020), '2018–2019 English Language Learner Demographic Report' [Demographic Report]. New York City Department of Education.

Garcia, A., and Cook, S. (2017, June 2), 'K-12 Teachers Are Disproportionately White and Monolingual. Here's One Way That Could Change', *Slate Magazine*. Available at: https://slate.com/human-interest/2017/06/paraprofessionals-can-help-diversify-the-k-12-teacher-workforce.html.

Gautam, S., and Hens, L. (2020), 'COVID-19: Impact by and on the Environment, Health and Economy', *Environment, Development and Sustainability*, 22(6): 4953–4. Available at: https://doi.org/10.1007/s10668-020-00818-7.

Gonzalez, N., Moll, L. C., and Amanti, C. (2006), *Funds of Knowledge: Theorizing Practices in Households, Communities, and Classrooms*. Oxfordshire: Routledge.

Gonzalez, T., Tefera, A., and Artiles, A. (2014), 'The Intersections of Language Differences and Learning Disabilities', in M. Bigelow and J. Ennser-Kananen (eds), *The Routledge Handbook of Educational Linguistics*, 145–57. Oxfordshire: Routledge.

Ijalba, E. (2015), 'Understanding Parental Engagement in Hispanic Mothers of Children with Autism Spectrum Disorder: Application of a Process-Model of Cultural Competence', *Journal of Multilingual Education Research*, 6(1): 91–110. Available at: http://fordham.bepress.com/jmer/vol6/iss1/6.

Institute of Medicine (US) Committee on Understanding and Eliminating Racial and Ethnic Disparities in Health Care. (2003), *Unequal Treatment: Confronting Racial and Ethnic Disparities in Health Care* (B. D. Smedley, A. Y. Stith, and A. R. Nelson, eds). Washington, DC: National Academies Press. Available at: http://www.ncbi.nlm.nih.gov/books/NBK220358/.

Kangas, S. E. N. (2014), 'When Special Education Trumps ESL: An Investigation of Service Delivery for ELLs with Disabilities', *Critical Inquiry in Language Studies*, 11(4): 273–306. Available at: https://doi.org/10.1080/15427587.2014.968070.

Kangas, S. E. N. (2017), '"That's Where the Rubber Meets the Road": The Intersection of Special Education and Dual Language Education', *Teachers College Record*, 119(7): 1–36.

Kantamneni, N. (2020), 'The impact of the COVID-19 pandemic on marginalized populations in the United States: A research agenda', *Journal of Vocational Behavior*, 119. https://doi.org/10.1016/j.jvb.2020.103439.

Levine, H. (2020, March 31), 'Parents and Schools Are Struggling to Care for Kids with Special Needs', *The New York Times*. Available at: https://www.nytimes.com/2020/03/31/parenting/kids-special-needs-coronavirus.html.

McKenna, L. (2019, April 16), 'District 75: "The Toughest Job You'll Ever Love"'. Edutopia. Available at: https://www.edutopia.org/article/district-75-toughest-job-youll-ever-love.

Moll, L. C., Amanti, C., Neff, D., and Gonzalez, N. (1992), 'Funds of Knowledge for Teaching: Using a Qualitative Approach to Connect Homes and Classrooms', *Theory into Practice*, 31(2): 132–41. Available at: https://doi.org/10.1080/00405849209543534.

Montelongo, A. (2015), 'Latino Parents' Perceptions of IEP Meetings', *McNair Scholars Journal*, 16: 109–30. Available at: http://www.csus.edu/mcnair/the-mcnair-experience/_2c-MSP-Journal/MeNair%20Scholars%20Journal%20-%20Volume%2016.pdf#page=58.

Oughton, H. (2010), 'Funds of Knowledge—A Conceptual Critique', *Studies in the Education of Adults*, 42(1): 63–78. Available at: https://doi.org/10.1080/02660830.2010.11661589.

Rodriguez, R. J., Blatz, E. T., and Elbaum, B. (2013), 'Strategies to Involve Families of Latino Students with Disabilities: When Parent Initiative Is Not Enough', *Intervention in School and Clinic*, 49(5): 263–70. Available at: https://doi.org/10.1177/1053451213513956.

Shapiro, E., and Harris, E. A. (2020, April 16), 'This Is Schooling Now for 200,000 N.Y.C. Children in Special Education', *The New York Times*. Available at: https://www.nytimes.com/2020/04/16/nyregion/special-education-coronavirus-nyc.html.

Tarasawa, B., and Waggoner, J. (2015), 'Increasing Parental Involvement of English Language Learner Families: What the Research Says', *Journal of Children and Poverty*, 21(2): 129–34. Available at: https://doi.org/10.1080/10796126.2015.1058243.

Trainor, A. A. (2010), 'Diverse Approaches to Parent Advocacy During Special Education Home–School Interactions Identification and Use of Cultural and Social Capital', *Remedial and Special Education*, 31(1): 34–47. Available at: https://doi.org/10.1177/0741932508324401.

Williams, R. B. (2017), 'Wealth Privilege and the Racial Wealth Gap: A Case Study in Economic Stratification', *The Review of Black Political Economy*, 44(3–4): 303–25. Available at: https://doi.org/10.1007/s12114-017-9259-8.

Wolfe, K., and Durán, L. K. (2013), 'Culturally and Linguistically Diverse Parents' Perceptions of the IEP Process', *Multiple Voices for Ethnically Diverse Exceptional Learners*, 13(2): 4–18. Available at: http://search.ebscohost.com/login.aspx?direct=true&db=eue&AN=95446094&site=ehost-live.

Yosso, T. J. (2005), 'Whose Culture Has Capital? A Critical Race Theory Discussion of Community Cultural Wealth', *Race Ethnicity and Education*, 8(1): 69–91. Available at: https://doi.org/10.1080/1361332052000341006.

Zhang, D., Katsiyannis, A., Ju, S., and Roberts, E. (2014), 'Minority Representation in Special Education: 5-Year Trends', *Journal of Child and Family Studies*, 23(1): 118–27. Available at: http://search.proquest.com.ezproxy.gc.cuny.edu/socscicoll/docview/1473940387/abstract/AC9AFCD9AC064A02PQ/2.

Zimmerman, A. (2019, January 7), 'NYC Spends $325 Million to Send Students with Disabilities to Private School'. Chalkbeat New York. Available at: https://ny.chalkbeat.org/2019/1/7/21106489/new-york-city-now-spends-325-million-a-year-to-send-students-with-disabilities-to-private-schools.

14

'We're in the Same Storm but NOT in the Same Boat': Searching for the Voices of Parents of Students with SEN in Covid-19 Times

Elisabeth De Schauwer, Inge Van de Putte and Geert Van Hove

Introduction

Flanders has been stuck with inclusive education for a very long time. Flemish education suffers from the syndrome of the inhibiting head start. Our highly developed special education system has poor quality reports and little connection to further education and/or inclusive employment, compounded by the inadequate knowledge and skills of those who implement inclusive education. Thus, we are confronted with an expert model and significant power differential. Lyotard described such a situation as 'le differend':

> A 'differend' would be a case of conflict, between (at least) two parties, that cannot be resolved for lack of a rule of judgement applicable to both of the arguments. One side's legitimacy does not imply the other's lack of legitimacy. However, applying a single rule of judgement to both in order to settle their 'differend' as though it were merely a litigation would be wrong (at least) for one of them (and both of them if neither side admits this rule). (*Differend, xi*, as cited in Young 2002: 72)

Lyotard offers a number of examples of differends, such as the relation of the colonizer and the colonized. Biesta (2015: 117) confirms that inclusion is usually colonial in nature, whereby a majority determines who is allowed to participate without questioning the basic ideas of the (educational) system. Inclusion is not seen as a real educational option.

In Flanders, this goes together with a superficial involvement of families with disabled children in regular education. Some students grow up in a supportive environment with a (larger) network; others are in more vulnerable situations due to socio-economic status, migrant background and single-parent families. Their parents are heavily dependent on regular schools regarding educational choices and are often vulnerable within the school system (Hodge and Runswick-Cole 2008; Zeitlin and Curcic 2014). Parents do not feel that education professionals really listen to them and have to motivate their choice for inclusive education repeatedly, with both teachers and support workers (Mortier et al. 2010). Choosing inclusive education requires substantive efforts from parents (Mortier et al. 2009). Their experience is that it demands a lot of energy to handle the constant danger of being thrown out of school each time difficulties arise, and they express feelings of loneliness in their responsibility to ensure their children have enough support (Van Hove et al. 2009).

In these tense circumstances, Flanders went in lockdown on 16 March 2020 because of Covid-19, unaware of what was to come. There is a lot of pressure to be flexible, to switch and shift rapidly. The impact was particularly hard for parents of disabled children due to the reduction or elimination of support, the isolation and the experience that inclusion remained conditional. How did they survive the first twelve months with Covid-19? We collected testimonies of parents choosing inclusive education in Flanders from March 2020 to March 2021. We have accessed these stories first-hand through the collaboration of the Support Network for Inclusion[1] with parents in schools and through the training of students at Ghent University, who provide support within the classroom.

The social debate around Covid-19 often misses the voices of parents of disabled. We follow Young's (2002) view that:

> Those who suffer a wrongful harm, or oppression lack the terms to express a claim of injustice within the prevailing normative discourse. ... Those who experience the wrong, and perhaps some others who sense it, may have no language for expressing the suffering as an injustice, but nevertheless they can tell *stories* that relate a sense of wrong. (Emphasis added, p. 72).

---

[1] Support Network for Inclusion originated from the parents' association, Parents for Inclusion. They offer information, make an inventory of thresholds and barriers that children and parents experience in regular schools, and give support to children and parents in inclusion situations in leisure time. The Support Network for Inclusion starts from individual questions, and tries to open them up to policy and focuses on sensibilization. (www.oudersvoorinclusie.be).

The stories teach that parents of disabled students have to fight even harder for inclusion in Covid-19 times, even to the extent that their gearbox is broken. This chapter seeks to have their voices heard through their testimonies.

Importance of Collecting Stories of Parents of Disabled Students

Young (2002) observes three modes of 'political communication': (1) greeting (public acknowledgement), making sure people do not feel ignored or, even worse, spoken about by others as though they were not there (57); (2) rhetoric, which is about privileging neutral, universal and dispassionate expression (63) and (3) narratives and situated knowledge, fostering understanding among members of a policy with very different experiences or assumptions about what is important (71). Storytelling is often the only vehicle for understanding the experiences of those in particular social situations – experiences not shared by those situated differently, but which they must understand to do justice (Young 2002: 73–4). Through stories, people can gain insight into the experiences, needs, projects, problems and pleasures of people in different social circumstances. Applying general normative principles to such insights is necessary to do justice (Young 2002: 74). We have long been interested in what we call the small stories of parents of disabled children. They give us access to education from a different perspective and allow us to experience inclusion and exclusion through the daily lived experiences. It is possible to see recurring lines, patterns and knots in parents' experiences. These can be used to critically examine our education system, inform our academic thinking and pinpoint areas for further development of inclusive education.

The small stories of parents help us have a more complex picture of what is working in our efforts towards inclusive education and where the obstacles are lying for students who want to participate and belong in regular education. On Covid-19 in the media and academic literature today, we see predominant voices of teachers, education boards and educational professionals concerned about students being disadvantaged, the pros and cons of working digitally and the organizational difficulties experienced across all levels of education. We rarely hear anything about special education or disabled children in regular education. When we do hear from parents, it is often about middle-class parents who find the combination of homework and following up on their children's schooling challenging. While we do not want to deny this, there is more. Edward Said talks in his work about contrapuntal reading, and this is what we want to do in this chapter:

> The goal of the contrapuntal reading is thus to not privilege any particular narrative but reveal the 'wholeness' of the text, the intermeshed, overlapping, and mutually embedded histories of metropolitan and colonized societies and the elite and subaltern. A contrapuntal reading is like a fugue which can contain 'two, three, four or five voices; they are all part of the same composition, but they are each distinct'. (Chowdhry 2007: 59–60)

We believe the experiences of parents of disabled students add something to the Covid-19 debate that is often overlooked or ignored too easily.

Why do we keep falling back on the stories of parents? To this end, we sought inspiration with Donna Haraway (in Le Guin 2019): 'Stories are capacious bags for collecting, carrying and telling the stuff of living ... to stitch, knot, weave and embroider both intimate and public peace, even as it unravels yet again' (3 and 10). It is a way for us to bring out stories that stay outside the big education picture and put a metaphorical horn to the voices of parents who are not being heard. We not only collect the stories themselves, we also continue to look at how to bring them out in the world. We see how parents try to stay afloat and keep looking for opportunities for their disabled children to offer them quality education in a society where the main narrative is still focused on special education. As Haraway notes, 'Le Guin taught us to keep telling the other story, the untold one, the life story' (in Le Guin 2019: 11). We see what is happening in the lives of these families, how what they want is different, and what they try to achieve every day, even when their children become adults:

> Conflict, competition, stress, struggle ... within the narrative conceived as carrier bag/belly/box/house/medicine bundle, may be seen as necessary elements of a whole which itself cannot be characterized either as conflict or as harmony, since its purpose is neither resolution nor stasis but continuing process. (Haraway 2016: 32)

It shows that inclusion cannot be defined, grasped and fixed straightforwardly; it is a continuous struggle (Allan 2007).

The stories of this process – captured in a big bag at many points, many moments and in great variety – continue to arouse our curiosity and inspire us. For Haraway, 'to carry, to wear, any of these bags is to enter into the knotting of capacities to respond, to become – with each other in the untold stories we need' (in Le Guin 2019: 12). The stories and experiences of parents of students with SEN continue to knock persistently on our door and demand responses. They prompt us to rethink how we look at education today:

> The urgent questions about how to tell stories that can help remake history for the kinds of living and dying that deserve thick presents and rich futures. In the spirit of Le Guin's insight that the fitting shape of a story is a sack, a hollowed-out container to hold things that bear meanings and enable relationships. (Haraway 2016: 11)

These stories of families ground us in lived realities in ways we recognize and connect with our own lives, while also seeing how education deals with difference and inclusion is realized in everyday lives. Next, we go to the stories and see what they can tell us about how parents have experienced the Covid-19 crisis, sometimes in unforeseeable ways, sometimes confronting familiar barriers.

What Do Parents of Disabled Students in Inclusive Education Have to Say?

We heard a lot about the pressure on parents' shoulders. It was something we all recognized, but here the weight was harder, deeper, more intense. It was also often unheard or underestimated. In Covid-19 times, the position of parents of children with SEN in the margins of our educational systems was confirmed. While we would like to start with a positive message about the resilient students, courageous parents, attentive teachers and creative support workers, the many stories forced us to start with the unbearable burden and far-reaching impact that led to frustrations and exhaustion. The Covid-19 crisis was a tough time for all of us, but certainly for parents of disabled children who choose regular education.

1. Covid-19 Measures Put Pressure on Parents

Parents who opt for inclusion make a choice outside the standard path. This choice for a (non-segregated) system often goes hand in hand with less support in schooling. In non-Covid-19 times, parents already do a lot of the work in finding support themselves – they are already vulnerable – but this was intensified by the crisis. Realizing optimal learning and opportunities for all children was a challenging task in Covid-19 times. It meant constant reorganization for everyone: schools switching to different codes (green, orange and red) with ever more far-reaching measures, periods of distance learning and online learning, parents working at home and students having to work more independently in their learning process. Parents of disabled children indicated that they were under pressure to keep everything running. During the various lockdowns, a lot was put 'on hold', including therapy, personal assistance and home support services. Consequently, even more of the burden fell on parents who could not utilize their usual (in)formal support network of family and friends:

> I am a teacher, a therapist, a breadwinner and also a little bit a parent. It feels that way. There seems to be no time for the latter or it is overshadowed by other tasks. Forcing your child to also finish the speech therapist's exercises is really not helping. (Parent of child, twelve years)

When Covid-19 contamination rates were less threatening, professional services opened or switched to online activities. The alternatives that gradually became available could not always adequately respond to the needs of the students and their families. In many situations, parents were unable to provide the support needed for a long time already. People were exhausted and felt they failed. The available alternatives also implied a great expectation on the part of parents. Parents combined these different roles and persevered for a long time, which took a lot of time and energy:

> The therapy could continue again, but online. Again I have to be around (operating the computer, checking the WIFI if the picture or sound is not working, scanning the exercises she has to write, sending them to the therapist …). My other tasks are again lying around, piling up and for my child it is also not nice that I am glued to her again. (Parent of child, eight years)

> I'm actually tired of being a therapist, being a taxi driver, being a support worker, doing all home tasks in the meantime … It's weighing on me, I'm starting to question everything. It also weighs on the family, and of course on her! She doesn't want to be so dependent on me. But at the moment, we still can't do otherwise. (Parent of child, nine years)

Parents experienced little support and felt they were on their own. Instead of getting more support in this challenging situation, they had to do with less. This was also the case for parents of disabled students in special education. They knew little about how things were done in the classroom, so they could not make adjustments or provide adequate support. In the case of online offers, parents indicated that they had to find out how things worked for themselves.

> What a jumble to find out about timetables and online classes. My child follows an individually adapted curriculum and joins different subjects in secondary education. We missed or came late to online classes, or were in the wrong online group. (Parent of youngster, fourteen years)

Parents constantly had the feeling of being in survival mode, and the mental pressures were very high. They had many considerations and doubts about whether their parenting was good enough and what they could expect for their child and family.

> Thinking in bubbles of two, three, four … is just not aligned with how we can run our family. Inclusion is work of many parties, of a large network and now we are expected to fold back completely on ourselves. (Parent of youngster, fourteen years)

Parents and children had been spending a lot of time together. This created challenges for parents: coming up with adapted activities, providing the necessary support, taking care of learning new skills and so on. Parents indicated that their own free time was slipping through their fingers. Tensions rose in families towards the other children as parents' energy drained. This experience was even more urgent for parents with a limited network, such as single parents:

> I am constantly filling up gaps and I am outdoing myself and our family in this. There is just no other option, we have no choice. (Parent of youngster, fifteen years)

Parents of children with SEN are already under pressure in normal circumstances. They often experience tensions to take on extra support and realize inclusive education. Due to the ongoing crisis, parents no longer got a break; their stress had become chronic and on different levels: emotionally, financially, physically and mentally:

> The past year I felt so alone as a single parent … It hurts me so much to find out that nobody, not the school, not the student counsellor, not the support worker, has even once asked how Tom was doing. (Parent of child, ten years)

> The physiotherapist recently sent me a list by email of activities I could do with my child. Very well intended, but I almost exploded. How am I supposed to add that on top of all the other roles? And how do I motivate him to do it again with Mum? (Parent of child, six years)

2. Covid-19 Measures Put Pressure on Inclusion in Regular Education

The first lockdown in the spring of 2020 was a shock for all of us. In those peculiar circumstances, the question for inclusive education arose (again) very suddenly and demanded much effort or evoked resistance (again). It shows that inclusive education is not an obvious choice in Flanders:

> We enjoyed relative peace. After four years at school you assume that some things have been built up. Corona seems to have turned everything upside down. The choice for inclusive education is questioned again. (Parent of child, eleven years)

> I read in the newspaper that some children were untraceable, my child's teacher and support worker were untraceable. After contact with the care coordinator, communication has been re-established. (Parent of child, nine years)

After the first lockdown, primary schools and the first grade of secondary education reopened at the end of May 2020. Covid-19 became the dominant window through which education had to be realized, which was not easy and required significant organization and respect for strict safety regulations. At the same time, starting up again did not mean simply picking up where we had left off. There was a different starting situation: students struggling with their well-being, no (suitable) teaching material, falling back on home education, teachers finding it more difficult to exchange information because of working in bubbles and minimal preparation of new teachers:

> We are already under pressure with all the measures, whether or not to switch to distance learning. To take on a person with these problems is really a bridge too far. We can't handle this as a school. That is what the care coordinator told us, when we wanted to return to school in May. (Parent of child, ten years)

When reopening, schools had to make extensive efforts to organize education safely. However, people are trying to mould the exceptional situation into known structures. We stubbornly clang to structures and procedures to handle Covid-19 in a school context. Rules and a technical approach to education took over, and the warm and supportive relations were threatened. In schools, we saw obstinate adherence to what was known and familiar. In contrast, the students who came to school needed additional flexibility, differentiation and focus on what was essential in the curriculum:

> Our child is also doing physical education in the fourth year. He likes it, enjoys the social contacts with the other children. But because of the current corona

measures this is no longer allowed. The school suggests that he goes to the care farm for half a day. We doubt that this would be better (aren't these extra contacts with people outside the school?) and are afraid that this will also make his place at school more questionable later on. (Parent of youngster, seventeen years)

Teachers and schools experienced tremendous pressure, and this went hand in hand with a narrow focus on academic learning. It was often about catching up on knowledge production, which did not always align with an appreciative and affirmative view of the efforts made by disabled students to move forward in their learning process. The focus on cognitive progress came at the expense of attention to participation and well-being at school:

The school has decided to replace the music lessons with two extra hours of language support. Then they set up remedial groups. My son is in three different groups. It was just announced. We have our doubts about whether this will be the solution or will have the opposite effect. (Parent of child, ten years)

Getting reasonable accommodations was difficult throughout Covid-19 pandemic. Adjustments were dropped, they were not 'translated' into an online lesson, or this only happened after the pupil or parents asked for it. The average student prevailed. Parents and students worried about the impact of not having reasonable adjustments in the final evaluations:

When I saw Louis's marks, I went to ask what support he was getting and what aids he could use. Only when I started thinking about this, they did start to consider how the adjustments should be translated to the online lessons. Since then, things have been going much better and there is also more mildness. The announcement of the orientation to another field of study was quickly buried. (Parent of youngster, thirteen years)

Ensuring inclusion in leisure time for disabled children is not easy under normal circumstances. Many children had to put their leisure time on hold during the year. Inclusion quickly faded into the background, support workers changed and needed change. We saw a lot of creativity in making free time possible – from fitness rooms to games in the garden – but this was no substitute for the real thing. The long period of no or limited supply significantly impacted families' quality of life, with empty diaries, few social contacts with peers and less connection in a group. Loneliness and social isolation weighed heavily on children and young people.

> Fortunately, there are four of them [in the family], because unfortunately there are not many other contacts. You can feel that this weighs heavily on them and that they miss it. Fortunately, the eldest can go for a walk with a friend, who is also of a certain age, but unfortunately the others cannot. All their leisure time is also taken away from them, given the risk … We really can't risk anything. (Parent of child, eleven years)

> We have built up a strong network over the years and he would have been able to continue seeing his friends in the basket and at the Chiro. Not so! Fortunately, the Chiro has started up again, but the basketball club already announced in December that they would not be starting up again, but you can feel that the connection is somewhat gone. (Parent of youngster, fourteen years)

3. Covid-19 Put Pressure on the Possibilities of Collaboration with Families

Consultation and communication at school was reduced to a minimum. Parents reported missing transparent collaboration, clear information and agreements, insight and flexibility in classwork and coordination around support. In some schools, a parent was not seen as an 'essential' actor in the educational process:

> In normal circumstances, I theoretically have 10 chances a week to briefly speak to the teacher. Now it is literally 0 out of 10, and there is no alternative. I notice that this weighs on the course. It's no longer about a month without a chat at the classroom door, it's about a whole school year in which this is not possible. (Parent of child, eight years)

However, there were some schools working creatively with consultations at a distance in gymnasiums or other large spaces, meetings on the playground or digital consultation. But most parents experienced that they were not invited to discuss and make shared decisions on the school trajectory. We noticed that the Covid-19 measures very abruptly draw a line through parents' position as full partners at school and in leisure time. Parents were (literally) not allowed in anymore, had to keep their distance and were forced to be excluded from the school environment. Parents indicated little thought was given to the impact of this missed communication:

> The school consultation about Ada went digitally. The support worker, teacher and special needs coordinator sat together at the computer. My connection was not always good, they couldn't hear me all the time. But they didn't pay attention,

I saw how they continued with the agenda and didn't wait for my input. I literally felt left out. (Parent of child, five years)

Parents not always found an ally in what was allowed, what was possible and what was required. This placed parents in the role of 'demanding' or 'difficult' parents. Parents became aware that collaborative teaming within the regular school context was not self-evident, and Covid-19 made this painfully clear. Shared care and support were shifted to a strongly individualized responsibility:

> Ward follows an individually adapted curriculum. This also means that his internship has a different content, both in terms of where he is doing it and in terms of the aims. Given the corona measures, he can no longer do an internship. The school did not respond to messages from the work place. As parents, we had to take the initiative to provide a meaningful alternative. Nobody asks us what the impact is for Ward, but also for us as a family. (Parent of youngster, seventeen years)

Parent contacts and consultations with educational professionals were organized digitally, often only when things were difficult and at very irregular times during the school year. Contact with the teacher became unintentionally fraught, with parents often having to ask or insist on consultation. Some parents were not able to connect digitally because of a lack of material and/or the technical skills required. Little thought was given to the accessibility of digital consultation for every parent:

> Normally in a physical consultation I get the space to briefly explain to parents in accessible language what was said and I notice a greater effort during the meeting by all partners. Now people talk so fast that there is no room for this, and they don't wait for me to explain. (Home-based counsellor)

Digital consultation also provided advantages. For example, no travel time meant it was easier to find a moment that suited all those involved, and the meeting felt more structured and efficient.

4. Covid-19 also Gave Perspective: Importance of Silver Linings in Families' Experiences

Parents of disabled students were masters at overcoming unforeseen hurdles on their inclusive pathway. They were resilient and could deal with stress and setbacks and sometimes came stronger. It is important to make room for positive aspects, share experiences and stories, and learn from them:

> The lockdown also gave us the opportunity to let go of all our obligations. What a relief! (Parent of child, eight years)

> Now working with the computer was applicable to every young person. Also for my son. He has never used the computer before, here a world has opened up. Also to group work and social relationships. (Parent of youngster, fifteen years)

Compulsory digital learning and more independent work also created future opportunities:

> Working at his own pace and alternating with movement is something we have tried to build into his program. Because those things made such a difference in the lockdown! (Parent of child, twelve years)

This period also provided opportunities to know children and young people differently. It gave parents energy and insight into the possibilities, interests and talents of their child. It offered opportunities for other, more informal learning (like working with a smartphone, baking a cake or listening to science podcasts), and insight into how to explore and approach what is needed. Parents became even more aware of what 'tailor-made' and 'at own pace' meant:

> We saw her doing tasks in the household that we didn't know she could already do independently. That was really the application of the lessons in practice. Babysitting the nephew, with an eye on him of course, went very well and she really enjoyed it. That gives a perspective on an internship and possible voluntary work in the future! (Parent of youngster, fourteen years)

Parents (re)wrote their child's 'own manual', based on this intense period of working together on schoolwork. Young people got to know their own 'user manual' better because of the new circumstances.

The small stories of parents provided moments of hope. Parents and teachers were forced to switch positions at times and put themselves in each other's shoes. Overall, they felt that explicitly focusing on well-being and the development of resilience was and is necessary:

> A very short email to check how Selma is doing during this period? Can Selma place everything? Can she keep some informal contact with her class? This email from a teacher felt like a world of difference. They thought about her. It is good not to be forgotten. Even though I realise that for teachers the rat race has started again. (Parent of child, eleven years)

We certainly wanted to pay attention to these small stories and practices that often helped parents politically resist dominant discourses of inferiority and exclusion at school and in society. It brought us closer to what really mattered to parents and children, and made the Covid-19 pandemic very clear. The difference was made over and over again in small nuances.

Conclusion

So, we can collect stories and these stories help to bring marginalized voices into the piece of music to enrich that music's wholeness and destabilize the conventional readings of the world. This is how we organize 'rupture', states Rancière (in Biesta 2015); this is how we choose the underrepresented. Further, it helps us expose 'the political' and gives attention to the power–knowledge nexus. We need what Latour (2004) outlines in connecting with families of disabled children: 'assembling and understanding that if something is constructed it means it is fragile and thus in great need of care and caution'. Small interventions, little support and a bit more time are not enough as solutions to the learning needs of disabled students. Parents' stories show us that we need more and to cut deeper. The interventions and support we provide must go to the bone and address the structure of regular education to make changes in the 'grammar of schooling', which Tyack and Tobin (1994) define as 'the regular structures and rules that organize the work of instruction' (454). They observed that schools have a set of grammatical rules and structures that feel very natural, are taken for granted and seem necessary for smooth operation. Covid-19 once more reinforced the importance of this grammar of schooling, which often went against the flexibility and openness necessary to create inclusive learning environments.

Currently, school is considered a series of places where boundaries are reinforced again. This leads to children being classified as either falling within these boundaries or out of them (Naraian 2017). There are always students who are seen as slow, dependent or incapable of learning (Deschenes, Cuban and Tyack 2001). Covid-19 made the boundaries more distinct and outspoken about more children not belonging in the regular school. So in the post-Covid-19 time, we need to support schools to make their borders more porous and create flexible learning environments for disabled students. We need more stories from students, and families, to help us re-imagine and rethink education and open up our repertoires of what we recognize and value as good schooling. As Haraway (2016: 115–16) asserts:

> Each time a story helps me remember what I thought I knew, or introduces me to new knowledge, a muscle critical for caring about flourishing gets some aerobic

exercise. Such exercise enhances collective thinking and movement too. ... We are all responsible to and for shaping conditions for multispecies flourishing in the face of terrible histories, but not in the same ways. The differences matter— in ecologies, economies, species, lives.

Differences are not only about *where* the student is educated but also *how* the student is educated. Educational relationships and power structures were hardly changed in Covid-19 times; indeed, we saw an even greater separation between professionals and parents. There was minimal communication and often only when problems arose. Teachers had a very technical relationship with their students to pass on the content. Instead, we need to develop warm relationships, as warm and supportive relationships are the true core of (inclusive) education. We should work from strengthening partnerships, paying attention to understanding each other's perspective, emergent listening and re-imagining what education could/should become. We can continue to learn from each other and shift our hierarchical positions. Inclusion requires an openness to keep looking for (little) opportunities and creative solutions each time to change the grammar of schooling in the long run:

> It matters what matters we use to think other matters with; it matters what stories we tell to tell other stories with; it matters what knots knot knots; what thoughts think thoughts, what descriptions describe descriptions, what ties tie ties. It matters what stories make worlds, what worlds make stories. (Haraway 2016: 12).

Stories will be the best possible vaccine to strive and re-imagine inclusive education for the future.

Acknowledgements

We want to thank Evelien Leyseele, Astrid Winderickx and Matthias Van Raemdonck, who captured with us a bag full of stories in working closely together with parents of children with SEN. We consider them allies and were able to bring in a lot of our shared conversations and work in this chapter. Thank you also for contributing to earlier versions.

References

Allan, J. (2007), *Rethinking Inclusive Education: The Philosophers of Difference in Practice* (Vol. 5). Rotterdam: Springer Science & Business Media.

Allan, J. (2020), 'Disability Studies and Interdisciplinarity: Interregnum or Productive Interruption'?, in L. Ware (ed.), *Critical Readings in Interdisciplinary Disability Studies*, 5–17. Cham: Springer.
Biesta, G. J. (2015). *Beautiful risk of education*. London: Routledge.
Chowdhry, G. (2007), 'Edward Said and Contrapuntal Reading: Implications for Critical Interventions in International Relations', *Millennium*, 36(1): 101–16.
Deschenes, S., Cuban, L., and Tyack, D. (2001), 'Mismatch: Historical Perspectives on Schools and Students Who Don't Fit Them', *Teachers College Record*, 103(4): 525–47.
Haraway, D. J. (2016), *Staying with the Trouble*. Durham, NC: Duke University Press.
Hodge, N., and Runswick-Cole, K. (2008), 'Problematising Parent–Professional Partnerships in Education', *Disability & Society*, 23(6): 637–47.
Latour, B. (2004), 'Why Has Critique Run Out of Steam? From Matters of Fact to Matters of Concern', *Critical Inquiry*, 30(2): 225–48.
Le Guin, U. K. (2019), *The Carrier Bag Theory of Fiction*. Ignota Books.
Mortier, K., De Schauwer, E., Van de Putte, I., and Van Hove, G. (2010), *Inclusief onderwijs in de praktijk.* Antwerpen: Garant.
Mortier, K., Hunt, P., Desimpel, L., and Van Hove, G. (2009), 'With Parents at the Table: Creating Supports for Children with Disabilities in General Education Classrooms', *European Journal of Special Needs Education*, 24(4): 337–54.
Naraian, S. (2017), *Teaching for Inclusion: Eight Principles for Effective and Equitable Practice*. New Yrok City: Teachers College Press.
Tyack, D., and Tobin, W. (1994), 'The "grammar" of Schooling: Why Has It Been so Hard to Change?', *American Educational Research Journal*, 31(3): 453–79.
Van Hove, G., De Schauwer, E., Mortier, K., Bosteels, S., Desnerck, G., and Van Loon, J. (2009), 'Working with Mothers and Fathers of Children with Disabilities: Metaphors Used by Parents in a Continuing Dialogue', *European Early Childhood Education Research Journal*, 17(2): 187–201.
Young, I. M. (2002), *Inclusion and Democracy*. Oxford: Oxford University Press.
Zeitlin, V. M., and Curcic, S. (2014), 'Parental Voices on Individualized Education Programs: "Oh, IEP Meeting Tomorrow? Rum Tonight!"', *Disability & Society*, 29(3): 373–87.

Conclusion

15

Out of Crisis the New Future: Concluding Thoughts on Inclusive and Equitable Education for All with a View from Scotland

David Watt

On 30 January 2020, the World Health Organisation declared the Covid-19 pandemic a public health emergency of international concern. The virus, transmitted across the globe, unfolding in stages and surges, infected tens of millions and resulted in deaths for over a half million people by June, then one million deaths by October 2020. States' responses varied across nations and jurisdictions. However, by the end of April, its effect was near total across the globe and within education systems. Schools closed in over 185 countries. According to the World Bank (2020) approximately 90 per cent of students were out of school. By May, over 1.5 billion children and young people were being affected. The pandemic's impact on school education was universal, systemic, inclusive of almost all – the new globalized education crisis.

Together with its systemic effects the pandemic uncovered and exposed already present structural and institutional inequalities within schooling. Such inequalities featured in different contexts and among specific groups of children and young people. The summary of the United Nations Educational Scientific and Cultural Organisation (UNESCO) report titled 'Reaching the Marginalised' recording progress towards their agenda of Education for All from 2010 stated:

> Failure to address inequalities, stigmatization and discrimination linked to wealth, gender, ethnicity, language, location and disability is holding back progress towards Education for All. (UNESCO 2010)

The UNESCO report warned that considering the global financial crisis of 2008

> Education is at risk and countries must develop more inclusive approaches, linked to wider strategies for protecting vulnerable populations and overcoming inequality. (UNESCO 2010)

In 2012, the OECD identified the need for equity and inclusion to feature in school systems:

> Equity in education means that personal or social circumstances such as gender, ethnic origin or family background, are not obstacles to achieving educational potential (fairness) and that that all individuals reach at least a basic minimum level of skills (inclusion). (OECD 2012:9)

Marginalized groups of learners already experienced poorer outcomes around factors linked to social background, gender, disability, ethnicity and sexual orientation and other characteristics. The OECD noted that:

> across OECD countries almost one of every five students does not reach a basic minimum level of skills to function in today's societies (indicating lack of inclusion). Students from low socio-economic background are twice as likely to be low performers, implying that personal or social circumstances are obstacles to achieving their educational potential (indicating lack of fairness). (OECD 2012:9)

As Covid-19 impacted, many of the marginalized learners were not fully supported during lockdowns, they could not participate in learning as they lacked access to suitable resources at home or digital technology was not readily available. The effect of Covid-19 was of a twin-track nature involving deschooling populations across education systems and further marginalizing groups of disadvantaged learners. In terms of social justice as conceived by Fraser and Olson (2008) such learners lacked parity of participation before and during Covid.

Within this text, practitioners offer examples of ways to engage with learners often misrecognized in education systems across the globe. Such examples include work with learners and parents in disadvantaged Roma communities in Romania (Drown) and refugee children in different settings (Barber, Bilgeri, McIntyre). Writers also identify the effects of maldistribution of resources in terms of inequalities (Spiteri) and highlight the need to ensure marginalized learners are represented and have a voice in education systems (Mowat). In their chapter based within the Austrian education system Lindner, Gitschthaler, Gutschik, Kast, Honcik, Corazza and Schwab highlight learners doubly disadvantaged being from a refugee background and intersecting with the challenges in learning the German language. Lindner and others identify that refugee children learning German encountered aspects of a system that imposed grade repetition and lack of progression through stages of their schooling. An emphasis of an intersectional approach was also part of the focus when considering the collaborative support for mothers of children and young people with emergent bilingual skills and disabilities within Cioè-Peña's chapter based on experiences of the Latinx community in New York, New York.

This concluding chapter proposes that regenerating our education systems entails addressing the twin-track effects of Covid-19, encompassing both its systemic and marginalizing consequences. In 2017, UNESCO published its guide to ensuring inclusion and equity. Here, inclusive education was defined as 'a process that helps overcome barriers limiting the presence, participation and achievement of learners'(UNESCO 2017). Inclusive education is now seen as a principle that welcomes diversity among all learners together with an aim to eliminate social exclusion (Ainscow 2020). Coming out of crisis, the new future needs to build back and beyond any version of the previous 'normal'. Injustices, injuries and insults that marginalize learners highlight the need to address all affected by such processes. The chapter considers a new future addressing inequalities and injustices through high-quality and equitable schooling provided with inclusive education at the system level and beyond.

Normality before Covid-19

In 2015, the World Education Forum (WEF) in Incheon, South Korea, brought together some 1,600 participants from 160 countries, including the United Nations Secretary-General, global education leaders and influential advocates from civil society and the private sector. WEF's final report, the Incheon Declaration (WEF 2015) articulated a new vision for education globally, thus:

> This new vision is fully captured by the proposed Sustainable Development Goal 4 (SDG 4) 'Ensure inclusive and equitable quality education and promote lifelong learning opportunities for all' and its corresponding targets. (67)

The new vision assumed an approach that was to be transformative and came with warnings about potential disruption to education.

> we note with serious concern that, today, … crises, violence and attacks on education institutions, natural disasters and pandemics continue to disrupt

education and development globally. We commit to developing more inclusive, responsive and resilient education systems to meet the needs of children, youth and adults in these contexts. (68)

In 2016, the United Nations Committee on the Rights of People with Disabilities (UNCRPD) published General Comment No.4 on the Right to inclusive education (UNCRPD 2016) setting out a strategic approach towards inclusive education.

In 2019, the UN Human Rights Council (UNHRC 2019) underscored the idea of inclusive education as a multiplier right in its 'Empowering Children with Disabilities' document. Each of these documents translated the vision of Sustainable Development Goal (SDG) 4 into necessary policy changes and practices to improve outcomes for marginalized groups including children with disabilities.

The guidance from the UNCRPD and UNHRC noted that situations of humanitarian emergencies and natural disasters disproportionately impact on the right to inclusive education with heightened risks for those with disabilities. Both documents proposed the need for change to the entire education system to include all students and stated that change was not solely about children with different needs adjusting to the standardized requirements of educational institutions.

In 2020, UNESCO planned for the publication of Global Education Monitoring (GEM) report. Its theme was to be inclusive education now with a broader meaning encompassing all learners.

Before Covid-19: The Complexities and Challenges of Inclusive Education – Drawing on Examples from the Scottish Education System

Given the broad definition of inclusive education, as yet no country in the world has implemented a fully inclusive system successfully. The UN has reported on the progress nation states have made on their approach to inclusive education. In 2019 (UNCRPD 2019) the Special Rapporteur welcomed the approach of the New Brunswick province in Canada:

> where all children with disabilities attend regular schools. In the view of the Special Rapporteur, that situation is one of the best in the world and should be taken as a role model. The government of New Brunswick adopted legislation

and policies requiring the inclusion of students with disabilities in general schools and the provision of support in an integrated and interdisciplinary framework.

In an extensive content analysis of the Committee's Concluding Observations 2011–2018 for seventy-two states, Byrne noted that over twenty different thematic areas of concern were expressed by the committee in their observations across seventy-two countries. In most reports concerns about educational placement, the presence of learners in local schools, were mentioned. While in terms of recommendations, twenty-four different proposals were made including recommendations in respect of staff training, reasonable adjustments, increased budgetary allocations, a more inclusive and quality education and compliance with SDG 4 (Byrne 2022)

While in 2017, the UN through its UNCRPD informed the UK of concerns about progress with inclusive education including rising numbers of children attending segregated special schooling. The Special Rapporteur recommended that the UK with its four education jurisdictions should 'develop a comprehensive and coordinated legislative and policy framework for inclusive education' (UNCRPD 2017:11) and 'adopt and implement a coherent strategy financed with concrete time and measurable goals on increasing and improving inclusive education' (UNCRPD 2017:11). At the onset of the pandemic no progress had been made within the four jurisdictions of the UK.

Among countries across Europe the European Agency for Special Needs and Inclusive Education (EASNIE), established in 1996, is an independent organization encouraging collaboration among its thirty-one member countries. It has aimed to work with its member countries towards more inclusive education systems. Their ultimate vision for inclusive education systems is to ensure that all learners of any age are provided with meaningful, high-quality educational opportunities in their local community, alongside their friends and peers (EASNIE 2015). EASNIE's array of projects has recently included

- Changing Role of Specialist Provision in Supporting Inclusive Education;
- Country Policy Review and Analysis;
- Raising the Achievement of All Learners in Inclusive Education;
- Supporting Inclusive School Leadership.

The agency notes that all European countries are committed towards ensuring more inclusive education systems. It recognized that nations do so 'in different ways, depending on their past and current contexts and histories'.

The complexity of being inclusive of all can be referenced in terms of examples from the Scottish education system drawn from disability, sexual orientation, social background and ethnicity. Examples from Scotland emphasize the complexity of the challenges across diverse contexts and groups.

Scotland has had a history of special education and special schools. It claims the establishment of a deaf school in Edinburgh at the end of eighteenth century. For most of the last twenty-five years as the developments of inclusive education progressed, the numbers of special schools and children and young people present in them have changed little in Scotland. About 2 per cent of school students attend special settings (Scottish Government 2020a).

The Scottish government regards the system as inclusive and has offered guidance on the presumption of mainstreaming (Scottish Government [2004], amended 2017). In recent years Scotland had three parliamentary debates on inclusive education over the period 2017-19. In January 2019, in the latest of three debates the Scottish Parliament agreed on a motion that mainstreaming, the Scottish policy towards a more inclusive education system, had 'laudable intentions' but that more consideration was to be given to placing children in special schools. Since then, more disabled children have been placed in special schools (Scottish Parliament Report, 2019).

In terms of inequality arising from social background and achievement, little progress has been made in narrowing attainment gaps among learners from areas of deprivation and those from more affluent areas. In the evaluation of three years of Scotland's attainment fund, the data showed a decline in attendance among children and young people from areas of greatest deprivation. The evaluation report concluded:

> Overall, the attainment data presents a mixed and complex picture of progress towards closing the poverty-related attainment gap. (Scottish Government 2019a)

The OECD (2007, 2015) has broadly reported Scotland as an inclusive system in terms of the socially equitable nature of its schooling at primary, especially, and secondary stages. Scotland has a small non-state private education sector with about 4 per cent of the school population attending about one hundred private schools, mainly in the cities.

Scotland has successfully implemented an aspect of inclusive education by addressing issues around sexual orientation through curricular inserts to promote education on Lesbian, Gay, Bisexual, Transgender and Intersex (LGBTI) education. After a campaign conducted to persuade politicians, almost all Members of the Scottish Parliament (MSPs) offered political will for the Scottish curriculum to be more inclusive and the government welcomed teaching and learning in schools about LGBTI issues. In briefly considering aspects of diversity in terms of social background, disability and sexual orientation it is clear that the progress in Scotland is one that does present 'a mixed and complex picture'.

Before January 2020, in a high-income country such as Scotland, children and young people faced inequality linked to disability or social background. In their chapter in this book Folostina and Patrascoiu map out the extent and impact of poverty on children in Romania. Fraser (2010) has defined such inequalities as leading to injustice and that overcoming 'injustice means dismantling institutionalised obstacles that prevent some people from participating on a par with others, as full partners in social interaction' (Fraser 2010). Such examples of misrecognition were evidenced in terms of the differing rates across inclusive themes of presence, participation and achievement encountered by groups of children and young people within school education. After March 2020, they were to be further amplified through the course of the pandemic.

During COVID-19: Shocks to Schools and Systems

The response to rapid transmission of the virus through populations across the globe led to wide-ranging impact on education systems. Governments and Ministries of Education moved to close schools, centres and universities, cancelled processes of national certification or external examinations, set up online learning and multi-platform approaches, managed risks to children's health and well-being and provided basic needs such as school meals.

The World Bank in its paper 'Shocks to Education and Policy Responses' (2020) set out that the world was already off track for meeting SDG 4 in terms of high-quality equitable and inclusive education and also its ambitious targets for example 'all girls and boys complete free, equitable and quality primary and secondary education' (Target 4.1). The 'Shocks to Education' paper identified other aspects of the world's learning crisis:

> The COVID-19 pandemic now threatens to make education outcomes even worse … The damage will become even more severe as the health emergency translates into a deep global recession. (5)

Back in 1971, Ivan Illich published 'Deschooling Society', which proposed that as institutions like schools were manipulative institutions, they should be ended with no need for obligatory attendance at such institutions. His definition of school was 'the age-specific, teacher related process requiring full-time attendance at an obligatory curriculum' (Illich 1971: 14). He went on to state:

> school is obligatory and becomes schooling for schooling's sake: an enforced stay in the company of teachers, which pays off in the doubtful privilege of more such company. (Illich 1971: 10)

The deschooled society, as envisaged by Illich, may well have rapidly emerged globally within the Covid-19 crisis of 2020. However, this view and Illich's vision neglect the wider role of schools in contributing to citizenship and health and well-being, beyond the certification gains of 'the company of teachers'. Schooling can establish an environment where 'the development of collective capabilities creates spaces where disadvantaged groups can gain ground', the focus of Bilgeri's chapter on possibilities of, and practice in, quality education for refugee children, even during a pandemic. Schools for many are places of safety, security and well-being. During the pandemic, staff in schools sought to ensure children were fed as well as attended to their learning and pastoral needs (as highlighted by Joan Mowat her chapter on mental well-being). While Mngaza in considering the historical context of Black children and young people in UK schools proposes that schooling with a trauma-informed approach could extend the possibility that schools can be a place of culturally relevant psychological support for all children.

In addition, Illich did not consider fully the role of the school as an agent of social change. The vision inherent in SDG 4 places a wider challenge on schooling than certification or the exam factory highlighted by Illich. By transforming the nature of schooling, we remove structural and institutional barriers within schools and challenge interpersonal attitudes that support inequity. Apple (2013) has asked the question: can education change society? His answer, with its conditions, was positive:

> The answer can be 'Yes.' But if and only if what we do is grounded in larger projects, respectful of our differences, connected to the process of building and defending decentered unities that will give us collective strength, and mindful that the path will be long and difficult ... there is a rich history of people and movements inside and outside of education who can provide sources of strength ... Keeping these traditions alive and pushing these impulses forward in educational institutions is even more important today. (Apple 2013)

As we have seen there has been little change in Scotland in moving resources from segregated settings to supporting inclusive education for children and young people with disabilities. The success in Scottish schools in promoting teaching and learning on LGBTI issues has encouraged teachers and young people to establish groups of Gay/Straight Alliances in some secondary schools. While aiming to reduce the gap in attainment linked to socio-economic background, the Scottish government allocated over £300 million through its Pupil Equity Fund and Scottish Attainment Challenge though it only led to success that is mixed and complex.

Yet no system of schools has been fully successful in going beyond a complex and mixed picture of engaging with the different contexts and specific groups that are marginalized or disadvantaged through schooling. This complexity and mixture of outcomes for groups occur within systems that lack the strategic approach to inclusive education at system level.

Yet globally, no education system has fully implemented inclusive education successfully. In combination with the strategic gap, no communities or schools are yet fully effective in reducing barriers to learning from diverse groups and different contexts. In 2007, the OECD offered a summary of the position in Scotland in regard to its journey towards being equitable and inclusive.

'Children from poorer communities and low socio-economic status homes are more likely than others to underachieve.' In terms of the place of diversity and identity in Scottish education the OECD stated, in terms of Fraser's misrecognition and maldistribution:

'In Scotland, **who you are** is far more important than **what school you attend**.'

In 2015 the mixed and complex picture was highlighted in the next OECD report, which praised Scotland's inclusive education highlighting the extent of students of different socio-economic backgrounds attending the same school, the achievement of immigrant students who achieve at higher levels than their non-immigrant peers and students of Asian origin, especially Asian Chinese, who achieve in school and gain positive follow-up destinations at higher levels than their white peers (OECD 2015).

The OECD reports replicated the mixed and complex nature in respect of diversity and offered no comment on children with disabilities, special schools or the inclusive education agenda of UNCRPD or UNESCO. Both reports indicated more positive outcomes for girls in respect of attainment data in most curricular areas at secondary school (OECD 2007, 2015).

Before and during Covid-19 no nation had successfully implemented a fully inclusive system. Without fully implementing inclusive education at system level, countries were not able to improve outcomes for all marginalized groups though successes for some specific groups were realized.

Responding to Covid-19: Learning at Home and the Digital Divide

In noting the shocks to the systems from the pandemic, the World Bank in their 'Shocks to Education' report (World Bank 2020) suggested a threefold approach involving coping, managing continuity and improving and accelerating. It warned not to look to a return to systems that generated inequalities previously but to build back better.

Scotland closed its schools on 23 March 2020 and made plans to set up an Education Recovery Group. By late April a data intelligence report (Scottish Government 2020b) identified vulnerable children with a multi-agency plan as about 10 per cent of the population of children aged 0–17, at 97,000. This definition of vulnerable or at risk excluded large numbers of children with additional support needs in Scotland.

During April, the attendance figure of vulnerable children with multi-agency plans attending schools and hubs was around five hundred, which was only about 0.5 per cent of those identified as vulnerable by the Scottish government. In addition, about five thousand attended a school or hub for a free school meal, about 5 per cent of those entitled to that provision. Over the following weeks, attendance levels slightly improved. However, most children and young people did not attend such hubs.

Teachers and pupils were able to access a national online learning platform, GLOW connect. Based on statistics published by the national education improvement agency, Education Scotland (Education Scotland 2020) over the three months of the pandemic between March and June, numbers of children and young people logging in to the systems increased from 211,618 in February to 351,905. The latter figure was approximately 50 per cent of children and young people in schools in Scotland. No disaggregated data on users were available from this national system in terms of disability, gender, social background, ethnicity, religion or other characteristics. During the pandemic almost all teachers had logged into the platform in May 2020.

For families, updates on provisions and changes to advice were being sought through online and social media. However, many families did not have access to smart phones or internet technology. Nevertheless, this led to links between home and school that were more collaborative within communities.

> The immediate response to the crisis, has involved extraordinary effort, from community groups and 3rd sector organisations, and from health and local

authority services. Many senior leaders have indicated, this has often been achieved by working with and alongside families, and 'not by doing things to them'. (Scottish Government 2020c)

In a similar development, Drown's chapter on research for a pilot project to promote digital access with Roma communities in Romania noted an additional benefit that

> parents understood more about the school system, which was operated by non-Roma teachers with a system designed by the majority culture of the country. This way they [parents] felt able to become more involved and confident about their children's education, therefore to engage with schools when they reopened.

Black (2020) highlighted concerns about different inequalities raised through a survey of teachers carried out by the main teachers' trade union, the Educational Institute of Scotland (EIS). Concerns were raised regarding access to internet, lack of working space at home and information about online learning in different languages for parents. The overall percentage of households in Scotland with internet access was 87 per cent. While 94 per cent of households in least deprived areas had internet access in the most deprived areas it was 82 per cent of households. (Scottish Government 2019b). The government committed additional funding to provide tablets to address the divide.

A study across the four nations of the UK identified an expected learning loss that varied according to social background and was marked within primary and secondary education.

> Socio-economic differences in the estimated education loss are marked.

> - For children in primary education, those from the most advantaged families will have lost on average 24% of a standard deviation across subjects by the time schools reopen in autumn, while children from the most disadvantaged families will have lost 31% of a standard deviation. (Pensiero, Kelly and Bokhove 2020)

By June, in Scotland, discussions considered dates for return to schooling, for the starting date of the new term of 11 August. By then, schools would have been closed for over seven weeks. In June, the government moved from a form of blended learning with part-time attendance towards fully opening schools for the middle of August in line with scientific advice. Additional resources were to be offered to ensure aspects of a digital divide could be narrowed. External examinations for 2021 were to be postponed with consideration of reviewing high-stakes external examinations in the future.

In their study of responses across three primary schools in Iceland Gunnþórsdóttir and Sigurðardóttir outline the changes in teaching practices for those children and young people with support needs and special education provision. Their chapter considers not only how teachers responded during the pandemic but also the potential long-term consequences of those children and young people in vulnerable positions.

Post Covid-19 – No Build Back 'Normal'

Covid-19 provoked disruption in the education systems of the world, a new crisis. Its effects will restrict any opportunity to build back better. A return to some pre-Covid normal would only mean that the problems of discrimination and exclusion from the past would be present. As shown, education systems, north and south, were not yet successfully achieving inclusive education for all learners. Going forward the roadmap out of the pandemic needs to take account of the need for systemic change and tackling inequalities faced by the marginalized. For instance, from the Italian perspective as shared by Guerini, Ruzzante and Travaglini, a set of changes to schooling – technological, organizational and pedagogic – are seen as necessary to build forward better in the twenty-first century beyond the after-effects of the pandemic.

In the last week of June 2020 as the pandemic continued to roll out across the world, UNESCO published its Global Education Monitoring Report 2020 on inclusion and education. The report noted that

> Characteristics commonly associated with inequality of distribution include gender, remoteness, wealth, disability, ethnicity, language, migration, displacement, incarceration, sexual orientation, gender identity and expression, religion, and other beliefs and attitudes. Some mechanisms contributing to inequality are universal while others are specific to social and economic contexts, as the Covid-19 pandemic has laid bare. (24)

Inclusive education, as broadly defined by the GEM report, offers a twin-track response to the pandemic – a transformative change that recognizes that structural and institutional inequalities are barriers that must be eliminated and crunched while targeting finance and resources to those marginalized and disadvantaged in a system that previously operated on a 'one-size-fits-most' approach.

In its introduction the report then asks

> whether it really is necessary to seek justifications for inclusive education to be pursued. It notes that debating the benefits of inclusive education can be seen as tantamount to debating the benefits of abolition of slavery or indeed of apartheid. (8)

The GEM report includes sections on laws and policies, data, governance and finance, curricula, textbooks and assessments, teachers and education support personnel, schools, students, parents and communities. All the themes are part of the landscape for a roadmap out of the crisis landscape of Covid-19, forging new inclusive and resilient education systems for all learners. It also places an importance upon an inclusive curriculum that tackles racism and discrimination including textbooks and assessment that take account of diversity.

In 2015 in response to another crisis after the terrorist attacks in France and Denmark, European education ministers in the Paris declaration of 2015, agreed at a national level to strengthen actions with a view to

> Ensuring inclusive education for all children and young people which combats racism and discrimination on any ground, promotes citizenship and teaches them to understand and to accept differences of opinion, of conviction, of belief and of lifestyle, while respecting the rule of law, diversity and gender equality. (European Commission, 2016)

During the pandemic, the death of George Floyd in Minneapolis led to collective action about #BlackLivesMatter, which crossed the world in a global campaign of marches and demonstrations. In terms of education, they sought an end to out-of-school exclusions to fight the school-to-prison pipeline for Black young people, more equitable school funding and a de-emphasis on standardized testing.

Beyond the 'New Normal': Shaping an Inclusive Future

The UNESCO GEM report commented in two of its key messages:

- Identity, background and ability dictate education opportunities;
- Teachers, teaching materials and learning environments often ignore the benefits of embracing diversity (UNESCO 2020: xviii–1).

Inclusive education is a way out of crisis, yet full commitment to improving outcomes for all is not always shared as a vision or supported by political will. As Slee (2014) has said communities need to recommit to the project of education. He comments on the ways that participants among 'school communities find spaces to establish inclusive and productive educational settlements capable of building worthwhile futures for all students' (Slee 2014). He also identified a further three emergences in a changing context: the limited role of standardized testing, a rethinking of ways to engage with achievement gaps and mounting financial pressures to funding regimes.

At community and school levels, such a recommitment and regeneration of inclusive education will require inclusive leaders. Oskarsdottir and others place the role of inclusive leaders within their school communities at levels from macro and international to micro and classroom based.

> Inclusive leaders are responsible for leading schools that build on the principles of equity to raise the achievement of all learners and their families in the local community. For inclusion to be fully embraced by the school, school leaders need to set a strategic vision and attend to both human and organizational development. (Oskarsdottir et al. 2020:532)

In curriculum-making, consideration needs to include all learners by offering experiences and outcomes that ensure the participation and achievement for all. Universal design for learning offers a way for schools to be responsive to diversity. The school adapts the learning environment towards its learners rather than expect learners to be school-ready. Bilgeri's chapter highlights the developments in use of digital tools to secure quality education for refugee children. Such approaches to design for learning are designed to represent all and not omit or misrecognize any. When Scotland's Curriculum for Excellence was developed, senior managers and staff from support services and special schools advised writing groups on approaches to include all learners. In recent years curriculum inserts were made available to shape engagement and discussion of the inclusive education about LGBTI matters. EASNIE in the follow-up study 'Raising the Achievement of All Learners in Inclusive Education' suggested leadership teams should involve all stakeholders to

> Consider annual plans for inclusion as part of all school improvement programmes. Such local planning should cover a wide range of inclusive practices in a sustainable way. (EASNIE 2019)

Teachers should be encouraged in their willingness to learn about diversity, and further supported as they struggle to be culturally responsive in their teaching. Moreover, as they embrace diversity, our teachers should be supported to develop their knowledge and skills, to become increasingly responsive to difference.

bell hooks writes of her experience in a chapter titled 'Embracing Change'

> When I first entered the multicultural, multiethnic classroom setting I was unprepared. I did not know how to cope effectively with so much 'difference'. Despite progressive politics, and my deep engagement with the feminist movement, I had never before been compelled to work within a truly diverse setting and I lacked the necessary skills. (hooks 1994: 41)

Smith, in an earlier chapter while discussing risk and vulnerability, argues that in engaging with difference we need to see beyond labels and consider how wider societal conditions create uncertain subjects. Such considerations should be engaged with through ethical discussion and debate about labels of risk and vulnerability attached to some learners and not to others. A wide range of materials now offer teachers ways to continue their training and learning on approaches to diversity (Education Scotland 2017, UNICEF 2015).

Finally, how will this be achieved in schools and classrooms? Teachers and learners need to engage together in developing inclusive education in a common learning environment. Munoz Martinez and Porter, writing about work in New Brunswick, noted that

> When students who experience obstacles to learning are engaged and included in schools and classrooms they have a better chance to take their place in communities and society. We believe common learning environments supported by integrated personal learning plans is an effective way to do this. (Martinez and Porter 2018)

Messiou and Ainscow offer the use of inclusive inquiry to promote inclusion in schools. They argue that dialogue among teachers and their students about how to make their lessons more inclusive are supportive of inclusion. Those are

> dialogues that can lead to transformations of practices and thinking, and the development of inclusive schools. Some of the challenges involved in using the approach are identified. (Messiou and Ainscow 2020)

The narratives of educational innovation and inclusion are numerous. The resources and guidance are clear. UNESCO 2020 highlights that it only needs the will to achieve this. Covid-19 is another crisis for education. Inequalities uncovered should no longer be ignored or passed on to others. In their chapter, De Schauwer, Van De Putte and Van Hove collated narratives of changing the grammar of schooling post-Covid-19 with a bag full of stories from Flanders. Such stories and the stories in other chapters in this text tell of the need to make worlds that re-imagine inclusive education for the future.

In 2019 participants interested in inclusive education gathered in the city of Cali, Columbia, to mark twenty-five years since the Salamanca statement on inclusive education. A quarter of a century of proposing inclusive education led to seeking to regenerate the broad definition of inclusive education. The Cali conference called for

> All children and young people should learn together, wherever possible, regardless of any difficulties or differences they may have. Inclusive schools and learning settings must recognize and respond to the diverse needs of their students. (UNESCO 2019)

Coming out of the pandemic, inclusive systems and inclusive schools must respond to diversity, end segregationist approaches and shape our new future. The aim will be to secure the participation and achievement of all, through high-quality inclusive and equitable education.

References

Ainscow, M. (2020), 'Promoting Inclusion and Equity in Education: Lessons from International Experiences', *Nordic Journal of Studies in Educational Policy*, 6(1): 7–16. Available at: https://doi.org/10.1080/20020317.2020.1729587.

Apple, M. (2013), *Can Education Change Society?* New York: Taylor & Francis.

Black, B. (2020), *Attainment and Disadvantage in Scotland's Schools: What May the Impact of Lockdown Be?* Research and Policy Briefing, Policy Scotland, 5 June 2020. Available at: https://policyscotland.gla.ac.uk/attainment-and-disadvantage-in-scotlands-schools-the-impact-of-lockdown-briefing (accessed September 2022).

Byrne, B. (2022), 'How Inclusive Is the Right to Inclusive Education? An Assessment of the UN Convention on the Rights of Persons with Disabilities' Concluding Observations', *International Journal of Inclusive Education* 26(3): 301–18.

Education Scotland. (2020), *GLOW Usage Statistics*. Available at: https://glowconnect.org.uk/about-glow/glow-usage-stats/. (accessed September 2022).

Education Scotland. (2017), *Introduction to Inclusive Education*. OpenLearn Create Website. Available at: https://www.open.edu/openlearncreate/course/view.php?id=3359 (accessed September 2022).

European Agency for Special Needs and Inclusive Education (EASNIE). (2015), *Agency Position on Inclusive Education Systems*. Odense, Denmark. Available at: https://www.european-agency.org/sites/default/files/PositionPaper-EN.pdf (accessed September 2022).

European Agency for Special Needs and Inclusive Education (EASNIE). (2019), 'Raising the Achievement of All Learners in Inclusive Education: Follow-Up Study'. (D. Watt, V. J. Donnelly and A. Kefallinou, eds). Odense, Denmark. Available at: https://www.european-agency.org/resources/publications/raising-achievement-follow-up (accessed September 2022).

European Commission/EACEA/Eurydice. (2016), *Promoting Citizenship and the Common Values of Freedom, Tolerance and Non-discrimination through Education: Overview of Education Policy Developments in Europe following the Paris Declaration of 17 March 2015*. Luxembourg: Publications Office of the European Union. Available at: https://op.europa.eu/en/publication-detail/-/publication/ebbab0bb-ef2f-11e5-8529-01aa75ed71a1 (accessed September 2022).

Fraser, N. (2010), *Scales of Justice: Reimagining Political Space in a Globalizing World*. New York: Columbia University Press.

Fraser, N., and Olson, K. (2008), *Adding Insult to Injury: Nancy Fraser Debates Her Critics*. London: Verso.

hooks, bell. (1994), *Teaching to Transgress: Education as the Practice of Freedom*. London: Routledge.

Illich, I. (1971), *Deschooling Society*. New York: Harper & Row.

Martinez, Y. M., and Porter, G. (2018), 'Planning for All Students: Promoting Inclusive Instruction', *International Journal of Inclusive Education*, 24(14): 1552–67.

Messiou, K., and Ainscow, M. (2020), 'Inclusive Inquiry: Student Teacher Dialogue as a Means of Promoting Inclusion in Schools', *British Educational Research Journal*, 46(3): 670–87.

OECD. (2007), *Quality and Equity in Scottish Schools*. Paris: OECD Publishing.

OECD. (2012), *Equity and Quality in Education: Supporting Disadvantaged Students and Schools*. Paris: OECD Publishing.

OECD. (2015), *Improving Schools in Scotland: An OECD Perspective*. Paris: OECD Publishing.

Óskarsdottir, E., Donnelly, V., Turner-Cmuchal, M., and Florian, L. (2020) 'Inclusive School Leaders – Their Role in Raising the Achievement of All Learners', *Journal of Educational Administration*, April 2020. Available at: https://www.emerald.com/insight/content/doi/10.1108/JEA-10-2019-0190/full/html.

Pensiero, N., Kelly, A., and Bokhove, C. (2020), *Learning Inequalities during the Covid-19 Pandemic: How Families Cope with Home-Schooling*. University of Southampton research report. Available at: https://eprints.soton.ac.uk/442619/1/Covid_paper_20.07.2020.pdf (accessed September 2022).

Slee, R. (2014), 'Discourses of Inclusion and Exclusion: Drawing Wider Margins', *Power and Education*, 6(1): 7–17.

Scottish Government. (2017), 'Additional Support for Learning: Statutory Guidance'. Available at: https://www.gov.scot/publications/supporting-childrens-learning-statutory-guidance-education-additional-support-learning-scotland/ (accessed September 2022).

Scottish Government. (2019a), 'Evaluation of Attainment Scotland Fund: Interim Report (Year 3)'. Available at: https://www.gov.scot/publications/evaluation-attainment-scotland-fund-interim-report-year-3/ (accessed September 2022).

Scottish Government. (2019b), 'Scottish Household Survey 2018'. Available at: https://www.gov.scot/publications/scottish-household-survey-key-findings-2018/pages/1/ (accessed Septemebr 2022).

Scottish Government. (2020a), *Pupils in Scotland Pupil Census: Supplementary Statistics*. Available at: https://www.gov.scot/publications/pupil-census-supplementary-statistics/ accessed September 2022.

Scottish Government. (2020b), *Coronavirus (COVID-19): Supporting Vulnerable Children and Young People Data Intelligence Report*. Available at: https://www.gov.scot/publications/supporting-vulnerable-children-young-people-data-intelligence-report/ (accessed September 2022).

Scottish Government. (2020c). *Poverty, Inequality and COVID-19*. Available at: https://www.improvementservice.org.uk/__data/assets/pdf_file/0013/16402/Poverty-inequality-and-COVID19-briefing.pdf (accessed September 2020).

Scottish Parliament Report. (30 January 2019), *Debate on Motion. Education (Presumption to Mainstream) S5M-15607*. Available at: https://shar.es/afu43k (accessed September 2022).

UNESCO. (2010), *Reaching the Marginalized: EFA Global Monitoring Report, 2010; Summary*. Paris: UNESCO.

UNESCO. (2017), *A Guide for Ensuring Inclusion and Equity in Education*. Paris: UNESCO. Available at: unesdoc.unesco.org/ark:/48223/pf0000248254.

UNESCO. (2019), *Final Report of the International Forum on Inclusion and Equity in Education – Every Learner Matters, Cali, Colombia, 11–13 September*. Paris: UNESCO. Available at: https://unesdoc.unesco.org/ark:/48223/pf0000372651.locale=en (accessed September 2022).

UNESCO. (2020), *Global Education Monitoring Report Inclusion and Education*. Paris: UNESCO. Available at: https://unesdoc.unesco.org/ark:/48223/pf0000373718 (accessed September 2020).

United Nations Committee on the Rights of Persons with Disabilities. (2016), *General Comment No. 4 (2016) on the Right to Inclusive Education*. CRPD/C/GC/4. New York: United Nations Available at: www.ohchr.org/EN/HRBodies/CRPD/Pages/GC.aspx (accessed September 2022).

United Nations Committee on the Rights of Persons with Disabilities (UNCRPD). (2017), *Concluding Observations on the Initial Report of the United Kingdom of Great*

Britain and Northern Ireland. (CRPD/C/GBR/CO/1) New York: United Nations. Available at: http://docstore.ohchr.org/SelfServices/FilesHandler.ashx?enc=6QkG1d%2fPPRiCAqhKb7yhspCUnZhK1jU66fLQJyHIkqMIT3RDaLiqzhH8tVNxhro6S657eVNwuqlzu0xvsQUehREyYEQD%2bldQaLP31QDpRcmG35KYFtgGyAN%2baB7cyky7 (accessed September 2020).

United Nations Human Rights Council (UNHRC). (2019), *Empowering Children with Disabilities for the Enjoyment of Their Human Rights, Including through Inclusive Education*. (A/HRC/40/27). New York: United Nations. Available at: https://undocs.org/Home/Mobile?FinalSymbol=A%2FHRC%2F40%2F27&Language=E&DeviceType=Desktop&LangRequested=False (accessed September 2022).

United Nations Human Rights Council (UNHRC). (2020), *Visit to Canada Report of the Special Rapporteur on the Rights of Persons with Disabilities*. (A/HRC/43/41/ADD2). Available at: https://www.undocs.org/Home/Mobile?FinalSymbol=A%2FHRC%2F43%2F41%2FADD.2&Language=E&DeviceType=Desktop&LangRequested=False (accessed September 2022).

UNICEF. (2015), *UNICEF ToT Modules on Inclusive Education*. New York: UNICEF. Available at: https://www.unicef.org/eca/sites/unicef.org.eca/files/2019-03/ToT_Intro_Module.pdf (accessed September 2022).

World Bank. (2020), *The COVID-19 Pandemic: Shocks to Education and Policy Responses*. Washington, DC: World Bank. Available at: https://openknowledge.worldbank.org/handle/10986/33696 (accessed September 2020).

World Education Forum. (2015), *Incheon Declaration. Education 2030: Towards Inclusive and Equitable Quality Education and Lifelong Learning for All*. Incheon, Republic of Korea: 19–22 May 2015.

Index

ableism 2, 225-6
absenteeism 93-5, 98, 105
abuse 14, 29, 115-16, 178
access to technology *see* digital accessibility
ACEs Adverse Childhood Experiences 116
adolescence 85, 113-15, 122
agency 13-23, 96-106, 119, 188, 199
   collective agency 14, 17-19, 22
   cross-agency childhood 30
   multi-agency plan 270
   relational agency 17-18, 22-3
   teacher agency 167, 179
anxiety 27-8, 113, 133, 169-70, 176-9, 208
   increase in 36, 112
   mental 237
   prevent 47, 54
   related disorders 117
Arendt, Hannah 4
ASN Additional Support Needs 114
asylum seekers 60, 167, 183, 185, 190
attachment 170, 190, 204-5, 207, 210
attendance 5, 28-9, 44, 48-9, 53-5, 83, 115, 174, 208, 266-71
autonomy 84-5, 119, 146, 213

background 104
   cultural background 129
   disadvantaged background 99-100, 105
   socio-economic background 20, 63, 80, 129, 262, 269
Basaglia, Franco 76
belonging 22, 81, 119, 16772, 175, 177, 179, 184-6, 190-7, 207, 212
bereavement 113, 116, 199-200, 206-7
best practice 168-9, 171
Bourdieu, Pierre 94, 96-7, 102-6, 225-6

CAMHS Child and Adolescent Mental Health Services 117

capability approach 13, 17, 19, 21-3, 96
   basic capabilities 101-2
   Collective capabilities 13-14, 18-23
   collectivist capabilitarianism 19
   External capabilities 20-1
   resilient capabilities 22-3
   resistant capability 22-3
capital 96, 99, 102-3, 104, 225-6, 236-8
   capital needs 99
   cultural capital 98-9, 102, 104-6, 226, 238
   economic capital 226
   financial capital 96, 102, 104-6
   human capital 15
   social capital 96-9, 102, 104-6, 118-19, 179, 225-6
Children's Rights 122, 130
citizenship 184, 268, 273
   active citizenship 81, 146
   cultural citizenship 184, 196
   inclusive citizenship 196
   social citizenship 196
colonialism 201, 243
communication 50, 82-3, 187, 231, 237, 250, 252
   barrier 72
   electronic 50, 53, 55
   online 131, 160
   political (Young) 245
compulsory schools 43-4, 46, 48, 53
contrapuntal reading 246
conversion factors 14, 20, 94, 96, 99, 102-6
culturally diverse 212
   CLD culturally and linguistically diverse families 236-8
culturally sensitive approaches 212
curricular
   adaptions 132
   changes 142-4, 146
   demands 96
   development 145, 236-7, 274

extra 142, 224
inserts 266
curriculum 61, 133, 184, 192–3, 250
  competencies 175
  full-time holistic 191
  Icelandic 46
  inclusive 273
  individually adapted 145, 249, 253
  obligatory 268
  Scottish 267–6, 274

democratic
  activities 54
  society 44
dependency relationship 35
depression 169–70, 178, 206, 208
development
  academic 224, 235
  of digital tools 23
  of inclusive education 2, 245, 266, 275
  institutional 132, 138, 140, 146
  learning 44, 70
  opportunity 94, 96, 103–6
  psychological 113
  psychosocial 171, 179
  socio-emotional/social and emotional 22, 115, 134, 146, 168, 238
diagnosis 36, 49, 52–3, 55, 71, 203
digital
  accessibility 67, 69, 72, 82–3, 132–3, 135–6, 138, 140–1, 156, 158, 162, 174, 192, 2–233, 253, 262, 270–1, 274
  devices 67, 69, 100–1
  divide 2, 20, 118, 270
  illiteracy 82
  skills 20
digitalization 20, 23, 63, 145
disabled students 76–7, 245–8, 251, 253, 255
disabilities
  learning 78
  students with 76–84, 223, 228, 265
disability
  related needs 227
  students with
DisCrit Dis/abilities critical race studies 225–6, 237

disease control rules *see* protective measures
distance learning 44–5, 62–3, 65–7, 75–7, 82, 95, 156, 159–62, 173, 223–33, 235, 237, 248, 250, 267, 271
divide 70, 162, 224
digital *see* digital

EASNIE European Agency for Special Needs and Inclusive Education 265, 274
EB emergent bilinguals 223
EBwDs emergent bilinguals with disabilities 223–7, 237–8
Education recovery plan 36
EFA Education for all 3, 14, 63, 129, 183, 261, 272–3
EHCP Education, Health and Care Plans 25
ELET early leaving from education and training 93
ELLs English Language Learners 175
emotional
  healing/recovery 200, 212
  intelligence 119
empowerment 21, 97, 190, 264
  family 145
ESRC Economic and Social Research Council 120–1
ethic of care 35, 168, 172, 178
  caring relation 172
ethnicity 60, 261–2, 266, 270, 272
  Black ethnic groups 199–206, 210–14
eugenicist world views 203
exclusion 2, 4, 11, 16, 25, 31, 59–61, 200, 202, 204, 224, 245, 255, 272–3
  digital exclusion 131
  educational 5–6
  micro-macro exclusion 77
  social exclusion 7, 130, 171, 263

fearful subject 27
feminism 172, 226, 275
financial situation 52, 102, 230, 233–4
Foucault, Michel 31
Freire, Paulo 78

gap
  digital 230
  of inequality 156

inequality 93–4, 104
  poverty-related attainment 266
  racial wealth 233
  social class and capital gap 104
  social gap 63, 78
GARs government-assisted refugees 169
GEM Global Education Monitoring 264, 272–3
gender 93, 176, 231, 261–2, 270, 272–3
gifted children 140, 145
grief 168, 204–9, 212

health
  health care 117, 151–2, 179, 208, 234
  health conditions 27, 37, 120, 199
  health mitigation measures *see* protective measures
  health-protective behaviour 27
home-schooling *see* distance learning
hospitalization 155, 202
HSCL Home School Community Liaison 94–106

ICF International Classification of Functioning 83
IEP individualized education plan 227
immigrant children 45
inclusion 59, 122, 129–30
  of Black students 203–5
  colonial nature of 243
  criteria 227
  educational 155, 275
  ethos of 169–71
  Index for (Booth, Ainscow) 81
  policy of 43, 145–6
  of refugees 171, 183–5
  of all students 167–8
  of students with SEN(D) 29, 245–51
  school 76–7, 81–4
  social 16, 32, 78–81, 155
inclusive
  education 4, 14–15, 30, 43–55, 59, 145, 185, 191, 243–50, 256, 263–9, 272–6
  school 45, 75, 83–4, 130, 265, 275–6
intergenerational 237
  impact 200, 202, 214
international conventions on the rights of children 53

international convention on the rights of the disabled 53
intersectionality 22, 121, 171, 223, 225–6, 237, 262–3
isolation 25, 115–16, 120, 162, 167, 178, 186, 224, 229, 244
  physical 192
  social 72, 113–14, 120, 133–4, 195, 235, 251

joint action 18
justice for all (Fraser) 191

Kittay, Eva Feder 35

labelling 5, 25–37, 204, 207–8, 223, 275
language
  abandon 153
  accessible 253
  barriers 71–2
  common 187
  competence 61–2, 69
  decoding 176
  discriminatory 154
  family 227
  first 59–60, 63–4
  foreign 50–1, 54
  GLSCC German Language Support Classes and Courses 59–72
  home 224–5, 227
  of instruction 60–1, 231
  issues of 20
  learning 70, 223, 227
  lessons 169
  minority 60
  needs 224
  primary 227
  proficiency 226
  refugees' 171
  Second 51, 71, 114, 223
  skills 61, 71, 167, 185
  support 61–2, 71, 251
  therapy 223
  of vulnerability and risk 28, 31
learning difficulties 71, 77, 95, 101–2, 133
legislation 29, 81, 83, 203, 264
  educational 60, 145
LGBTI Lesbian, Gay, Bisexual, Transgender and Intersexual 266–7, 269, 274

LGBTQ2 lesbian, gay, bisexual,
    transgender, queer, two-spirited
    169
lifelong learning 129, 263
linguicism 225
literacy 99, 169, 174, 229
    digital 104
    digital illiteracy 82
    hygiene literacy 168
    Illiteracy 78, 156
lockdown 28–9, 36, 103, 112, 114–18, 168,
    171, 205, 230–7
    in Austria 63–4, 69
    in Canada 167, 173, 178
    in Flanders 244, 248, 250, 254
    in Italy 81–3
    in UK 79, 117, 183–4, 186, 192–4,
        201, 208
loss 199–200, 204–12, 234–6
    capital 96–7
    career 71
    of contact 100, 115
    economic 235
    education 271
    of housing 2
    income 2, 113, 230, 233
    job/work 112, 136, 230
    learning 6, 96–7, 115, 236, 271
    of loved ones 168, 204, 207
    resilience to 207
    of rites/routines 113, 117, 204

mask(s) 156, 160, 162, 184–5
meaningful location (Creswell) 190
medical care *see* health care
medical model of disability 77, 83
mental health 2, 113–15, 117–20, 167–8,
    176, 179, 191–2
    of adolescents 122
    caretakers'/mothers' 236–7
    issues 117, 167, 177
    needs 204
    services 117, 121
    specialists 4
    support 117, 237
mental illness 208
migration 2, 59–61, 153, 163, 272
    biography 59, 71–2
    forced 13, 18, 22, 59–60, 63, 168, 185–6

journey 168, 170
migrant/migration background 7, 244
pre-migration experiences 194
Milani, Don 78–9
Montessori, Maria 78
multicultural workers 177
municipality 44, 46, 136, 141–2

neglect 14, 32, 80, 115–16
network 54, 186, 244, 249, 252
    cultural 175
    extended 224
    Family 118–19
    of relations (Foucault) 31
    of (extended) support 115, 118–19
    social 79
    Support 49, 53, 55, 115, 248
new normal 122–3, 183–5, 195, 273
Noddings, Nel 172, 178
Nussbaum, Martha 15, 101

OECD 117, 129, 132, 145, 262, 266, 269
Ofsted 5
online schooling *see* distance learning
ontology 34
    ontological vulnerability 35
open learning 85
opportunity development 94, 96, 103–5
otherizing 33

participation 13–14, 31, 54–5, 76, 81, 83,
    146, 169, 184, 188, 195, 197, 251,
    263, 267, 274, 276
    effective 132–3
    Participatory parity (Fraser)/parity of
        183–8, 191–2, 262
    progressive 76
    social 62
personal assistance 248
    face-to-face 23, 171, 185
    Interaction 27, 36
    lack of 133
    with parents 237
    peer 114
    personal 23
    Physical social interaction 114–15
    with the place 197
    of protective and risk factors 122
    social 19, 50, 115, 170, 267

place-making methods 184, 186–92, 196
policy
   changes 264
   child welfare 29
   deployment of vulnerability in (Brown) 25
   education(al) 30, 43–5, 103, 203, 266
   framework 265
   implications for 119
   interventionist 26
   paternalistic 34
   preven(ta)tive 30, 94
   programmes 96–7, 105
   social integration 154
   socially just 104
   support 94
poverty 22, 81, 94, 111–21, 130, 151–7, 162, 174, 178, 206
   child 131
   educational 76–9, 82, 85
   illnesses 151
   maintenance of 129–31
   material 76
   related attainment gap 266
pre-service teachers 70
protection 25, 32–5, 60, 81
   child 116, 142
   disability-inclusive social 144
   legal 28, 36
   need for 27
   and participation 13–14
   Protective measures 36, 48–9, 95, 115, 176, 247–8, 250
   rhetoric of (safety and) 29, 36–7
pull and push phenomena (Demo) 77, 82

racism 200, 204, 213, 225, 273
   and ableism 226
   anti-Black 202, 214
   ecological nature of 210
   institutional 204
   medical 202
   structural 201–2
   systematic 201
racial
   discrimination 202
   disparities 201
   lack of racial diversity 204
   and linguistic barriers 225

wealth gap 233
reciprocal knowledge building (Comber) 190
recovery plan
   of the European Union 85
   UK government 36
refugee
   biography 69–72
   children 13–23, 167–71, 177, 184–5,
   education 20, 167–8, 183–5, 195–7
   students 59–63, 167–70, 174–9
remote instruction/schooling/teaching *see* distance learning
resilience 14, 118, 199, 213, 236, 247, 253–4, 264, 273
   building/developing 121–2, 171, 254
   emotional 114, 116
   increased 213
   levels of 205
   to loss 207
   methods of 209
resilient
   capability 22–3
   communities 80, 119, 121–2
   education systems 264, 273
   parents 253
   students 247
   teachers 144
resumption of ordinary life (Kohli) 183–5
right to education 15, 22, 130–1, 145
risk
   assessment 26–9
   being at risk 25
   discourse 26, 32
   factor model 30
   health 96, 116, 141–2
   management 25–9

Salamanca statement 14–15, 276
salient adults 94–9, 103, 106
SBAF Sen-Bourdieu Analytical Framework 94–106
school closure 3, 33, 36, 46, 59, 64, 70, 77, 81, 93, 112, 131, 155–6, 168, 261, 267
school recovery 204, 212
SDG 4 Sustainable Development Goal 4, 263–5, 267–8
self-care 175–6, 235

self-efficacy 78, 170, 207
SEN special educational needs 26, 71, 129, 132–8, 140–5, 243–7, 256
  special education 45, 223, 243–8, 266, 272
  special needs students 175
  special needs teachers 49–55
Sen, Amartya 16–17
SEND special educational needs or disabilities 25–37, 114
sexual orientation 176, 262, 266–7, 272
social
  background 45, 262, 266–7, 270–1
  distancing 27–9, 36, 62, 113–16, 135, 156, 159–60, 171, 175, 184–5, 193–4, 224
  (and economic) justice 4, 19, 43–5, 53, 78, 93, 192, 262
  media 118, 120, 227, 270
socio-economic
  background 20, 63, 80, 262, 269
  classes 173
  status 202, 262, 269
socio-emotional
  development 22, 113–14, 134, 137, 145
  needs 23
  situation 72
  support 238
stress 155, 177, 229–37, 235, 253
  adult 120
  and anxiety/anxiety and 112, 179, 208
  economic 234, 237
  emotional
  financial 233
  household 114
  levels 2, 229
  management 200
  manifestation of 235
  mothers' 230, 232, 235
  post-traumatic 117, 208
  social 237
stressors 113–18, 177
summer programmes/schools 36, 70, 95
support
support teachers 4, 75, 81–4, 134, 145
  additional support 43–8, 52–6, 114, 134, 270

teacher professionalism 45, 53–4, 119, 140, 275
teacher training *see* teacher professionalism
therapy 248
  art 209
  behavioural 142, 209
  model 210
  music 209
  narrative 213
  occupational 113
  physio 113
  play 142, 209
  psycho 209
  speech and language 113, 223
transition 29, 61–2, 71, 155–7, 170, 185
trauma 14, 22, 60, 117, 170, 176, 199–200, 210
  trauma-informed (school) approach 210–14, 268
  collective trauma 210–11, 213
  PTG post-traumatic growth 213–14
  PTSD post-traumatic stress disorder 169, 179, 186, 235
Tree of Life approach 212–14

UDL Universal Design for Learning 20, 84, 274
UN united nations 20
UNCRPD Committee on the Rights of People with Disabilities 264–5, 269
UNESCO Educational, Scientific and Cultural Organization 3, 122, 261–4, 269, 272–6
UNHCR High Commissioner for Refugees 13–14, 20–1, 169
UNHRC Human Rights Council 264
UNICEF Children's Fund 80, 111–13, 123, 131
UNICEF RA Rapid Assessment 131
universal/whole-system approach 210–11, 214

violence 14, 116, 168, 170, 178, 263
vulnerability
  clinical vulnerability 27
  educational vulnerability 138
  emotional vulnerability 138
  social vulnerability 133, 138, 145
  vulnerable label 26, 28, 31

WEF World Education Forum 263
welfare services 32, 116
well-being 3, 14–17, 111, 135, 171, 251, 268 14ff, 21, 46, 54, 97, 100ff, 113f, 118ff, 120, 123, 135, 137f, 145, 171, 177, 179, 192, 224, 235, 250f, 254, 267f
  and agency 99–103, 106
  of Black children 199–214
  children's 17, 36–7, 46–7, 113–14, 118, 120, 145–6, 235, 267
  emotional 163, 175, 199–200, 207–10, 214, 235
  families' 96, 100, 118
  freedom and 97, 101, 103
  of a group 22
  individual 21
  learner 177
  mental (and physical) 117, 209
  mothers' 224, 234
  psychological 114, 120, 160
  of refugee children 22
  of salient adults 99
  social 160, 175
  socio-emotional 111, 163
  students' 93, 96, 100, 106
  of young people 192
WhatsApp *see* social media
WHO world health organisation 152, 168, 261
Whole-school approach 94–106
World bank 144, 261, 267, 270

www.ingramcontent.com/pod-product-compliance
Lightning Source LLC
Chambersburg PA
CBHW071806300426
44116CB00009B/1219